Deterministic Artificial Intelligence

Edited by Timothy Sands

Published in London, United Kingdom

IntechOpen

Supporting open minds since 2005

Deterministic Artificial Intelligence
http://dx.doi.org/10.5772/intechopen.81309
Edited by Timothy Sands

Contributors
Matthew Cooper, Kyle Baker, Emmanuel Oyekanlu, Azura Che Soh, Behzad Vaferi, Raheni T D, P Thirumoorthi, Tatiana Mikhaylovna Zubkova, Brendon Smeresky, Alexa Rizzo

First published in London, United Kingdom, 2020 by IntechOpen
IntechOpen is the global imprint of INTECHOPEN LIMITED, registered in England and Wales, registration number: 11086078, 7th floor, 10 Lower Thames Street, London, EC3R 6AF, United Kingdom
Printed in Croatia

British Library Cataloguing-in-Publication Data
A catalogue record for this book is available from the British Library

Additional hard and PDF copies can be obtained from orders@intechopen.com

Deterministic Artificial Intelligence
Edited by Timothy Sands
p. cm.
Print ISBN 978-1-78984-111-4
Online ISBN 978-1-78984-112-1
eBook (PDF) ISBN 978-1-83880-728-3

An electronic version of this book is freely available, thanks to the support of libraries working with Knowledge Unlatched. KU is a collaborative initiative designed to make high quality books Open Access for the public good. More information about the initiative and links to the Open Access version can be found at www.knowledgeunlatched.org

For EU product safety concerns:
IN TECH d.o.o., Prolaz Marije Krucifikse Kozulić 3, 51000 Rijeka, Croatia, info@intechopen.com or visit our website at intechopen.com.

Meet the editor

Dr. Timothy Sands graduated from Columbia University, Stanford University, and the Naval Postgraduate School. He is an International Scholar Laureate of the Golden Key International Honor Society, a Fellow of the Defense Advanced Research Projects Agency, a panelist of the National Science Foundation Graduate Research Fellowship program, and an interviewer for undergraduate admissions at Stanford University. He has published prolifically in archival journals, conference proceedings, books, and book chapters, in addition to giving plenary, keynote, and invitational presentations; he holds one patent in spacecraft attitude control. He is currently the Associate Dean of the Naval Postgraduate School's Graduate School of Engineering and Applied Science having previously served as a university chief academic officer, dean, and research center director.

Contents

Preface

This book is immersed in the ubiquitous understanding of artificial intelligence with an overview of *stochastic* artificial intelligence followed by four chapters on such algorithms. A particularly important contribution prepares readers for the deterministic (non-stochastic) treatment of the topic: namely, deterministic algorithms can be used in stochastic artificial intelligence, but the approach remains stochastic. Deterministic artificial intelligence is examined next in three chapters that apply the approach to disparate facets of mechanical motion control.

Deterministic artificial intelligence applied to motion control typically necessitates analytic expressions of desired motion displacement, velocity, and acceleration. The first two chapters of the section of this text examine methods of autonomous generation of such trajectories. The final chapter utilizes the prerequisite material to enumerate and critically evaluate the deterministic approach compared to nominal methods, including optimal and classical feedback methods.

The text is meant for basic scientifically inclined readers who possess the basics of mathematics (while calculus certainly aids the reader to get more out of the chapters). The topics learned from reading this text will prepare students and faculty to investigate interesting problems, while readers able to understand and abstract the general method will be able to apply it to any area whose defining principles can be found, either by adherence to a natural law or by using the certainty equivalence principle to assert self-awareness following system identification. This claim is buttressed by the disparate nature of illustrative systems. The first chapter in the second section applies the methodology to the famous forced van der Pol equation (an electromechanics example), while the second applies the method to sinusoidal trajectories for mechanical motion. The final chapter uses Euler's moment equations for deterministic self-awareness, allowing rigid bodies to be aware of the existence in the context of knowledge of the natural laws that govern its behavior. It is the fondest hope of the editor and authors that readers enjoy the book.

Dr. Timothy Sands
Columbia University (CVN),
USA

Naval Postgraduate School,
Stanford University,
USA

Section 1

Stochastic Approaches

Chapter 1

Stochastic Artificial Intelligence: Review Article

T.D. Raheni and P. Thirumoorthi

Abstract

Artificial intelligence (AI) is a region of computer techniques that deals with the design of intelligent machines that respond like humans. It has the skill to operate as a machine and simulate various human intelligent algorithms according to the user's choice. It has the ability to solve problems, act like humans, and perceive information. In the current scenario, intelligent techniques minimize human effort especially in industrial fields. Human beings create machines through these intelligent techniques and perform various processes in different fields. Artificial intelligence deals with real-time insights where decisions are made by connecting the data to various resources. To solve real-time problems, powerful machine learning-based techniques such as artificial intelligence, neural networks, fuzzy logic, genetic algorithms, and particle swarm optimization have been used in recent years. This chapter explains artificial neural network-based adaptive linear neuron networks, back-propagation networks, and radial basis networks.

Keywords: artificial intelligence, artificial neural network, functions, weights, bias, Adaline network, back-propagation network, radial basis network

1. Introduction

In day-to-day life, artificial intelligence (AI) has brought further advantages to pattern features and human expert systems. Based on experience and through learning, it continues to gain further potential in industrial growth. The primary elements for a neural network are the neurons, which are special types of brain cells. The neuron has the ability to retain, realize, and execute the previous existence of every action.

A neural network is an analytical model that is inspired directly by biological neural networks. An artificial neural network (ANN) is an information processing system and is capable of processing nonlinear relationships between inputs and outputs. The network consists of interconnected neurons and functions to produce an output pattern of a given input pattern [1]. The learning process of a neural network takes place by itself, which means the network learns by examples that make it more powerful, so there is no need to devise an algorithm to perform a particular task. Because of the above reasons, a neural network has no internal mechanism to perform a specific task [2].

The network consists of nodes that are connected by weights and obtains knowledge through variations in the node weights that are being exposed as samples. Every neuron is linked to other neurons by a network link, and the network link is associated with the weights that contain instructions in the input signal. In addition, each neuron has a centralized state of its own. The centralized state is the activation level of the neuron that serves as input to the neurons. The activation level of the neuron is imparted to the other neurons. To make the neural process more beneficial, mainframe computers are used. Various computational tasks are developed using ANNs at a more rapid rate than traditional systems.

2. Biological neural network

Human brains consist of neurons with a number of connections. The basic element of a neural network is called a neuron. The biological neural network consists of axons, dendrites, and a cell body (soma). Each cell performs relatively simple computations, whose nature is indistinct from slow-style networks. Dendrites are tree-like structures (dendrite trees) that accept signals from the neighboring neurons, and each branch is connected to one neuron. The tree-like dendrite structure is connected to the main body of the neuron called the soma (cell body). The cell body is a cylindrical shape that sums the incoming signal. Dendrites are connected by a synapse. A synapse is a structure that allows a nerve cell to pass electric signals to another nerve cell. An axon is a thin cylindrical cell that carries the impulse of the nerve cell. A single nerve cell has 1000 to 10,000 synapses, while 100 billion neurons are present in our brain, and every neuron has 1000 dendrites. The processing of a biological neural network is a slow process and the learning process is uncertain [3].

The simple biological neural network architecture is shown in **Figure 1**.

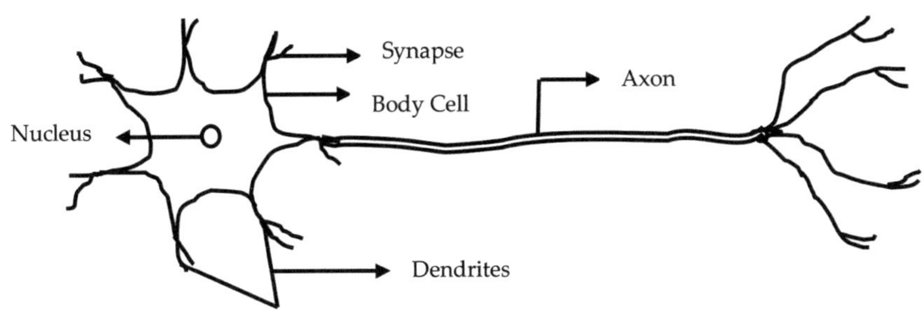

Figure 1.
Biological neural network—Simple biological neuron architecture.

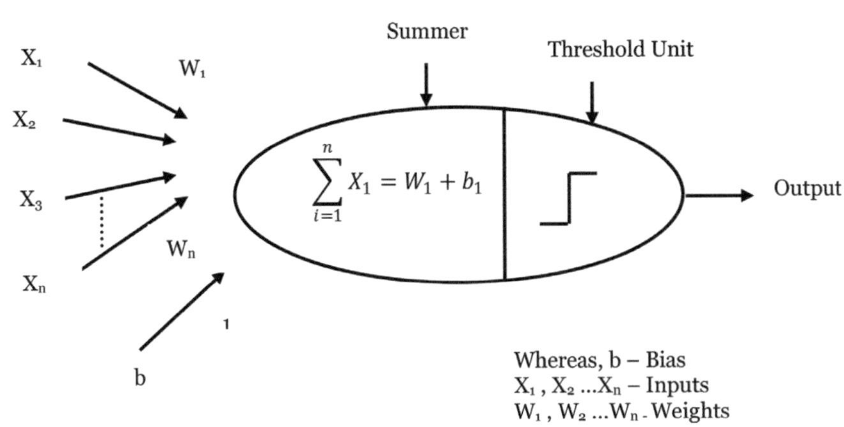

Figure 2.
ANN model.

2.1 Model and elements of an artificial neural network

The network is observed as weighted direct graphs in which the directed edges of corresponding weights are connected to input and output neurons. The network receives the input in the form of a pattern and image in point (vector) form. The inputs are mathematically assigned by the notation $x(n)$ for "n" number of inputs. An ANN model is shown in **Figure 2**.

Every input is multiplied by its corresponding weights. To solve a problem with the network, weight is used and correspondingly weight is represented as the strength of connections between the neurons. If the weighted sum is zero, then bias is added to make the output not zero. Bias has the weight in which the input is always equal to 1 [4].

3. Classification of a neural network

Neural networks are classified on the basis of patterns to determine the weights correspondingly. The neurons are arranged in the form of layers and have the same activation function. Neural network processing depends on the following segments:

i. Network topology

ii. Learning methods

iii. Adjustment of weights and activation functions

The networks are arranged by connecting the points or with connecting lines. Depending on the topology of the network, it is classified as follows:

i. Single-layer feed-forward network

ii. Multilayer feed-forward network

3.1 Single-layer feed-forward network

In this network, the signals or the information move only in a forward (one) direction from the input nodes, through the hidden nodes and to the output nodes. A single-layer network does not require cycles or loops. The network consists of output nodes in a single layer, while the inputs are directly fed to the outputs through a series of interconnected weights. Every node is calculated by its sum of the product of the weights. If the value is above threshold (above zero), then the activated value is 1 (positive), and if the value is below threshold (below zero), then the activated value is -1 (negative) [5]. The above network functions such that input nodes are connected to the corresponding hidden nodes with different weights and result in a series of output per node. It consists of multiple neurons that are interconnected to form a single-layer network. The two layers, namely input and output layers, are used. In the input layer, the neurons pass data from one node to the other node and the inputs are scattered and perform no calculation. Each input layer $a_1, a_2, a_3, \dots, a_n$ is linked to each neuron in the output layer through the connection weight. Each output neuron value such as $b_1, b_2, b_3, \dots, b_n$ is calculated according to the set of input values. Based on the connection weights the values of the output layer are varied accordingly. This type of network is widely used in applications like computer vision, speech recognition, and pattern classification problems. A single-layer neural network is shown in **Figure 3**.

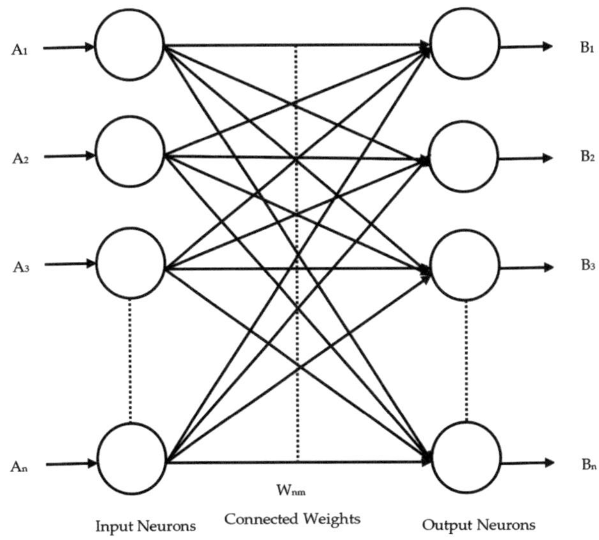

Figure 3.
Single-layer neural network.

3.2 Multilayer neural network

A multilayer neural network is an interconnection of signals in which the inputs and calculations flow forward from the input nodes to the output nodes. The number of signals in a neural network is the number of layers in the network. It consists of more layers for estimated units, and usually the connections are interdependent in the forward path. Every neuron in a single layer is interconnected with neurons of the consequent layer. Multilayer networks use other learning algorithms such as back propagation, Hopfield, Adaline (adaptive linear neuron), etc. In this network, if a layer is connected to the input, then the layer is a hidden layer. The multilayer network is shown in **Figure 4**.

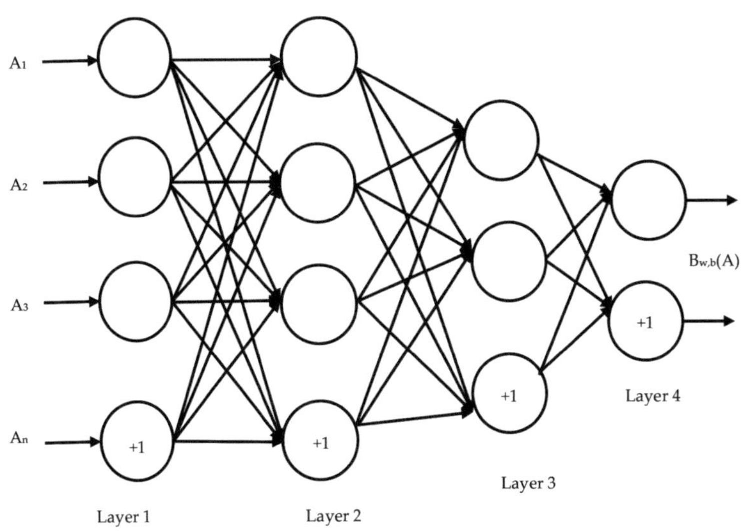

Figure 4.
Multilayer neural network.

The network consists of input layers $A_1, A_2, \ldots, A_n$. To train the network we require training layers, i.e., input layers $\{(a(1), b(1)) \ldots (a(m), b(m))\}$ of m training sets. To train the network, the gradient descent method is one of the best methods. This method seeks to find the minimum function in the network set.

3.3 Learning methods of a neural network

The key aspect of a neural network is the ability to learn by itself. Training or learning methods help the neural network adapt itself by making appropriate adjustments and good responses. To train the network according to custom needs, there are three types of learning. Once a network has been designed for a precise application, then the network is equipped to be trained. To begin these processes, the initial weights are chosen randomly. Then, the training or learning process begins with the following techniques:

i. Supervised learning

ii. Unsupervised learning

iii. Reinforcement learning

3.3.1 Supervised learning

Supervised learning is one of the learning methods in which the data, observations, and measurements are defined with predefined classes. It is similar to how a "teacher" explains content to students. The pairing of each input vector with the target vector determines the desired output. Training pairs mainly deal with the input vector and the corresponding target vector. The training process takes place when the input vector is applied, resulting in an output vector. If the actual response differs from the target response, the network will obtain an error signal. The corresponding error signal is used to calculate the adjustment of weights so that both the actual and target outputs match.

A supervised algorithm in a neural network encompasses classification and regression types for learning processes [6]. In the classification type, outputs are confined to a finite set of data, whereas in the regression type, the output may contain analytical data within the given limits. The best execution process for error minimization is the supervised learning algorithm. Input and output data are used to train the mapping function of the network and are given by the following relation:

$$B = f(a) \tag{1}$$

where $f(a)$ is the function of input a.

The aim is to provide an approximate mapping function so that new input data (a) help to predict the output (B). The supervised learning algorithm is shown in **Figure 5**.

The purpose of supervised learning is to vary its weights according to the input/output samples. After executing this network, input-to-output mapping with minimum error has been achieved. Without proper training sets, performance is no longer determined, while it seems stochastic in either case.

3.3.2 Unsupervised learning

Unsupervised learning is the type of machine learning function that describes the hidden layer from the unviable data. The unviable data explain the classification and measurements that are not included in the observations. Because of unviable data, there can be no calculation to reach an accuracy level.

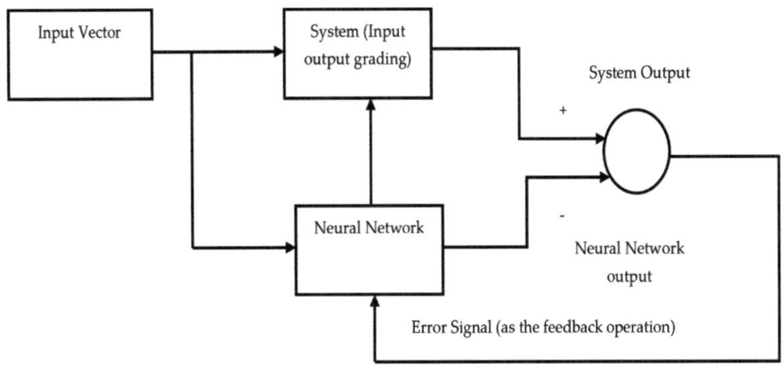

Figure 5.
Supervised learning.

Unsupervised learning is utilized in self-organizing neural networks, and this type of learning does not require a teacher to teach the network [7]. To train the network, data sets used in the supervised model are used along with the synaptic weights, which are assigned as:

$$\text{Unsupervised training} = \frac{1}{\sqrt{\text{Number of input attributes}}} \quad (2)$$

It has the ability to solve complex problems and analyze the changes that occur in undefined data. It is widely used for preprocesses in the network of a supervised learning algorithm. A block diagram of unsupervised learning is shown in **Figure 6**.

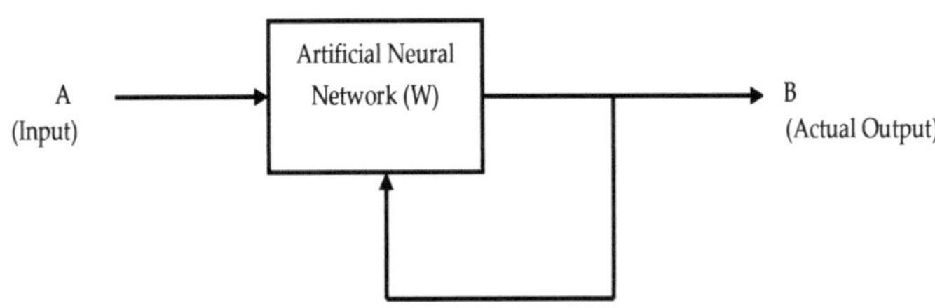

Figure 6.
Unsupervised learning.

Unsupervised learning methods can be further grouped into clustering and association problems.

Clustering is a basic method to analyze the data that occur in the network. It spots some inherent structures present in a set of objects based on a similarity measure. The clustering technique is based on statistical model identification or competitive learning. It is widely used for feature extraction, vector quantization, image segmentation, function approximation, and data mining [8]. The association learning rule is a machine learning method to create relations between variables in large databases, and the approach to unsupervised learning is of two types, namely:

- Anomaly detection
- Neural networks learning—Hebbian learning method

Anomaly detection is used for analyzing events and observations. The system is broadly classified into three types such as unsupervised anomaly detection, supervised anomaly detection, and semisupervised anomaly detection. It preprocesses the data sets and detects the faults that occur in the system.

The Hebbian method is a learning rule that determines the weight of the two different units either to increase or to decrease the weight to activate the function. Learning is performed by varying the synaptic gap between the weights. The weight of the vector increases gradually with respect to the input. The Hebbian rule for updating the weight is given by:

$$w_{a(\text{new})} = w_{a(\text{old})} + C_a * B \tag{3}$$

where $w_{a(\text{new})}$ is the new weight equal to the sum of the old weight and the learning method $C_a * B$.

3.3.3 Reinforcement learning

This learning is identical to supervised learning and the difference in operating the network from its actual output for about 50%. In supervised learning, for each output data, the simultaneous input data are known when compared to reinforcement learning. Due to the absence of a training data set, reinforcement learning learns from its experience.

The trial and error process is designed to maximize the expected value of a criterion of functions and actions followed by an improvement, so it is referred to as reinforced learning. The reinforcement signal and the corresponding input patterns depend on the previous data of the stochastic unit. Gaussian processes combine the neural networks for model-based reinforcement learning [9]. A block diagram of reinforcement learning is shown in **Figure 7**.

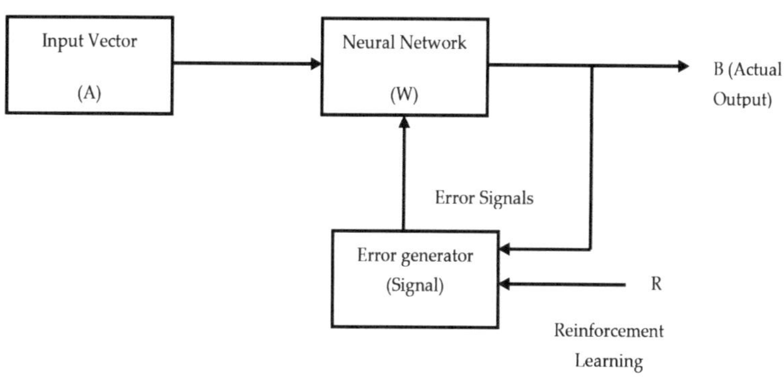

Figure 7.
Block diagram of reinforcement learning.

3.4 Activation functions of a neural network

3.4.1 Weights

$W_1, W_2, \ldots, W_n$ are the factors of the weight that are associated with each node to determine the quality of input row vector $Y = [Y_1, Y_2, \ldots, Y_n]T$. Every single input is multiplied by a related weight by connecting the activation function. **Figure 8** shows the basic elements of a neural network.

3.4.2 Threshold

The internal threshold is the offset that marks the activation function of the output node Z and is given by:

$$Z = \sum_{i=1}^{n} (X_i W_i) - \theta_k \tag{4}$$

Threshold function may be either binary type or bipolar type, respectively. The output of a binary threshold function is given by:

$$Z = f(p) \tag{5}$$

$$\text{condition is}''0''\text{if } p < 0\text{s}$$

$$\text{condition is}''1''\text{if } p \geq 0$$

3.4.3 Linear activation function

Linear function fulfills the superposition concept. The activation function performs mathematical operations on a signal output, and the equation for linear activation function is given by:

$$Z = f(p) = \alpha.p \tag{6}$$

where α is the slope of the linear activation function. The linear activation curve is shown in **Figure 9**.

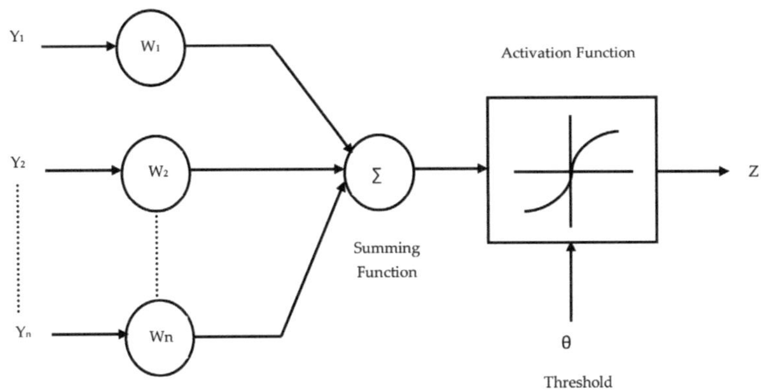

Figure 8.
Basic elements of a neural network.

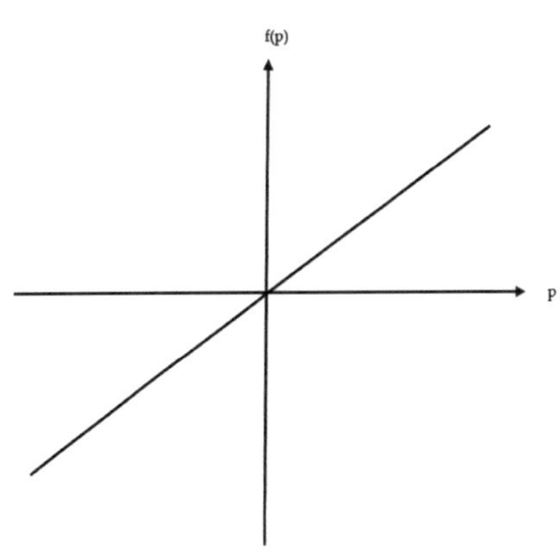

Figure 9.
Linear activation curve.

Slope 1 is the identity function. The output Z of the identity function is equal to the input function (p).

4. Methods of implementing a neural network

The methods of implementing a neural network are the adaline method, back-propagation method, and radial basis method.

4.1 Adaptive linear neuron network

The Adaline model was developed by Widrow Hoff. It is a single-layer network consisting of other nodes. The network is classified by varying the weights in such a manner that it diminishes mean square error for every iteration. An Adaline network is shown in **Figure 10**.

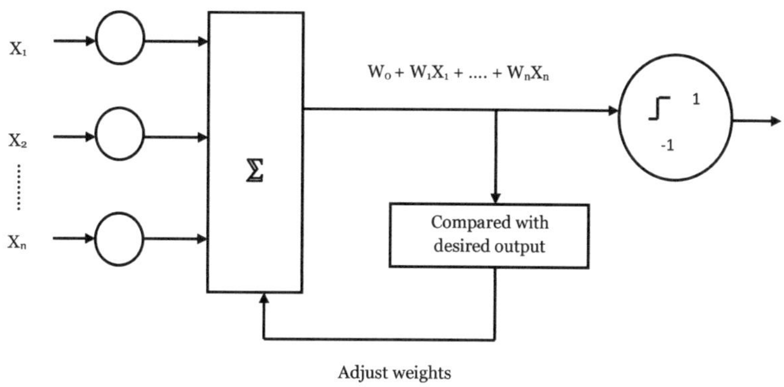

Figure 10.
Adaline network.

Each node acquires a number of inputs and propagates a single output. The input and output signals to the Adaline network use bipolar activation function. When compared to other types of networks, the input and output function of the Adaline network is linear. The weights are bounded by the input and varied accordingly to the user's choice. The bias in the network acts as an adjustable weight where the activation function is always 1. The output function of the Adaline network has one output unit and the network is a trained delta rule. This rule is otherwise known as the least mean square rule. This type of learning rule is used to decrease the mean squared error between the output and activation function [10]. An Adaline network is implemented by using the three steps, which are shown in **Figure 11**.

i. **Initialize**: assume random weights to all the links that are connected to the network.

ii. **Training**: initialize the input weights and arrange the known inputs in a random sequence. Compare errors between input and output by simulating the network. This forms an error function and by adjusting the weights, learning function takes place. Repeat the process until the total error is less than $\sum$.

iii. **Thinking**: in the thinking process, the network will respond to input nodes. Even for trained inputs, it does not provide a good result. By defining an error

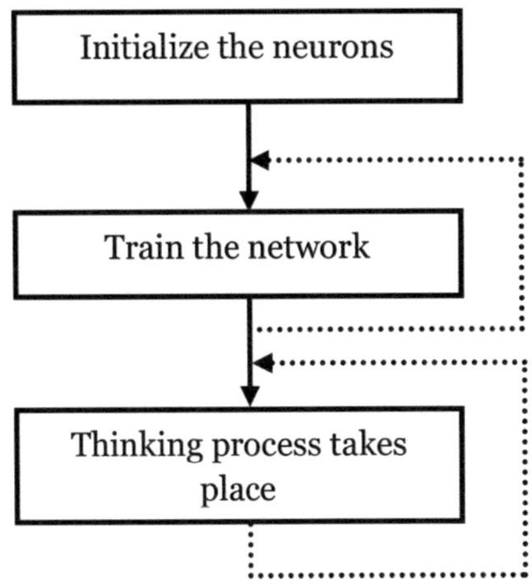

Figure 11.
Steps—Adaline network.

function, it measures the performance in terms of weights. The derivative of the function with respect to weights is obtained by varying the weights, and error in the system is decreased. A block diagram of an Adaline network is shown in **Figure 12**.

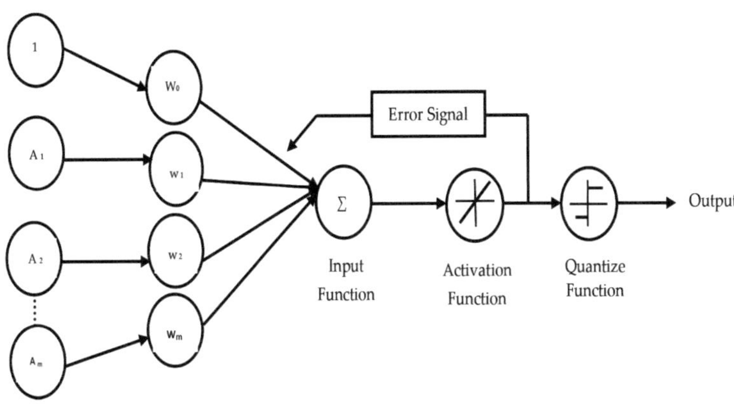

Figure 12.
Block diagram of an Adaline network.

The input to the neural network is represented as A.

$A = [1\, A_1, A_2, \ldots, A_m]$, whereas $1 = A_0 =$ bias.

$W = [W_0, W_1, W_2, \ldots, W_m]$ represents the weight in the network.

Initially, weights are chosen in a random manner. The value of −1 and 1 is taken. The weighted sum of input neurons, including a bias term, is calculated by comparing with output neurons. Based on the delta rule, the weights are adjusted. The output equation for the network is given by:

$$C = \sum_{k=1}^{n} a_k w_k + \alpha \tag{7}$$

where a is the input vector, w is the weight of the vector, n is the number of inputs, α is a constant, and C is the output vector.

By assuming $a_0 = 1$ and $w_0 = \alpha$, the output equation is further minimized to:

$$C = \sum_{k=0}^{n} a_k w_k \tag{8}$$

4.1.1 Adaline learning algorithm

The learning algorithm of a network is a delta rule but its base is different. To reduce variation between the input and output, the delta rule is preferred and improves the weight between the connections. The main objective is to reduce error that occurs in overall training networks [11, 12]. The updated weight in the network is given by the following equation:

$$w \leftarrow w + \delta(t - C)a \tag{9}$$

where δ is the learning rate of the network, C is the model output, and t is the desired target output.

The Adaline network merges with the least square error and the equation is given by:

$$E = (t - k)^2 \tag{10}$$

where E is the least mean square error.

According to the input response, the system is activated and training is started. Consider Y as an input and W is the weight. Let us assume $x_{n+1} = 1$ and x_{n+1} as the bias weight. Therefore, the weighted sum "S" is a dot product of the function given in the equation:

$$S = W.Y = \sum_i w_i y_i \tag{11}$$

The identity function of the network is chosen as $I = S$ and considered as an activation function. The squared error $E = (O - I)^2$ is the error function. The network defines error function and determines performance of input, weight, and desired output. Adaline networks are used in net input values and noise correction. The following are the steps for learning the Adaline algorithm:

Step 1: Assume the synaptic weight values in the range from -1 to $+1$.
Step 2: Set activation functions of the input units:

$$A_0 = 1 \text{ and } A_i = S(i = 1, 2, 3, \ldots, n)$$

Step 3: Compute the net input to the neuron as:

$$S = W.Y = \sum_i w_i y_i$$

Step 4: Update the corresponding bias and weights:

$$W_0 \text{ (New)} = W_0\text{(Old)} + \alpha\left(t - y_{in}\right) \tag{12}$$

$$W_1 \text{ (New)} = W_i\text{(Old)} + \alpha\left(t - y_{in}\right)x_i \tag{13}$$

where $i = 1, 2, 3, \ldots, n$.

Step 5: If the following conditions are satisfied, then the network is stopped or else:

The steps from the initial conditions are repeated.

Adaline network example:

By using an Adaline network, train the AND, NOT gate function with bipolar inputs and targets performs one epoch of training. The input values are given as:

X_1	X_2	t
1	1	−1
1	−1	1

Solution:

The initial weights are taken to be $W_1 = 0.1$, $W_2 = 0.2$, $b = 0.4$, learning rate $\alpha = 0.6$.

The weights are calculated until the least mean square is obtained.

First input:

$X_1 = 1; X_2 = 1; t = -1; b = 0.4; W_1 = 0.1; W_2 = 0.2; \alpha = 0.6$.

$Y_{in} = b + W_1X_1 + W_2X_2 = 0.7$.

$(t - Y_{in}) = -1.7$ not equal to zero, then update the weights,

W_1 (New) $= W_1$ (Old) $+ \alpha(t - Y_{in})X_1 = -0.42$.

W_2 (New) $= W_1$ (Old) $+ \alpha(t - Y_{in})X_2 = -0.82$.

b (New) $= b$ (Old) $+ \alpha(t - Y_{in}) = -0.62$.

$\Delta W_1 = \alpha(t - Y_{in})X_1 = -0.102; \Delta W_2 = \alpha(t - Y_{in})X_2 = -0.204;$

$\Delta b = \alpha(t - Y_{in}) = -1.02$.

To compute the error, $E = (t - Y_{in})^2 = 2.89$.

Similarly, for the second input:

$X_1 = 1; X_2 = -1; t = 1; W_1 = -0.41; W_2 = -0.82; b = -0.62$.

$Y_{in} = b + W_1X_1 + W_2X_2 = -0.24$.

$(t - Y_{in}) = 1.24$ not equal to zero.

Update the weights:

W_1 (New) $= W_1$ (Old) $+ \alpha(t - Y_{in})X_1 = 0.324$.

W_2 (New) $= W_1$ (Old) $+ \alpha(t - Y_{in})X_2 = -1.564$.

b (New) $= b$ (Old) $+ \alpha(t - Y_{in}) = 0.124; E = (t - Y_{in})^2 = 1.5376$.

Epoch 1: For the first input, $Y_{in} = b + W_1X_1 + W_2X_2 = -1.116$.

$(t - Y_{in}) = 0.116$; update the weights W_1 (New) $= W_1$ (Old) $+ \alpha(t - Y_{in})$ $X_1 = 0.3936$.

W_2 (New) $= W_1$ (Old) $+ \alpha(t - Y_{in})X_2 = -1.4944$; b (New) $= b$ (Old) $+ \alpha(t - Y_{in}) = 0.1936$; $E = (t - Y_{in})^2 = 0.01345$; $\Delta W_1 = \alpha(t - Y_{in})X_1 = 0.0696$.

$\Delta W_2 = \alpha(t - Y_{in})X_2 = 0.0696; \Delta b = \alpha(t - Y_{in}) = 0.0696$.

So now the error for two inputs varies from 2.89 to 0.013435.

Mean error = 2.89 + 0.01345 = 3.0245.

4.2 Back-propagation network

A back-propagation network is a common method of training a neural network. The training method is used for a multilayer neural network. The network consists of processing elements with continuous differentiable activation function. In this network, a gradient descent method is used for minimizing the total squared error of the network. Training the network of a given set of input/output pairs is identified and the network has a procedure for changing the weights to classify given input patterns correctly. This is the network where the error is propagated back to the hidden unit [13]. A back-propagation network is a sensitive approach for dividing the contribution to each weight. The two differences between updating the rule are as follows:

i. Activation of the hidden unit/neurons is used instead of activation of the input value or input neuron.

ii. The rule contains a gradient descent for the activation function to operate.

The back-propagation network is the reformation of the least mean square algorithm and varies the network weights to minimize mean squared error between the actual and desired outputs of the network. The network is trained and exerted using training samples of respective inputs and desired outputs are fetched. The algorithm consists of input and output layers to vary weights and analyze the arrangements of input in an acceptable manner. This algorithm takes a unique set compared to other techniques—during the learning period itself the weights are calculated [14]. The error signal is calculated by taking the difference between the calculated and target output. The result is measured in the output layer.

In the back-propagation network, the testing of data is implemented in the feed-forward path. While executing the network, it has the ability to operate in other hidden layers and is more efficient than operating with one hidden layer. The training process requires further time to train the network but the net result of the network during the training process produces a better result. The network is disintegrated into three categories, namely: (i) computation of the feed-forward network, (ii) back propagation to the output and hidden layer, and (iii) updating of weights. The algorithm will be terminated as the error value approaches a negligible numerical value.

The feed-forward computation network undergoes two processes. The first process receives the values of the hidden layer nodes, and in the second process the value from the hidden layer is used to compute the values of the output layer. Once the hidden layer values are determined, the network produces values from the hidden layer to the output layer. The hidden layer is observed once when the error from the output layer is propagated to the hidden layer. Weights are updated only if all the errors in the network are calculated. Further iterations help the network to train and produce a good training result. Block diagram of back propagation network is shown in **Figure 13**.

To calculate the derivative function for the squared error with respect to the weights of the network, the gradient descent method is used in the back-propagation network. The squared error function is defined by:

$$E = \frac{1}{2}(t - c)^2 \tag{14}$$

where E is the squared error, t is the target output for a given sample, and c is the actual output of the output neuron.

The constant (1/2) is included, while the differentiating constant is canceled. A limitation of using the back-propagation algorithm is that the input vectors are not normalized and because of that, its performance is not improved. The network identifies only the local minimum values not the global minimum function to determine the errors.

There are two types of back-propagation networks, namely static and recurrent neural networks. The static network produces a mapping of static input for static output. It helps to solve static classification issues like optical character recognition. The recurrent type is a feed-forward network, until a fixed value is obtained.

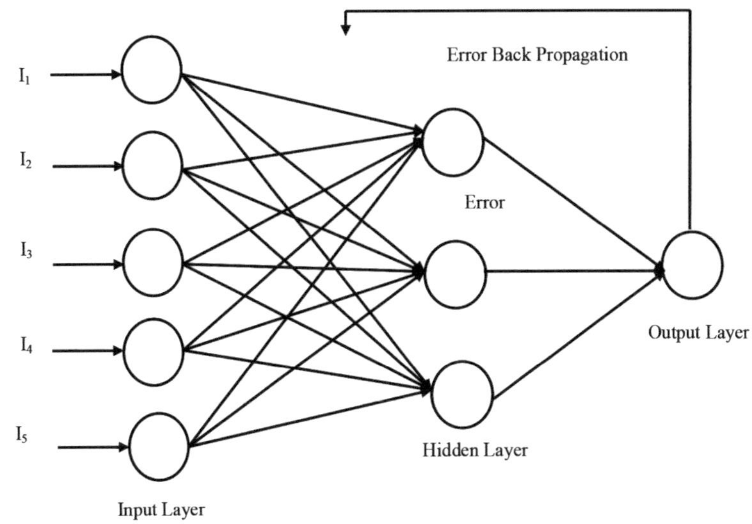

Figure 13.
Block diagram–Back propagation network.

The error is computed and propagated backward. Mapping of the recurrent network is nonstatic.

4.2.1 Learning process of the back-propagation network

Each neuron is composed of two units. The primary unit sums the product of weight coefficients and input signals. The secondary unit realizes the nonlinear function, in which the neurons are transferred to the activation function. Signal e is the adder output signal, and $Y = F(e)$ is the output signal of the nonlinear element. Signal y is also the output signal of the neuron. **Figure 14** shows the learning process of the network.

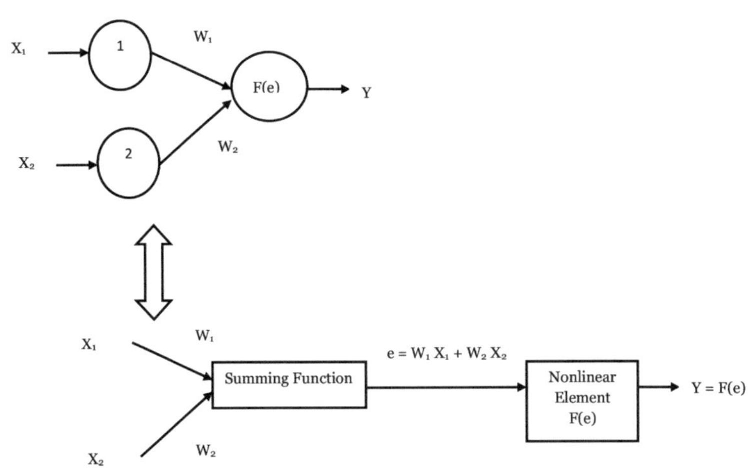

Figure 14.
Learning process of the back-propagation network.

A training data set is required to instruct the neural network. The training data set consists of input signals (X_1 and X_2) assigned to corresponding target output. The training network is an iterative process, and for each iteration, weight coefficients of nodes are changed using new data from the training data set. Each training step starts by forcing both input signals from the training set. It is possible to determine the output signal values for each neuron in every network layer.

Training steps of the back-propagation algorithm:

Step 1: The network of random weights is initialized.
Step 2: The training process takes place using the following steps:

i. Initially, training values are given as input to network and calculate the output of the network.

ii. The training process (i.e., starting with the output layer, back to the input layer):

   a. Compares the network output with the correct output (an error function).

   b. Adapts the weights in the current layer.

Step 3: By using the gradient descent method, the error is minimized.

Step 4: The propagating delta rule is used to adjust the error backward from the output to the hidden layer to the inputs. The back-propagation network is shown in **Figure 15**.

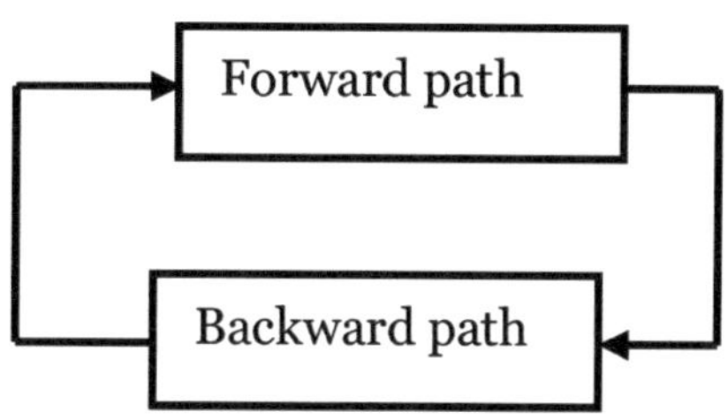

Figure 15.
Layer of back-propagation network.

Back-propagation neural network example problem:

By using the back-propagation network, train the input vectors for the following functions: $X_1 = 0.15$; $X_2 = 0.10$; $b_1 = 0.45$; $b_2 = 0.80$; $t_1 = 0.10$; $t_2 = 0.85$. The example of back propagation network is shown in **Figure 16**.

Solution:

Initialize the weights as $W_1 = 0.35$; $W_2 = 0.50$; $W_3 = 0.75$; $W_4 = 1.25$; $W_5 = 0.80$; $W_6 = 0.56$; $W_7 = 0.45$; $W_8 = 0.56$.

Activation function, $H_1 = \frac{1}{1+e^{-H1.}}$

Forward pass:

$H_1 = b1 + W_1X_1 + W_2X_2 = 0.55215$

Out $H_1 = \frac{1}{1+e^{-H1}} = 0.6346$

$H_2 = b1 + W_3X_1 + W_4X_2 = 0.6875$

Out $H_2 = \frac{1}{1+e^{-H2}} = 0.66541$

Now, for calculating Y_1:

$Y_1 = \text{Out } H_1 * W_5 + \text{Out } H_2 * W_6 + b_2 = 1.6803096$

Out $Y_1 = \frac{1}{1+e^{-y1}} = 0.842945$

In the same way:

$Y_1 = \text{Out } H_2 * W_8 + \text{Out } H_1 * W_7 + b_2 = 1.45819$

Out $Y_2 = \frac{1}{1+e^{-y2}}$ = 0.811255

Calculating total error:

$E_{\text{Total}} = \sum \frac{1}{2}(\text{Target} - \text{Output})^2 = \frac{1}{2}(T_1 - \text{Out } Y_1)^2 + \frac{1}{2}(T_2 - \text{Out } Y_2)^2 = 0.27665$

Backward pass:

To update weights, consider W_5

Error at $W_5 = \frac{\Delta E_{\text{Total}}}{\Delta W_5} = \frac{\Delta E_{\text{Total}}}{\Delta \text{Out}_{Y1}} * \frac{\Delta \text{Out}_{Y1}}{\Delta Y_1} * \frac{\Delta Y_1}{\Delta W_5} = 0.07035$

Updating W_5, $W_5 = W_5 - \eta * \frac{\Delta E_{\text{Total}}}{\Delta W_5}$

η is the learning rate = 0.1; W_5 = 0.7929

In the same way, calculations are done for updating the weights for W_6, W_7, and W_8. In a similar manner, the weights are updated for W_1, W_2, W_3, and W_4 by using hidden layers in the network.

Advantages of the back-propagation network:

i. The network is fast, simple, and programming code is easy when compared to other networks. It supports high-speed applications.

ii. It does not require any parameters to tune except for the number of inputs, and the network does not require prior knowledge to implement.

Disadvantages of the back-propagation network:

i. The network consumes more time for training and is stuck in local minima resulting in suboptimal solutions.

ii. A broad amount of input and output data is required, so there exists a complexity when solving a problem. The network is quite sensitive for noisy data.

iii. A major drawback occurs in a single-layer signal and the network cannot learn the process. It approximates nonlinear separable tasks and functions.

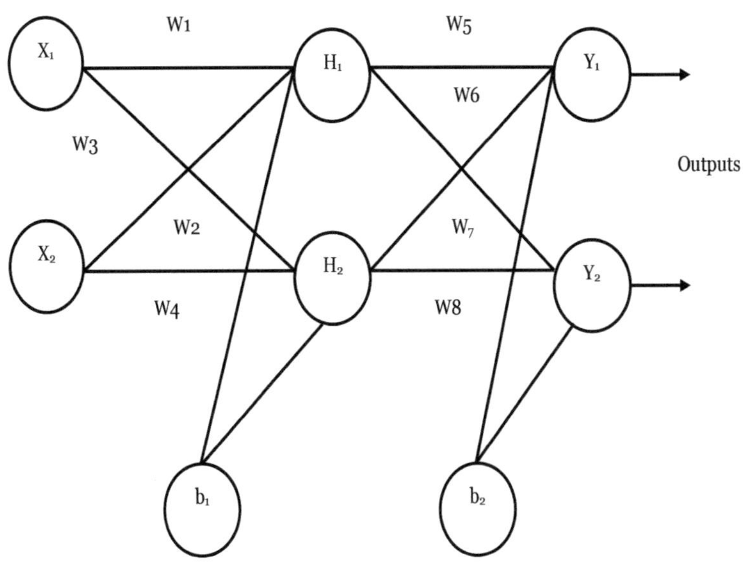

Figure 16.
Back-propagation network.

Applications of the back-propagation network:

The network is especially useful for machine learning processes, face recognition systems, image or speech recognition, classification, function approximation, time series prediction, etc.

4.3 Radial basis function

The radial basis function is a three-layer feed-forward neural network. The transfer function of the hidden layer is the radial basis function. It is derived from function approximation theory. In a neural network, the radial basis function is modeled by the narrow-tuned feedback that is viewed in biological neurons [15]. This type of tuned response is found in several parts of nervous systems. In a feed-forward network, one hidden layer is required for the design of simple structures of lower computational cost. A radial basis network is a nonlinear type that makes the bias function change. The network is used to create regression-type problems.

The radial basis function is composed of three layers, namely input layer, hidden layer, and output layer. The sigmoid type of activation function is not used as in the case of the back-propagation algorithm, whereas the radial basis network uses Gaussian function as an activation function. The input layer consists of neurons with a linear activation function given to the hidden layer. The connection between input and hidden layers is not observed, which means that input neurons received from each hidden neuron remain the same in the network [16]. The Gaussian activation function is determined by:

$$F(d) = \exp\left(-d^2/\mu^2\right) \tag{15}$$

where μ is the real parameter value and d is the distance between the input and intermediate vector (the distance is usually measured in terms of Euclidean norm).

Consider the input vector for a period of "m" time denoted by:

$$Y(m) = \left[y_1(m), y_2(m), y_3(m) \ldots ..y_n(m)\right]T \tag{16}$$

The intermediate vector for each hidden neuron is denoted by B_i (for i = 1, 2, 3, ..., k), where "k" is the number of neurons in the hidden layer. The output of each neuron in the radial basis function is given by:

$$h_i(n) = F_i(\| Y(m) - B_i\|), \text{for } i = 1, 2, \ldots, k \tag{17}$$

Operation of the radial basis network is based on a least mean square algorithm and the local minima values are used for training the neural network. The training process requires a longer computation time but the learning period is less in the network [17]. Schematic representation of the radial basis network is shown in **Figure 17**.

Every neuron in the radial basis function stores a sample vector from the training set. The neuron in the network compares the input vector with its sample vector, and outputs a value between 0 and 1. If the input is equal to the sample vector, then the output of that neuron will be 1. The neuron's response value is called the activation value.

Every neuron in the radial basis function computes a measure of the similarity between input and sample vector. The values are obtained from the training set. Input vectors are similar to sample vectors and return a value closer to 1. There are different possible choices of similarity functions, but the most popular is based on

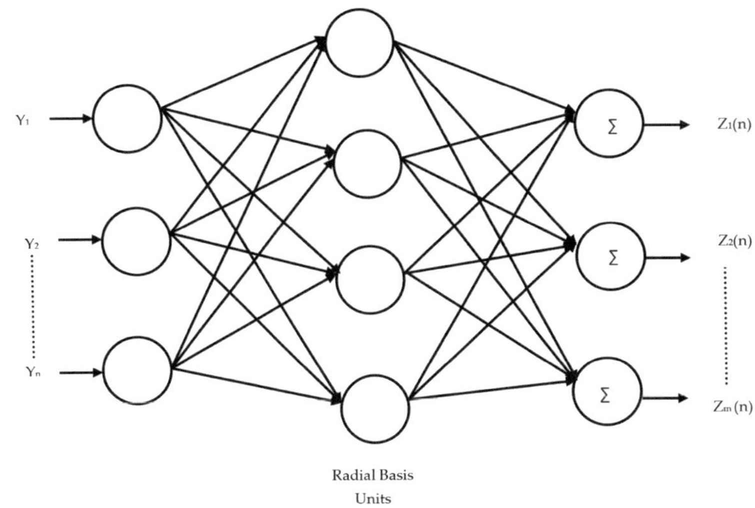

Figure 17.
Radial basis network.

the Gaussian function. The equation for a Gaussian function with a one-dimensional input is given by:

$$F(x) = \frac{1}{\sigma\sqrt{2\Pi}} e^{-\frac{(x-\mu)^2}{2\sigma^2}} \tag{18}$$

where x is the input, μ is the mean, and σ is the standard deviation.

Training steps of the radial basis function:

Step 1: Initialize the input vector Y from the obtained training set.

Step 2: Determine the output of the hidden layer.

Step 3: Compute the output Z and compare with the desired value. Adjust each weight W accordingly:

$$Z = W_{ij}(n+1) = W_{ij}(n) + \eta\left(y_j - z_j\right)y_i \tag{19}$$

Step 4: Repeat the steps from 1 to 3 for each vector in the training set.

Step 5: Repeat the steps from 1 to 4 unless the error is smaller than the maximum acceptable limit.

Applications of the radial basis function:

Applications of the radial basis function are function approximation type, classification, interpolation, and time series prediction. These applications provide various industrial uses like stock price prediction, fraud detection in financial transactions, and anomaly detection of data.

5. Conclusion

This chapter encompassed the learning algorithms of neural networks such as adaline, back-propagation, and the radial basis network. Of all the learning methods, the back-propagation network is effective in training because of its mature back-propagating mechanism. The training process of the radial basis function is rapid and almost matches the ability of the back-propagation network. The radial basis function is a good substitute for the back-propagation network. When the selected features are clear enough, then the back-propagation network produces satisfactory results. The study of neural network has been slow, but now computers have better processing power. The back-propagation network effectively solves the exclusive-OR problem.

Author details

T.D. Raheni* and P. Thirumoorthi
Kumaraguru College of Technology, Coimbatore, Tamilnadu, India

*Address all correspondence to: raheni92@gmail.com

References

[1] Sivanandam SN, Paulraj M. Introduction to Artificial Neural Networks. Delhi, India: Vikas Publishing House Pvt. Ltd.; 2011

[2] Deepa SN, Sivanandam SN. Principles of Soft Computing. 2nd ed. Delhi, India: Wiley India Pvt. Ltd.; 2011. ISBN 10: 8126527412/ISBN 13: 9788126527410

[3] Zurada JM. Introduction to Artificial Neural Systems. 1st ed. Eagan, USA: Jaico Publishing House; 1992. ISBN 10: 0314933913/ISBN 13: 978-0314933911

[4] Eluyode OS, Akomolafe DT. Comparative study of biological and artificial neural networks. European Journal of Applied Engineering and Scientific Research. 2013;**2**(1):36-46. ISSN: 2278–0041

[5] Fausett L. Fundamentals of Neural Network Architectures, Algorithms and Applications. Florida Institute of Technology. Singapore: Pearson Education; 1994. ISBN: 978-81-317-0053-2

[6] Sathya R, Abraham A. Comparison of supervised and unsupervised learning algorithms for pattern classification. International Journal of Advanced Research in Artificial Intelligence (IJARAI). 2013;**2**(2):34-38

[7] Khanum M, Mahoob T. A survey on unsupervised learning algorithms for automation, classification and maintenance. International Journal of Computer Applications. 2015;**119**(13): 34-39

[8] Du K. Clustering: A neural network approach. Neural Networks. 2010;**23**(1): 89-107

[9] Nagabandi A, Kahn G. Model-Based Reinforcement Learning with Neural Network Dynamics. California, USA: Berkeley Artificial Intelligence Research; 2017

[10] Ali Zilouchian and Mo Jamshidi. Intelligent Control Systems Using Soft Computing Methodologies. CRC Press LLC; 2001. ISBN: 0–8493–1875–0

[11] Widrow B, Lehr MA. Artificial Neural Networks of Perceptron, Madaline and Back Propagation Family. Neurobionics. Germany: Elsevier Science Publishers; 1993:133-205

[12] Maind SB, Wankar P. Research paper on the basics of artificial neural networks. International Journal on Recent and Innovation Trends in Computing and Communication. 2014; **2**(1):96-100. ISSN: 2321–816 9

[13] Kishore R, Kaur T. Backpropagation algorithm: An artificial neural network approach for pattern recognition. International Journal of Scientific & Engineering Research. 2012;**3**(6):1-4. ISSN: 2229–5518

[14] Joshi SC, Cheeran AN. MATLAB based back-propagation neural network for automatic speech recognition. 2014; **3**(7):10498-10504. DOI: 10.15662/ijareeie.2014.0307016. ISSN (Print): 2320–3765; ISSN (Online): 2278–8875

[15] Karkalos NE, Markopoulos AP. Surface roughness prediction during grinding: A comparison of ANN and RBFNN models. WSEAS Transactions on System and Control. 2016;**11**:384-389. E-ISSN: 2224–2856

[16] Wong KP. Artificial intelligence and neural network applications in power systems. In: IEEE 2nd International Conference on Advances in Power System Control, Operation and Management, Hongkong. 1993

[17] Mohamad H. Hassoun. Fundamentals of Artificial Neural Networks. 1st ed. MA, USA: MIT Press Cambridge; 2010. ISBN: 978-81-203-1356-9

Chapter 2

Simulated Real-Time Controller for Tuning Algorithm Using Modified Hill Climbing Approach Based on Model Reference Adaptive Control System

Ahmed Abdulelah Ahmed, Azura Che Soh, Mohd Khair Hassan, Samsul Bahari Mohd Noor and Hafiz Rashidi Harun

Abstract

In this chapter, an intelligent algorithmic tuning technique suitable for real-time system tuning based on hill climbing optimization algorithm and model reference adaptive control (MRAC) system technique is proposed. Although many adaptive control tuning methodologies depend partially or completely on online plant system identification, the proposed method uses only the model that is used to design the original controller, leading to simplified calculations that do not require neither high processing power nor long processing time, as opposed to identification technique calculations. Additionally, a modified hill climbing algorithm that is developed in this research is specifically designed, configured and tailored for the automatic tuning of control systems. The modified hill climbing algorithm uses a systematic movement when searching for new solution candidates. The algorithm measures the quality of the solution candidate based on error function. The error function is generated by comparing the system response with a desired reference response. The algorithm tests new solution candidates using step signals iteratively. The results showed the algorithm effectiveness to drive the system response. The simulation results illustrate that the method schemes proposed in this study show a viable and versatile solution to deal with controller tuning for systems with model inaccuracies as well as controller real-time calibration problem.

Keywords: real-time controller, auto-tuning algorithm, optimization, modified hill climbing approach, model reference adaptive control system (MRAC)

1. Introduction

The increasing complexity of industrial processes is always pushing for advancements and innovations in technologies involved in industrial processing, including control systems engineering. The invention of computers paved the way for new and intelligent possibilities in control system technologies [1]. The last four decades witnessed a rapid movement towards the field of intelligent control [2–5]. This movement was being coupled with what were already growing new ways and paradigms of applying automatic control for even more decades prior to computer inception [6]. Control systems advanced from having a sensor-actuator relationship moulded together in feedback paradigm to complex multilayer interrelated sets of systems [2].

In designing control systems, system modelling can be considered the backbone of the design process. Many modelling techniques were introduced by researchers through time. The introduction of computers pushed towards better models [7]. However, no matter how good modelling techniques are getting, whether being based on analytical analysis or identification methods, no model would be a perfect match to the system it is depicting. There would always be an accuracy factor affecting the model quality.

The controller design is dependent upon the system model. As a result, the end-product controller quality is hugely dependent upon the model quality, and, to a degree, the model mimics the behaviour of the system it represents [8]. However, due to the vast and deep complexity of most systems humans encounter in the world, whether physical, economical or any other types of systems, humans tend to build mathematical models for control purposes as simplified as possible in order to simplify the controller design process. That simplification comes with a major flaw, which is a decreased accuracy of system presentation by the model. The effects of this flaw, however, are often not important or of insignificant consideration for the control system. However, sometimes it is effective to a degree of generating a degraded control quality over the system. That is especially present when models encounter even more degradation in quality due to system parameter fluctuation over time due to various operational effects.

However, sometimes control strategy should be built to deal with a high or variable model inaccuracy. Complex systems would often be represented with simplified models to reduce calculation time and efforts [9], which result in less accurate models [8], while in many cases, the model accuracy degrades over time due to either sudden system variable change due to undisclosed reasons or gradual variable change from normal wear and tear of system components [10].

Due to control system design procedures being highly dependent on the mathematical model of the controlled plant [9], a high model quality and accuracy is critically needed. However, in some dynamic systems, it is very difficult (or even impossible) to have models with good accuracy that are sufficient to predict the plant behaviour in a way that an acceptably controlled performance can be produced.

On the other hand, sometimes even if mathematical models are sufficiently accurate in a way that a good controlled performance can be obtained, long-term operation (or even short term in some cases) gradually increases the difference between the plant and its dynamical model, which, in turn, would lead to a degraded performance.

It is a common task in industrial applications to recalibrate the control system periodically, as the plant parameters suffer various fluctuations from their original values that were used in designing the control system. The calibration procedure usually requires professional attendance, which adds up to more maintenance costs. Also, the experimental nature of the manual calibration often requires at least part of the plant operations to be halted [2, 11].

Instead of relying on manual calibration, this research proposes an automatic tuning scheme and algorithm specifically designed for control systems to deal with model inaccuracies and parameter fluctuations during real-time operation without the need to halt plant operation.

2. Model reference adaptive control (MRAC)

Adaptive control systems were among the first techniques in automatic control to tackle the problem of parameter fluctuation [12]. The various techniques required a continuous system observation or identification to improve the model quality while adapting the controller parameters according to the new model [13, 14]. However, the general approach of adaptive control is different to that of real-time optimization. Real-time optimization techniques attempt to tune or optimize the control system generally by changing the operating conditions in order to get the desired response. There is no online modelling involved. It was introduced mainly in chemical processes and plants to deal with the autonomous calibration problem [15]. However, it is possible to generalize its framework to deal with other types of control systems [16].

Model reference adaptive control (MRAC) is one of the most important adaptive techniques in control engineering [12, 13], as it provides a good viewpoint to thoroughly analyse adaptive systems [12].

The MRAC system structure is generally considered to have two feedback loops [12, 17], an inner feedback loop that is the ordinary feedback that is compared with the set point and fed to the controller and an outer feedback loop that modifies controller parameters based on the adaptation mechanism. In this technique, a reference response is to be followed by the system. The reference response is generated by using a prebuilt reference model [12]. The controller parameters are adjusted based on the difference error between the reference model response and the controlled process response as shown in **Figure 1**.

The adaptation algorithm adjusts the controller parameters so that the error is reduced to zero [12]. Parameter estimation or process measurements help in forming the adaptation rule that the controller would be adjusted according to.

MRAC uses one of three mechanics to adjust controller parameters by finding an adaptation law. The Massachusetts Institute of Technology (MIT) rule is a gradient method that was the first used mechanic [12]. However, the MIT rule could sometimes lead to unstable system response [13]. Later, the Lyapunov stability theory and the passivity theory were also used to generate the adaptation law that was proved to be robust and stable [12, 13].

It should be noted that there is a large correlation between MRAC and self-tuning regulator (STR). Actually, some STRs can be considered as MRAC and vice versa [12, 17].

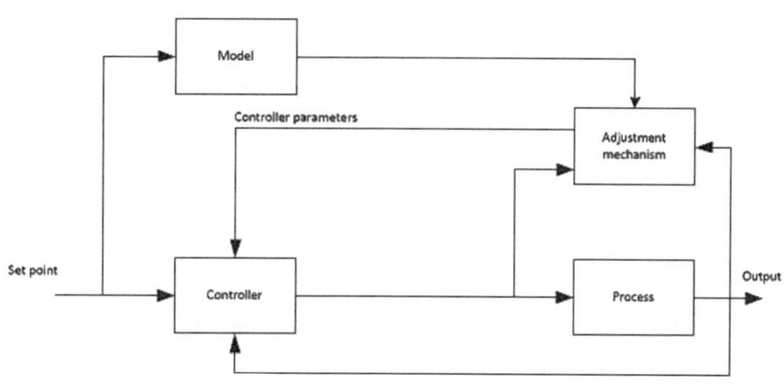

Figure 1.
Model reference adaptive control schematic diagram [12–13, 17].

3. Overview of hill climbing algorithm

It was proved that although process models are often inaccurate, they are sufficient to provide general knowledge for real-time optimization problem [18], while real-time optimization problem can be solved iteratively [16, 19]. The tuning operation includes searching for new actuator settings (e.g. gains) to achieve the desired performance [16]. Many optimization algorithms are available, but most of these algorithms are not suitable for real-time tuning due to several reasons such as time-consuming calculation or the algorithm's inability to provide a transitional solution until a satisfactory solution is found [20]. Obviously, the latter is essential for real-time operation.

In this research, a real-time controller tuning algorithm based on the principles of hill climbing optimization algorithm is proposed. The algorithm is suitable for controller automatic tuning in real-time. Hill climbing is one of the oldest traditional optimization algorithms. The procedure begins by selecting an arbitrary solution in the searching space and then testing the surrounding solutions, one at a time. If the algorithm finds a better solution than the currently selected solution, the better solution is selected, and the procedure is done again until the algorithm cannot find a solution that is better than the currently selected one, and at that point, the optimization stops, and the best found solution is considered the best solution [21].

In **Figure 2**, searching for a maximum height point is assumed. Let's suppose that the arbitrary starting point was point a. When the optimization starts, hill climbing would check the sides of point a and decide to move in the shown direction, since the left side gives a larger (height) value than the value of point a. On the other hand, the algorithm would not select to move to the right, since the value is less than that of point a. This movement would continue until the selection reaches the maximum point denoted as 'maximum height (global)' at which the optimization is considered finished and the selected point is the optimum, since no more movement is possible because points on both sides hold less value than the selected one.

However, starting arbitrarily at point b of **Figure 2** would result in the optimization to stop when reaching the point denoted as 'maximum (local)'. When the optimization starts from point b, the selection would take the direction shown in the figure. But that movement would stop upon reaching the local optimum point because the algorithm would be trapped at a point that is better than all its neighbours, although that point is not the overall best point of the search space.

The above example demonstrates a major flaw of the hill climbing algorithm, which is that the choice of the first solution at beginning of optimization can lead to a huge impact on the final result in case the function being optimized has multiple

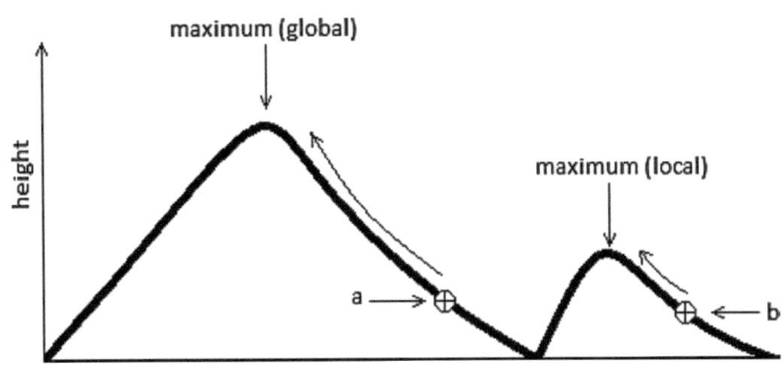

Figure 2.
An illustration of how hill climbing works.

optimum points [22, 23]. Therefore, hill climbing can easily be trapped in local optimum if applied to functions with non-uni-model landscapes [21]. In the same way, it can be trapped in plateaux or ridges also [21–23].

Even with its shortcomings, hill climbing is considered one of the best local searching algorithms [21] because it tends to move towards the local optimum quite fast [21, 23]. Therefore, many modifications to simple hill climbing were proposed by researchers to overcome its negatives and making it usable for a wider scope [21].

Stochastic hill climbing uses a random choice on the next uphill movement, which can give better results in some cases. Another variant is first-choice hill climbing, which is a modified form of stochastic hill climbing. In this algorithm, random steps are generated, and the movement occurs when a solution better than the current solution is found [21]. One of the other modifications is random-restart hill climbing. In this algorithm, simple hill climbing is used but with restarting from a new arbitrary point after each local search finds the optima. Hence, the probability of finding the global optimum is increased after several repetitions [21, 23].

Hill climbing, at its simple form, is very useful for real-time controller tuning, since the algorithm moves in the search space with small steps by changing one variable at a time while promoting a transitional solution until a final solution can be found [6, 10, 20]. On the other hand, all modifications to hill climbing that could be used to overcome its shortcomings are based on a random selection or movement in the search space [21]. Therefore, these variants produce the same consequences of genetic algorithms regarding controller tuning in real time. Unpredictability and instability of the response are not far from being possible.

4. The modified hill climbing algorithm

A systematic movement modification to hill climbing algorithm is suggested. Our modification is targeted at real-time tuning of control systems.

The main concept suggested as modification is to keep exploring the neighbourhood of the current best solution and keep moving candidates further from the best solution in both directions alternately (moving towards a bigger and a smaller value for each variable, one variable at a time), even if the surrounding candidates yield a degraded quality, until a satisfactory solution is found after searching for best values to all the elements of the controller. This is done by changing one variable at a time and testing the system by applying a testing step input iteratively [16].

An offset value must be specified that represents the minimum movement size from the current best value to the next candidate. This offset will be used as the discretization interval to find the movement amount for each variable in each iteration. That is done by simply increasing the movement amount by the value of the offset. **Figure 3** shows the general tuning operation workflow.

Instead of moving in one direction when searching for new candidates in classic hill climbing (the direction of the best neighbourhood of starting position), and keeping on moving until no further improvement in the fitness function is met, searching in the proposed algorithm would keep moving alternately between two directions and will not stop at maxima points. The searching for new candidates would stop when fitness (error function result) achieves the designer's requirements.

To demonstrate the moving mechanics when searching for candidates, it will be assumed that a function that has a single variable parameter is required to be tuned in order to achieve certain function fitness. It is also assumed that an arbitrary starting value of 'a' is assigned to the variable parameter, which gives a fitness value

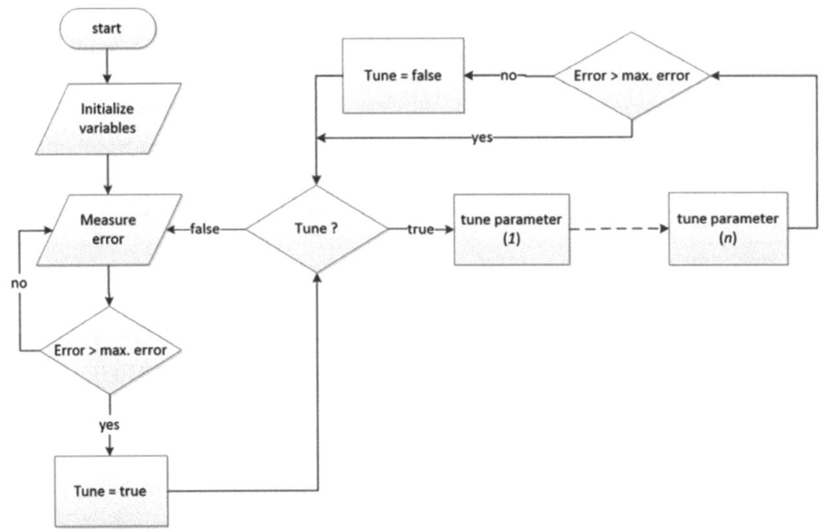

Figure 3.
Tuning algorithm schematic diagram for system with (n) variables.

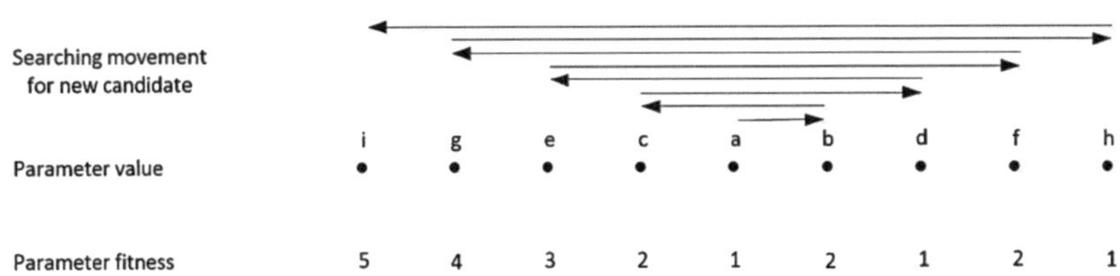

Figure 4.
Demonstration of movement when searching for new candidates.

of '1', as demonstrated in **Figure 4**. It is also assumed that the performance would be acceptable if fitness is equal or greater than '4', and therefore, tuning will stop if a fitness value of '4' or greater is reached, regardless if that value is the best value possible or not.

Each point in **Figure 4** is larger than the point to its left by an amount, called 'offset', and smaller than the point to its right by the same amount. The offset is the smallest movement the tuning algorithm is allowed to move when searching for candidates. The offset value must be determined by the designer depending on the system sensitivity to gain changes.

Considering tuning the function of **Figure 4** again, if the tuning started from point 'a', where tuning is required due to it having fitness of '1', the algorithm moves the candidate selection to the right by the amount of offset, so point 'b' is chosen as the new candidate. When testing fitness of point 'b', the algorithm finds it better than that of point 'a', and therefore, point 'b' will be promoted as the current best solution. However, fitness is still less than the minimum required value of '4'; hence, tuning continues. The movement amount is increased by the amount of offset and reversed in direction, which will result in selecting point 'c' as the new candidate. Testing the fitness of point 'c' shows that it is equal to the current best fitness, and as a result, no promoting is required, since no advantage will be acquired. Next, the movement amount is increased by the amount of offset again and reversed in direction.

The next candidate will therefore be point 'd', which has fitness less than the current best fitness, so this point will not be promoted. Increasing the movement amount by offset and reversing direction will select point 'e' as the next candidate.

There is still a fitness of point ‘b’ as the best, so point ‘b’ remains promoted as the best parameter value until now, even though it doesn’t satisfy the design requirements. When checking the fitness of the last selected candidate, point ‘e’, the algorithm finds that this fitness is better than the last best fitness. Therefore, point ‘e’ is promoted as the best current solution, although it also doesn’t satisfy the design requirements. The performance of point ‘b’ (and all other points other than the best point) is forgotten and won’t be memorized. The same procedure will continue until a parameter value with a satisfactory fitness is found (point ‘g’ in this example) by the algorithm, and then the tuning will stop, and the last best parameter selection is fixed to the system. If fitness is degraded for any reason once again, the tuning procedure will start again until it finds new satisfactory parameters. It is noticed that the algorithm doesn’t necessarily lead to finding the global best solution (point ‘i’ in the example), but if a solution exists, then it will be found, since the algorithm would theoretically pass through every possible candidate unless a solution is found.

Steps being done when tuning consists of the following:

1. Calculate variable candidate according to the following equation:

$$newV_c = oldV_c + (V_{md} * V_m) \tag{1}$$

2. Store current variable value as the best.

3. Change the variable value to the candidate value.

4. Check performance.

   i. If not improved, restore the best value to the variable, and set flag to change next variable.

   ii. If improved, reset all other variables movements around their best values.

5. Calculate the next direction of movement.

$$newV_{md} = -1 * oldV_{md} \tag{2}$$

6. Calculate the next amount of movement.

$$newV_m = oldV_m + offset \tag{3}$$

7. Check flag to decide on what variable to tune.

Notes
V_c: variable candidate
V_m: variable candidate movement amount
V_{md}: variable candidate movement direction

The following **Figure 5** below demonstrates operations to be done when tuning each single variable.

Like most optimization algorithms in general, and hill climbing specifically, the use of the algorithm does not guarantee the best solution for certain systems under certain conditions. However, if some solutions do exist, it is guaranteed that this modified algorithm will find one of them. The solution under the same circumstances would always be unique assuming similar starting conditions. However,

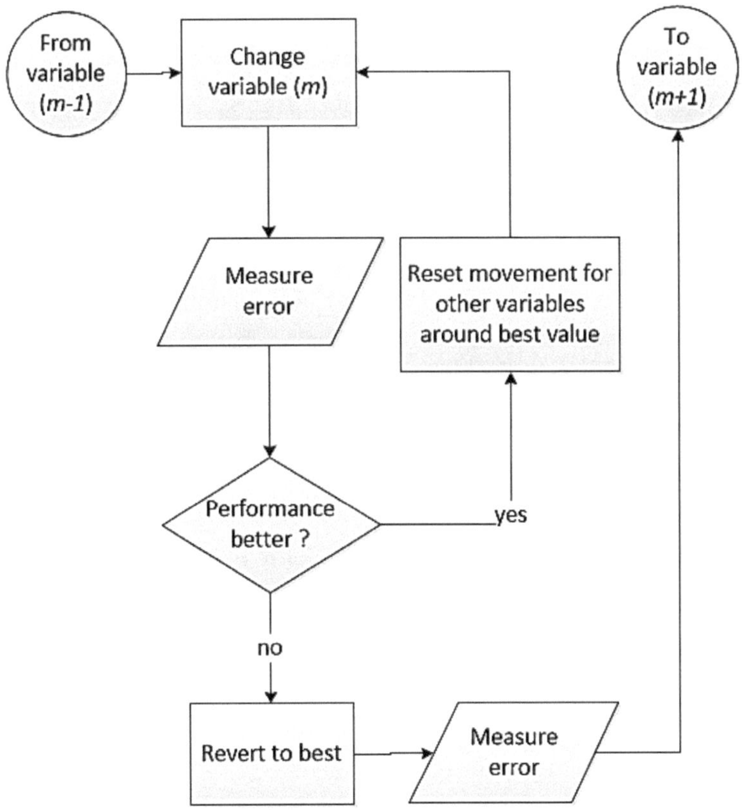

Figure 5.
Operations when tuning the m-th variable.

during the experiments at least one solution was assumed to be available within a certain error margin.

5. Control paradigm

The suggested control paradigm is to compare the actual system response with a desired reference response and then generate an error function that decides on whether to tune the system controller or not as demonstrated in **Figure 6**. This paradigm is inspired by the adaptive control paradigm, although it is not a complete replication, since no parameter estimation is involved. The desired reference response is generated by designing a controller for the system model.

The tuning drives the actual system response to act the same way as that of the modelled system. This is to be done by tuning the actual system controller [24].

In order to make a decision on whether it is required to tune the process controller or to check whether the latest modification improved the performance, a comparison between the desired reference response and the process response must be conducted.

This comparison generates an error signal using the error function block in **Figure 5**. If the error signal is smaller than the maximum allowed error, then tuning is not needed. If the error signal is larger than the maximum allowed error, then tuning is needed. This is also done after each tuning iteration. If the error signal becomes smaller than the maximum allowed error after making a tuning pass over all the tuneable parameters, tuning will stop. Otherwise, tuning will continue.

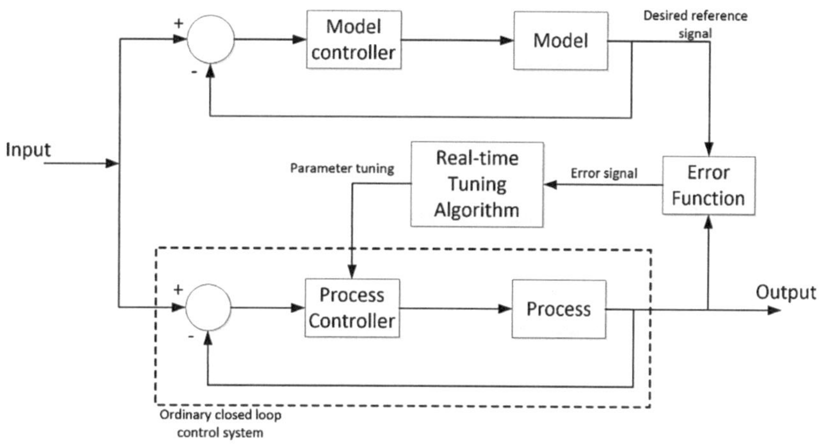

Figure 6.
Schematic diagram of the proposed design.

The error function itself is not a mere subtraction equation. In order to get sufficient clarification about the amount of the difference between the process response and the desired reference response, the designer needs to consider a period that covers both transient response to the experimental step input change and a steady-state response. Consequently, the designer must specify an inspection period so error measurements can be collected. Next, the error function can be the average value of the errors measured over a specified period of time, or it can be the summation of those error values or any other suitable function. The period can be identified from prior knowledge of the system, since the designer has a model of the process; though not accurate, it can give a general assessment of the required period. Meanwhile, error reading should be put in discrete form as pairs of model and process outputs that were taken simultaneously.

Hence, it can be considered that the error function is a cost function that is to be minimized below a certain value. That value is the maximum allowed error, which is also to be specified by the designer, reflecting the closeness required between process response and the desired reference response.

If tuning is needed (when the error generated by the error function is larger than the maximum allowed error), then the tuning algorithm will start to change the controller variables (e.g. Kp, Ki and Kd in a PID controller) one by one and measure the error after each single variable change. If the error is reduced, the algorithm would keep the new value for the variable and move on to change the next variable. Otherwise the algorithm would reset the variable to its best value and move on to change the next variable.

If a value substitution happened (when finding a better value for one of the variables), the movement amount for each other variable is reset to the minimum, which is the offset value. This is to make sure that the algorithm would search the neighbourhoods of the best values of variables again when any change happens to one of them in order to find the best possible values for them, since they could be strongly related to each other dynamically. For example, if we have a PID controller being optimized and the value of Kp is increased, then the system will be faster but will generate a higher overshoot. So, Kd should be tuned a little to lower the overshoot.

This procedure should be repeated until the error becomes less than the maximum allowed error. Then, the tuning will be stopped until the error fluctuates outside the allowed margins again. The model controller can be of any type.

5.1 Algorithm properties

To emphasize the advantages and usability of the proposed modified hill climbing algorithm, this section discusses the properties of the algorithm under real-time controller tuning considerations.

Firstly, the algorithm uses very simple calculations during system monitoring and controller tuning. All equations involved in the design consist of basic combinations of principal operations such as addition or division only. Therefore, the algorithm retains high applicability for real-time execution, since the calculation time of such simple equations can be considered irrelevant in current electronics; hence, it is very easy to be implemented using embedded computer systems. The shear simplicity of the calculations is largely attributed to the lack of online parameter estimation and to the simplicity of searching for a candidate mechanism which is partly inherited from hill climbing.

Secondly, due to its hill climbing inheritance, the algorithm is very applicable to tune multivariable controllers. Dealing with controller variables one at a time is one of the core principles taken from hill climbing that serves very well to overcome the tuning task in a systematic and procedural approach, without the need for randomness in candidates' selection which nullifies the ability to tune the controller based on the dynamic relation between the controller variables.

Thirdly, in principle, the algorithm is not tied to a specific type of controller. Any type of controllers can be tuned theoretically, using any heuristic tuning method. Although certain algorithms can be more suitable for certain types of controllers than to others, some controllers are better not be tuned heuristically. However, in the case study included in this paper, PID controllers were used. This is a result of PID controllers themselves being suitable for heuristic controller tuning in general, and real-time tuning specifically, as PID has few parameters to tune, reducing tuning time and effort.

Fourthly, an important property of the proposed algorithm, which is also inherited from classic hill climbing, is the ability to promote transitional solutions until a satisfactory solution can be found. In fact, this transitional solution is part of the overall tuning procedure, since the proposed algorithm repeatedly compares last candidate performance with the last best available solution performance. This property is essential for real-time tuning, as it keeps the controller running with the best possible variable selection periodically between new candidate testing instances, sustaining the best possible output performance for the furthest possible period and, in turn, reducing the chances of instability or other undesirable possibilities.

5.2 Important aspects to consider when applying the proposed design

Many design considerations should be taken during the design of any control system. These considerations are dependent on the performance requirements and design methodology. Here the concentration is put on the considerations that are related to the real-time controller tuning paradigm using the modified hill climbing algorithm.

Quality of the controller (model controller in **Figure 6**) used to generate desired reference response is a very sensitive aspect. Great care should be taken as this step will decide the shape of the response that we are aiming for. The desired reference response should be physically viable (within an allowed error margins).

The error function must be made so that it can detect the variable changing effect on the response. That is also directly related to the maximum error value and how the error is (difference between model and process outputs) being recorded (the period being considered after the change and the timing of collecting the signal). Consequently, the period spent on recording the outputs of the model and process should start from, or before applying, the experimental step input and end sometime after reaching a steady state.

The offset value should be chosen in the middle ground between the system sensitivity to variable or gain changes and the speed at which the candidates will move in the search space. To clarify this, it should be noted that the larger the offset value, the faster the algorithm reaches a solution, since the offset value would affect the new candidate movement amount. However, that would be on the expense of a reduced fine tuning accuracy, since no smaller steps than the offset is possible, which could mean missing a better parameter value point close to a relatively good point.

If necessary, some simple conditions can be applied to avoid well-known undesired candidates (e.g. negative gains for PID controller).

6. Simulation experiment

In order to demonstrate the design success, it was applied to a twin rotor MIMO system (TRMS). The results were obtained using simulations on MATLAB and Simulink software. The TRMS system used in the experiment is provided by Quanser [25]. This system is a two degree of freedom (2-DOF) mechanical system. It resembles a helicopter system using two rotors, one as a main rotor and one as a tail rotor, as seen in **Figure 7**.

It has two degrees of freedom: one for pitch angle and one for yaw angle. The device manual includes a linearized state-space model of the system [25], while the software bundled with the device includes a nonlinear Simulink model of the system. The linearized model was used to generate the desired reference signal, which was used for tuning the nonlinear model controller in Simulink.

Figure 7.
Quanser 2-DOF helicopter [25].

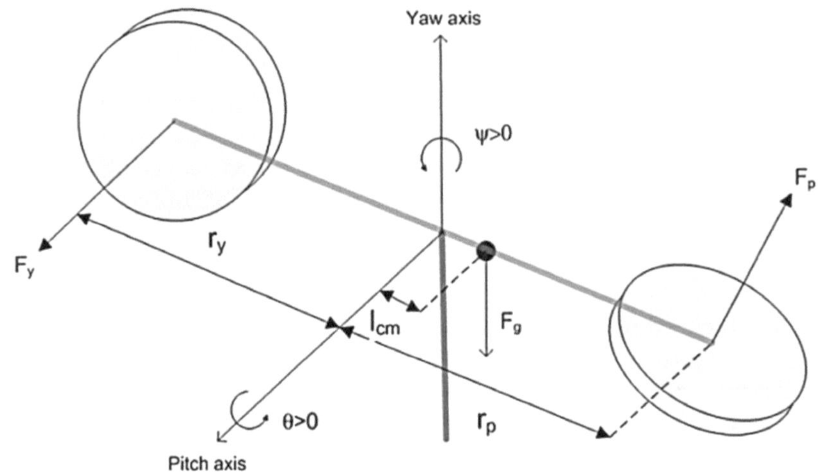

Figure 8.
Free-body diagram of Quanser helicopter [25].

Each degree of freedom is driven using a DC motor. The front head of the helicopter moves in the pitch angle and is driven by a 24 volt motor. The tail of the helicopter moves in the yaw angle and is driven by a 12 volt motor. The process is a highly nonlinear system with a very strong cross coupling between pitch and yaw angles.

The model uses the free-body diagram of **Figure 8** below.

The following modeling conventions were assumed [25]:

- The helicopter is horizontal when $\theta = 0$.
- The pitch angle increases positively, $\frac{d\theta(t)}{dt} > 0$ when rotating in the counter-clockwise direction.
- The yaw angle increases positively, $\frac{d\psi(t)}{dt} > 0$ when rotating in the clockwise direction.
- The pitch angle increases when pitch thrust force is positive, $F_p > 0$.
- The yaw angle increases when the yaw thrust force is positive, $F_y > 0$.

The model is a state-space representation of the system using the standard form of

$$\dot{x} = Ax + Bu \tag{4}$$

$$\dot{y} = Cy + Du \tag{5}$$

where the state vector and output vector are defined by

$$x^T = [\theta, \lambda, \dot{\theta}, \dot{\lambda}]$$

$$y^T = [\theta, \lambda]$$

where ***A, B, C*** and ***D*** are defined as (all parameters are defined in [25]):

$$A = \begin{bmatrix} 0 & 0 & 1 & 0 \\ 0 & 0 & 0 & 1 \\ 0 & 0 & -\dfrac{B_p}{J_{eq\_p} + m_{heli} l_{cm}^2} & 0 \\ 0 & 0 & 0 & -\dfrac{B_y}{J_{eq\_y} + m_{heli} l_{cm}^2} \end{bmatrix}$$

$$B = \begin{bmatrix} 0 & 0 \\ 0 & 0 \\ \dfrac{K_{pp}}{J_{eq\_p} + m_{heli} l_{cm}^2} & \dfrac{K_{py}}{J_{eq\_p} + m_{heli} l_{cm}^2} \\ \dfrac{K_{yp}}{J_{eq\_y} + m_{heli} l_{cm}^2} & \dfrac{K_{yy}}{J_{eq\_y} + m_{heli} l_{cm}^2} \end{bmatrix}$$

$$C = \begin{bmatrix} 1 & 0 & 0 & 0 \\ 0 & 1 & 0 & 0 \end{bmatrix}$$

$$D = \begin{bmatrix} 0 & 0 \\ 0 & 0 \end{bmatrix}$$

The system exhibits a high cross coupling between the pitch and yaw angles. The main feature of the suggested controller is to use two separated PID controllers, one for each degree of freedom, so that a simple design procedure can be applied.

Each of the fuzzy controllers, a PID controller and an LQR, was used to generate the desired reference response in order to tune PID controllers that govern the nonlinear model for both pitch and yaw. In all the cases, an arbitrary PID was used in the beginning. The values of Kp, Ki and Kd were all set to a gain value of 1. Both the fuzzy controller and PID controller were designed for the system, while the LQR is taken from a suggested design in the device manual [25].

7. Results and discussions

In addition to observing how much the process will follow the desired reference response in the twin rotor system, it will be checked whether the decoupling strategy is successful enough, since the twin rotor system inherits strong coupling between pitch and yaw angles.

In all the following cases, the initial parameter values of the process PID controller were set arbitrarily to 1 before the start of the tuning process. Stable responses were already achieved but with unacceptable performances. The performances of the initial PID controllers are shown when compared to the tuned systems below.

7.1 TRMS process controller tuning using PID controller to generate the desired reference response

In this case, a huge improvement was achieved in the process response after tuning. The tuning algorithm steered the process output to follow the desired reference response closely. Pitch angle controller tuning results are shown in **Figure 9**. The tuning results for the pitch were nearly perfect.

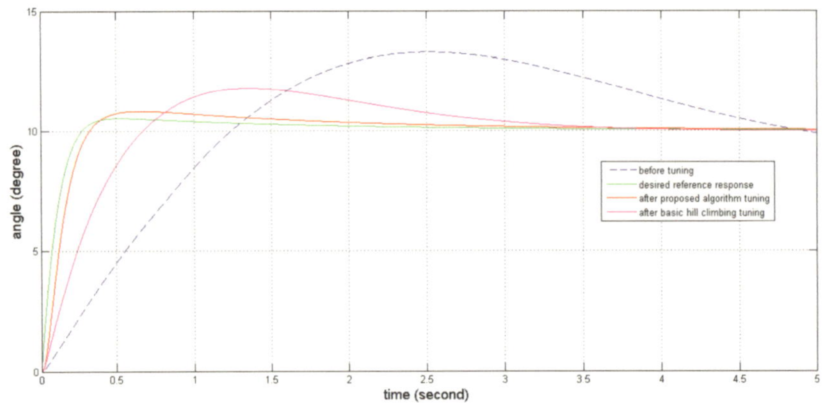

Figure 9.
TRMS pitch angle response before and after tuning with desired reference response generated by PID.

Tuning using the basic hill climbing did not achieve the same level of success in following the reference response; although the overshoot was reduced, the system response was slower in comparison.

The above result was achieved because the desired reference response was physically viable and that, in turn, it helped to relatively reduce the maximum allowed error margins; therefore, a very close following was achieved. The final tuned parameters for pitch angle PID were 1.9 for proportional gain, 1.2 for integral gain and 0.2 for derivative gain.

Figure 10 shows the error signal (difference between desired reference response and process output) for the pitch angle before and after tuning. The excellent tuning results are obvious in the error signal graph.

The yaw angle controller tuning also achieved very good results in bringing the process response closer to the desired reference response than the initial response, as seen in **Figure 11**.

Following the reference response was very good, and the overshoot was reduced dramatically, although not perfectly as in the pitch response. The small overshoot seen at the fifth second is due to coupling. This brings the researcher to mention that the yaw angle looks more difficult to be stripped from coupling effects than the pitch angle. Hence, there is no considerable effect when changing yaw angle on pitch angle; however, changing the pitch angle still has a small effect on the yaw

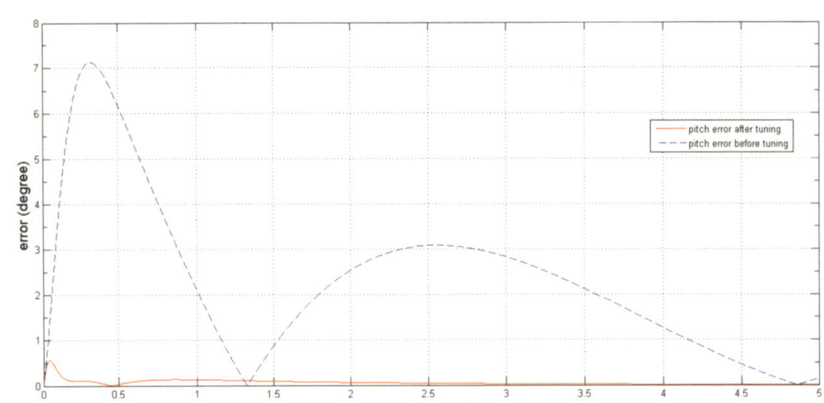

Figure 10.
Pitch angle response error signal to step set-point change before and after tuning when using PID to generate the desired reference response.

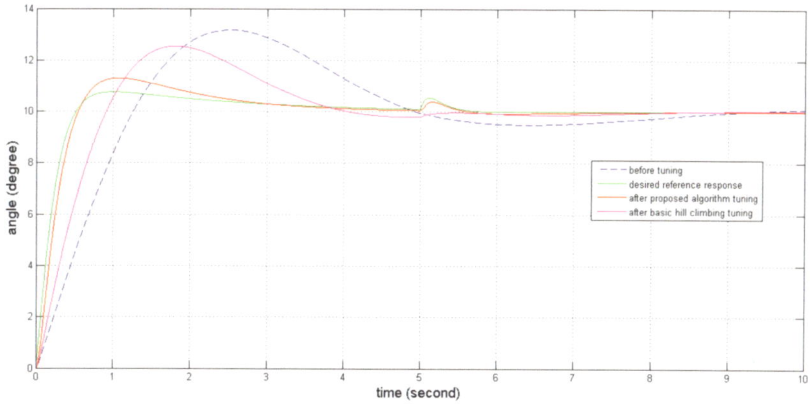

Figure 11.
TRMS yaw angle response before and after tuning with desired reference response generated by PID.

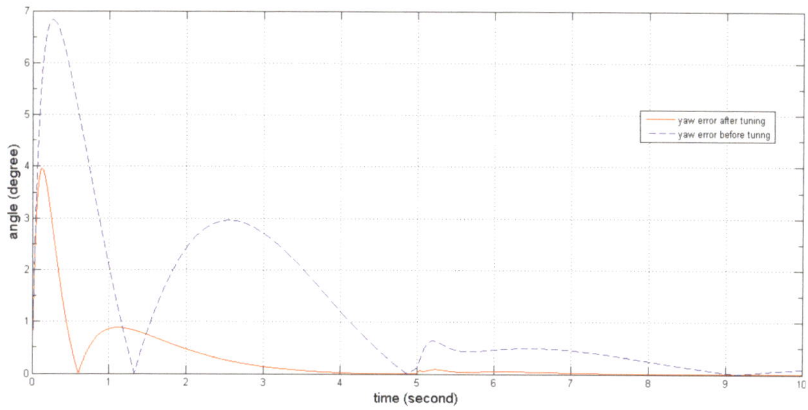

Figure 12.
Yaw angle response error signal to step set-point change before and after tuning when using PID to generate the desired reference response.

angle. The effect is very minimal, and the system decoupling efforts can be considered marginally successful. The final tuned parameters for the yaw angle PID were 1.7 for proportional gain, 1.2 for integral gain and 0.4 for derivative gain.

The error signal for the yaw angle before and after tuning is shown in **Figure 12**, where improvement in the response can clearly be seen.

7.2 TRMS process controller tuning using fuzzy controller to generate the desired reference response

The pitch angle response tuning, when using the fuzzy controller, was successful, as expected. Since the researchers had designed the desired reference response with an emphasis on reducing the overshoot with high speed performance, the tuned response of the process followed the design guidelines properly. It can be observed in **Figure 13** below how the process response moved from the initial PID controlled response to the final tuned PID controlled response quite well.

The result shows successful tuning of the process controller using the proposed algorithm. The effects of coupling were unnoticed, denoting the successful decoupling strategy that was designed, which was suggested earlier. The final parameters for the pitch angle process PID after tuning were 2.1 for proportional gain, 0.4 for integral gain and 0.7 for derivative gain.

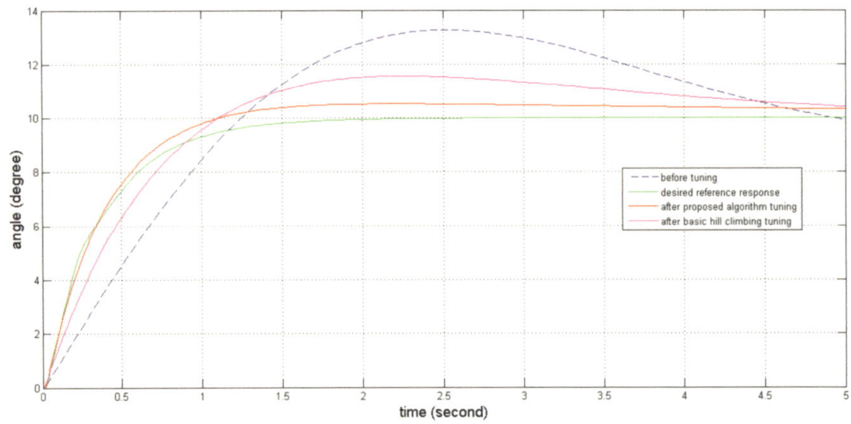

Figure 13.
TRMS pitch angle response before and after tuning with desired reference response generated by fuzzy controller.

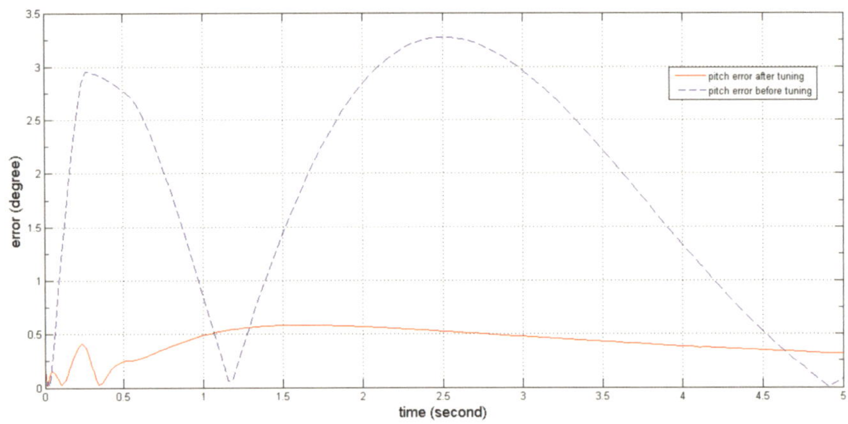

Figure 14.
Pitch angle response error signal to step set-point change before and after tuning when using fuzzy controller to generate the desired reference response.

The error signal between the desired reference response and the process response was reduced largely by the tuning algorithm. **Figure 14** shows the error signal graph of the pitch angle, both before and after tuning.

The yaw angle controller tuning did steer the process response from the initial towards the desired reference response, resulting in better performance; however, the response did not follow the reference perfectly. Namely, the response did have a considerable overshoot, unlike the desired reference response, as shown in **Figure 15** below. This came as a result of pushing the desired reference response beyond the physical nature of the actual process. The actual yaw angle system is inherently highly under-damped. Consequently, obtaining a well-damped response with decent speed seems unrealistic.

The final parameters for the yaw angle process PID after tuning were 1.7 for proportional gain, 0.7 for integral gain and 0.9 for derivative gain.

The error signal between the desired reference response and the process response was reduced by the tuning algorithm. A sizable error can be observed from the start of second second until the fourth second in **Figure 16**, showing overshoot difference as observed above. However, the error function was low enough to grant the response as acceptable, since the error at other areas is minimal.

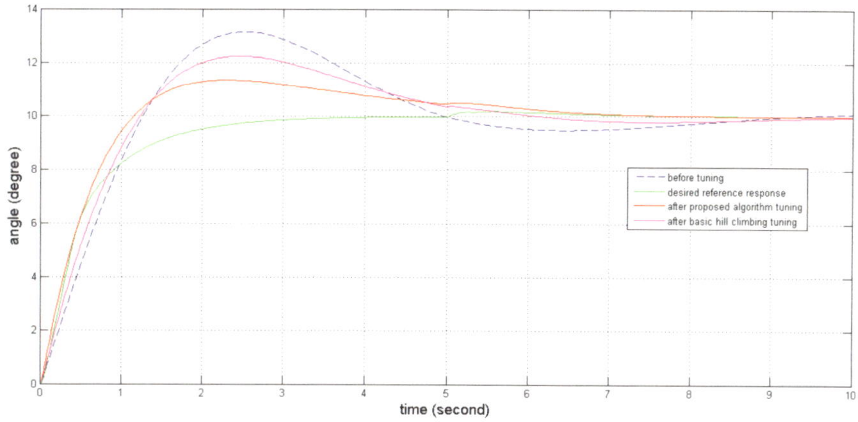

Figure 15.
TRMS yaw angle response before and after tuning with a desired reference response generated by fuzzy controller.

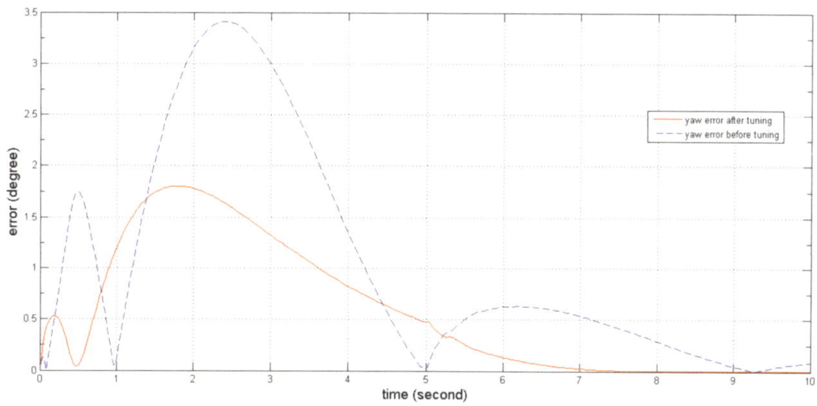

Figure 16.
Yaw angle response error signal to step set-point change before and after tuning when using fuzzy controller to generate the desired reference response.

Both pitch and yaw outputs that were tuned using the basic hill climbing gave an acceptable response speeds, but the overshoot amounts were high comparatively.

7.3 TRMS process controller tuning using LQR to generate the desired reference response

The tuning algorithm, as in other cases, succeeded in reshaping the process response so that it followed the desired reference response closely. This case gives evidence that the performance of the tuned process controller is highly determined by the performance of the desired reference response. In **Figure 17**, it can be seen that the tuned response exhibits a relatively high overshoot with slow response, because the desired reference response gave similar results.

The final PID parameters for pitch angle process after tuning were 1.5 for proportional gain, 0.6 for integral gain and 0.9 for derivative gain.

Although the response was not the best when compared to the other cases, the approach has again proven to be successful, as the error plot in **Figure 18** shows the improvement in reference following from the initial non-tuned response to the final tuned response. Tuning will always depend on error to the reference response, regardless of acquired performance, as shown in this case.

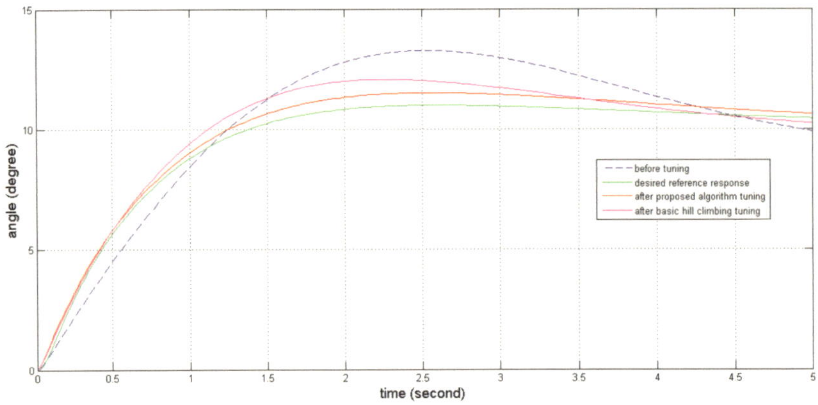

Figure 17.
TRMS pitch angle response before and after tuning with desired reference response generated by LQR.

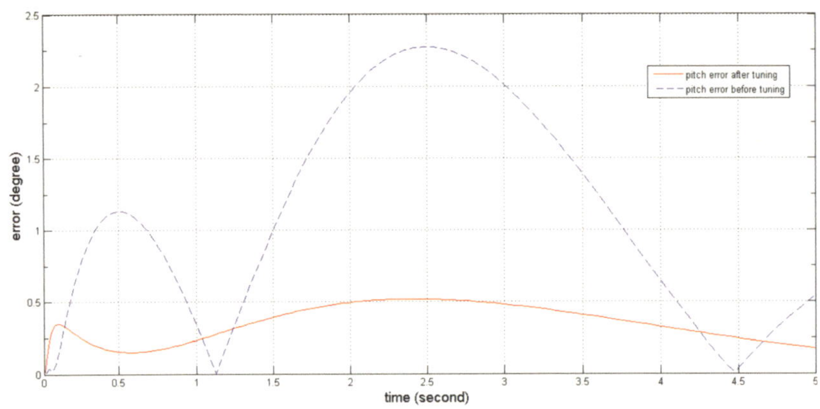

Figure 18.
Pitch angle response error signal to step set-point change before and after tuning when using LQR to generate the desired reference response.

The yaw angle response can be found in **Figure 19**.

The response is no different from the observations taken from the pitch response, as the low-quality model controller generated a low-performance desired reference response that, in turn, shadowed the performance of the tuned process

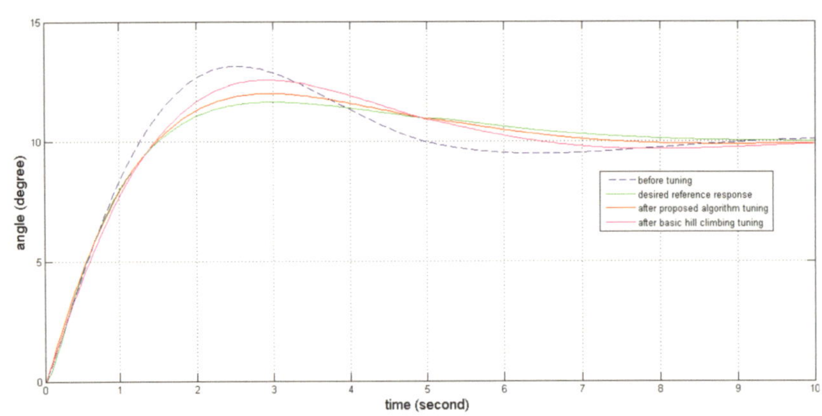

Figure 19.
TRMS yaw angle response with desired reference response generated using LQR.

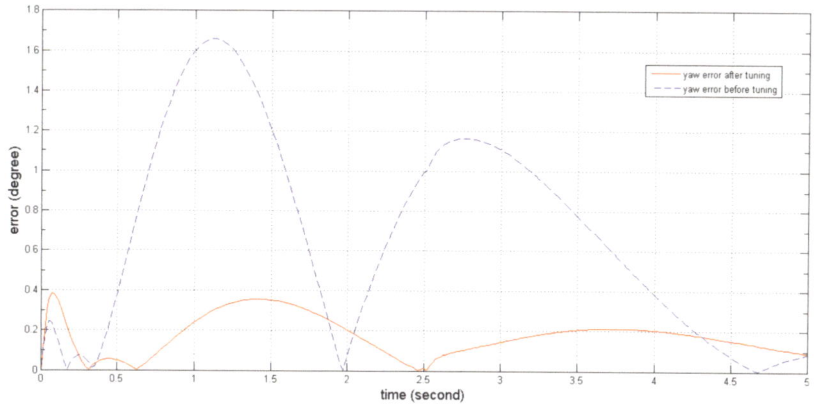

Figure 20.
Yaw angle response error signal to step set-point change before and after tuning when using LQR to generate the desired reference response.

PID controller. The final PID parameters for the yaw angle process after tuning were 1.4 for proportional gain, 0.7 for integral gain and 1.2 for derivative gain.

The error plot of the response before and after tuning is shown in **Figure 20**.

Although the responses tuned using basic hill climbing were very close to the desired reference response, they always lagged behind the proposed modified hill climbing algorithm responses in almost every performance index.

7.4 Comparison among the TRMS cases

In all the cases presented for the TRMS, which is a highly nonlinear, strongly inherited coupling system, the tuning algorithm proved to be highly successful, regardless of the desired reference response performance in each case. The tuning always brought the process response to act in a similar fashion to that of the desired reference response. Therefore, the process controller performance expectations should be relevant to the model controller performance on the one hand and to the applicability of that model controller performance to the process controller on the other hand. That can be clearly evident when checking the comparative results in **Table 1**.

Generally, the performance values have shown improvement on that of the initial response, except for the LQR case, where some performances were lower due to the low quality of the desired reference response (settling time for pitch and rising time for yaw). This, once again, confirms the importance of the desired reference response preparation to achieve the best possible results.

By examining **Table 1**, it can be seen that forcing the system to achieve a certain milestone in one area may lead to degradation in quality in other areas. For example, when using a fuzzy controller as a model controller, the desired reference response was pushed to the extreme to fully eliminate overshoot. Although overshoot in the model responses was eliminated, the results were different for the actual process. For the pitch angle, the overshoot was decreased by 3.2 degrees when using a fuzzy controller as a model controller, compared to using PID controller as model controller. However, both rising time and settling time were increased by 0.77 and 1.13 s, respectively. Here, it is up to the system designer to make a decision on which path to take, according to the operation preferences. For the yaw angle, however, the outcome is different. As the yaw angle in the actual process is naturally highly under-damped, trying to force it to achieve non-overshooting response brought negative effects. All performance indexes were

System		Model controller type	Final process PID gains			Model controller performance			Process controller performance		
			P	I	D	Rise time	Settling time	Overshoot (%)	Rise time	Settling time	Overshoot (%)
Pitch	Before tuning	N/A	1	1	1	N/A	N/A	N/A	1.25	4.5	33
	After tuning	PID (max. error = 0.2)	1.9	1.2	0.2	0.3	0.71	5.1	0.33	1.47	8.2
		Fuzzy (max. error = 0.5)	2.1	0.4	0.7	3	1.1	0	1.1	2.6	5
		LQR (max. error = 0.4)	1.5	0.6	0.9	1.3	4.7	10	1.25	5.35	15
Yaw	Before tuning	N/A	1	1	1	N/A	N/A	N/A	1.26	6.75	31.6
	After tuning	PID (max. error = 0.3)	1.7	1.2	0.4	0.48	0.35	4.6	0.54	2.43	13
		Fuzzy (max. error = 0.5)	1.7	0.7	0.9	5	2	0	1.15	4.85	13.4
		LQR (max. error = 0.2)	1.4	0.7	1.2	1.5	6.3	16.5	1.5	6	20

Table 1.
Comparative results of TRMS cases.

System	Model controller type	Improvement in	
		Overshoot (%)	Settling time (s)
Pitch	PID	9.6	1.34
	Fuzzy	10.5	2.15
	LQR	5.8	−0.86
Yaw	PID	12.3	1.02
	Fuzzy	9	−0.05
	LQR	5.6	−0.38

Table 2.
Performance improvement when using the proposed design in comparison to the basic hill climbing with TRMS cases.

reduced in quality in comparison to using a PID controller as model controller, even the overshoot itself. Rising time and settling time were increased by 0.92 and 3.88 s, respectively, while overshoot was increased by 0.4%. This sheds some light on the priority of not straining the process with unachievable performances.

In order to compare the proposed algorithm performance with that of basic hill climbing, the following **Table 2** is created.

Some of the settling time performances are slightly slower than basic hill climbing (<1 s), but that was a result to reducing the overshoot amount significantly. This is because the proposed modified hill climbing algorithm followed the reference response better than the basic hill climbing.

8. Conclusions

In this chapter, a paradigm for real-time tuning of control systems is proposed. The proposed paradigm facilitates the application of a tuning algorithm based on simple error cost function calculations. Additionally, a modified hill climbing algorithm is developed. The control paradigm allows the system controller to be tuned iteratively to enhance the control performance using the suggested tuning algorithm. The algorithm does not require complex calculations to move in the searching space looking for suitable candidates. The algorithm always promotes the best solution to be used until a better one is found, which makes it suitable for real-time tuning problem. Simulation results clearly showed that the system response is following the desired reference response after tuning. However, the reference response should always be physically viable within an acceptable error margins.

Results have shown that the algorithm provides a very useful tool for control systems' engineers and specialists. The proposed system, overall, was proved to be quite successful in driving controlled plant response by using an inaccurate model of that plant. Therefore, the proposed design is suitable for tuning controllers based on inaccurate models or for calibrating controllers of systems with parameters deviation automatically.

This research introduced a very effective methodology to tune or calibrate control systems in real time, without the need to intervene with the system's operation. The proposed methodology is very flexible and can be used to achieve various performance targets. It was implemented with control systems specifically in mind; hence, the depth of achievement possibilities is high.

Acknowledgements

This work is financed by Universiti Putra Malaysia, Grant Putra (GP-IPS/2013/9399830).

Appendix A

List of parameters that were used in expressing example models with their values (if available) is presented in this appendix (**Table A**).

Parameter	Brief explanation	Value
θ	Pitch angle	
ψ	Yaw angle	
F_p	Pitch thrust force	
F_y	Yaw thrust force	
B_p	Equivalent viscous damping about pitch axis	0.8 N/V
J_{eq_p}	Total moment of inertia about pitch axis	0.0384 kg m^2
m_{heli}	Total moving mass of the helicopter	1.3872 kg
lcm	Centre of mass length along helicopter body from pitch axis	0.186 m
B_y	Equivalent viscous damping about yaw axis	0.318 N/V
J_{eq_y}	Total moment of inertia about yaw axis	0.0432 kg m^2
K_{pp}	Thrust force constant of yaw motor/propeller	0.204 N m/V
K_{py}	Thrust toque constant acting on pitch axis from yaw motor/propeller	0.0068 N m/V
K_{yp}	Thrust toque constant acting on yaw axis from pitch motor/propeller	0.0219 N m/V
K_{yy}	Thrust toque constant acting on yaw axis from yaw motor/propeller	0.072 N m/V
α	Angle of attack	
q	Pitch rate	
δ	Elevator deflection angle	
μ	$\frac{\rho S\bar{c}}{4m}$	
ρ	Density of air	
S	Platform area of the wing	
$\bar{c}$	Average cord length	
m	Mass of the aircraft	
Ω	$\frac{2U}{\bar{c}}$	
U	Equilibrium flight speed	
C_D	Coefficient of drag	
C_L	Coefficient of lift	
C_w	Coefficient of weight	
C_M	Coefficient of pitch moment	
γ	Flight path angle	
σ	$\frac{1}{1+\mu C_L}$	

Parameter	Brief explanation	Value
i_{yy}	Normalized moment of inertia	
η	$\mu\sigma C_M$	
$V(t)$	Motor input voltage	
$e(t)$	Back electromotive force	
L_a	Motor armature electric inductance	0.15 H
$i(t)$	Electric current	
R_a	Motor armature electric resistance	0.2 Ohm
$T_m(t)$	Mechanical torque	
K_m	Motor torque constant	9.14×10^{-5} N m/A
K_b	Electromotive force constant	0.055 V/rad/sec
$w(t)$	Angular velocity of motor shaft	
$T_L(t)$	Load torque	
J_m	Moment of inertia of the rotor	1.36×10^{-5} kg m^2
B_m	Motor shaft viscous friction coefficient	0.5×10^{-5} N m sec

Table A.
List of parameters used in example models.

Author details

Ahmed Abdulelah Ahmed[1,2], Azura Che Soh[1*], Mohd Khair Hassan[1], Samsul Bahari Mohd Noor[1] and Hafiz Rashidi Harun[1]

1 Control System and Signal Processing (CSSP) Research Centre, Department of Electrical and Electronic Engineering, Universiti Putra Malaysia, Selangor, Malaysia

2 Faculty of Engineering, University of Kufa, Iraq Kufa, Najaf Governarate, Iraq

*Address all correspondence to: azuracs@upm.edu.my

References

[1] Jantzen J. Foundations of Fuzzy Control. New Jersey, USA: John Wiley & Sons; 2007

[2] Thomas BS. Telerobotics, Automation, and Human Supervisory Control. 1st ed. Cambridge, UK: MIT Press; 1992

[3] Sands TA. Physics-based control methods. In: Ghadawala R, editor. Advancements in Spacecraft Systems and Orbit Determination. Rijeka: In-Tech Publishers; 2012. pp. 29-54

[4] Sands T. Space system identification algorithms. Journal of Space Exploration. 2017;**6**:138

[5] Sands T. Nonlinear-adaptive mathematical system identification. Computational Engineering, Special Issue of Computation. 2017;**5**(4):47

[6] Ogata K. Modern Control Engineering. 5th ed. New Jersey, USA: Prentice Hall; 2010

[7] Reedy J, Lunzman S, Mekari B. Model-based design accelerates development of mechanical locomotive controls. Off-Highway Engineering. 2011;**19**(2):18-22

[8] Ogata K. System Dynamics. 4th ed. New Jersey, USA: Prentice Hall; 2015

[9] Miller TW. Modeling Techniques in Predictive Analytics. 1st ed. New Jersey, USA: Pearson Education, FT Press; 2013

[10] Burns R. Advanced Control Engineering. 1st ed. Oxford, UK: Butterworth-Heinemann; 2001

[11] Sands T. The catastrophe of electric vehicle sales. Mathematics. 2017;**5**:46

[12] Astrom KJ, Wittenmark B. Adaptive Control. 2nd ed. New York, USA: Dover Publications; 2008

[13] Ioannou PA, Sun J. Robust Adaptive Control. 1st ed. New York, USA: Courier Dover Publications; 2012

[14] Wittenmark B. Adaptive Dual Control. In: Control Systems, Robotics and Automation. Encyclopedia of Life Support Systems (EOLSS), Developed under the auspices of the UNESCO; 2002

[15] Kartik BA, Krstic M. Real-Time Optimization by Extremum-Seeking Control. 1st ed. New Jersey, USA: Wiley-Interscience; 2003

[16] Bunin GA, François G, Bonvin D. A real-time optimization framework for the iterative controller tuning problem. PRO. 2013;**1**(2):203-237

[17] Mosca E. Optimal, Predictive and Adaptive Control. 1st ed. New Jersey, USA: Prentice Hall; 1994

[18] Bonvin D, Srinivasan B. On the use of models for real-time optimization. In: Chemical Process Control-VIII, No. EPFL-CONF-181259; 2012

[19] Tan KK, Zhao S, Xu J-Z. Online automatic tuning of a proportional integral derivative controller based on an iterative learning control approach. IET Control Theory and Applications. 2007;**1**(1):90-96

[20] Kuo BC, Golnaraghi F. Automatic Control Systems. 9th ed. New Jersey, USA: John Wiley & Sons; 2009

[21] Russell SJ, Norvig P. Artificial Intelligence: A Modern Approach. 3rd ed. New Jersey, USA: Prentice Hall; 2010

[22] Katalin MH, Lakner R, Gerzson M. Intelligent Control Systems: An Introduction with Examples. Dordrecht, Netherlands: Kluwer Academic Publisher; 2004

[23] Charbonneau P. An Introduction to Genetic Algorithms for Numerical Optimization. Boulder, Colorado: NCAR Technical Note, Institute of Global Environment and Society (IGES); 2002

[24] Naysmith MR, Douglas PL. Review of real time optimization in the chemical process industries. Developments in Chemical Engineering and Mineral Processing. 1995;**3**(2):67-87

[25] Quanser. 2-DOF Helicopter. Reference Manual: Quanser, revision 2.11

Chapter 3

Random Forest-Based Ensemble Machine Learning Data-Optimization Approach for Smart Grid Impedance Prediction in the Powerline Narrowband Frequency Band

Emmanuel Oyekanlu and Jia Uddin

Abstract

In this chapter, the random forest-based ensemble regression method is used for the prediction of powerline impedance at the powerline communication (PLC) narrowband frequency range. It is discovered that while PLC load transfer function, phase, and frequency are crucial to powerline impedance estimation, the problem of data multicollinearity can adversely impact accurate prediction and lead to excessive mean square error (MSE). High MSE is obtained when multiple transfer functions corresponding to different PLC load transfer functions are used for random forest ensemble regression. Low MSE indicating more accurate impedance prediction is obtained when PLC load transfer function data is selectively used. Using data corresponding to 200, 400, 600, 800, and 1000 W PLC load transfer functions together led to poor impedance prediction, while using lesser amount of carefully selected data led to better impedance prediction. These results show that artificial intelligence (AI) methods such as random forest ensemble regression and deterministic data-optimization approach can be utilized for smart grid (SG) health monitoring applications using PLC-based sensors. Machine learning can also be applied to the design of better powerline communication signal transceivers and equalizers.

Keywords: random forest, regression, impedance, data quality, prediction, ensemble, machine learning, smart grid, deterministic artificial intelligence

1. Introduction

The utilization of powerline communication (PLC) as a tool for actualizing a smart grid (SG) has grown beyond its traditional uses for two-way SG communication, advanced metering infrastructure (AMI) applications, demand response, and power system control. As shown in **Figure 1**, cameras that can transmit data using

Figure 1.
Powerline communication is being deployed for numerous smart grid applications including remote asset monitoring using PLC-based cameras.

PLC are now being used for monitoring of power system assets installed in remote locations [1]. PLC is also being extensively used for broadband Internet applications [2], consumer home automation applications [3], facilitating grid-wide artificial intelligence (AI) applications [4–10], monitoring grid health using PLC modems as sensors [11], etc.

Despite these uses, there are still numerous challenges militating against a more effective deployment of PLC for SG applications. The powerline being primarily designed for power transmission is a harsh environment for communication. As such, there exist the problems of varying impedance, numerous white and different nonwhite noise types, and excessive frequency-dependent attenuation [12–15]. To ameliorate these problems and make PLC more useful for the SG, different parts of the powerline used for PLC as shown in **Figure 2** can be optimized from the transmission (TX) end to the receiving (RX) end [16].

For PLC to be particularly useful for grid health monitoring, many researchers worldwide have focused on the problem of powerline impedance estimation. Powerline impedance is a very important parameter in the design of PLC transceivers and in installing a modem grid architecture [17]. In PLC, to achieve maximum power transfer between the PLC transmitting and receiving ends, powerline TX (**Figure 2**), transmission line, and RX impedance must always be known by the impedance matching network [17]. PLC impedance however is time varying since electrical loads are always being connected to and disconnected from the PLC networks, thus leading to the problem of PLC network impedance mismatches [18]. Accurate and real-time impedance information can be used to match impedance variables in PLC couplers to decrease PLC data attenuation [19]. Also, online and real-time knowledge of PLC network impedance is essential to overall grid health monitoring of the SG. In addition, real-time PLC-based impedance information

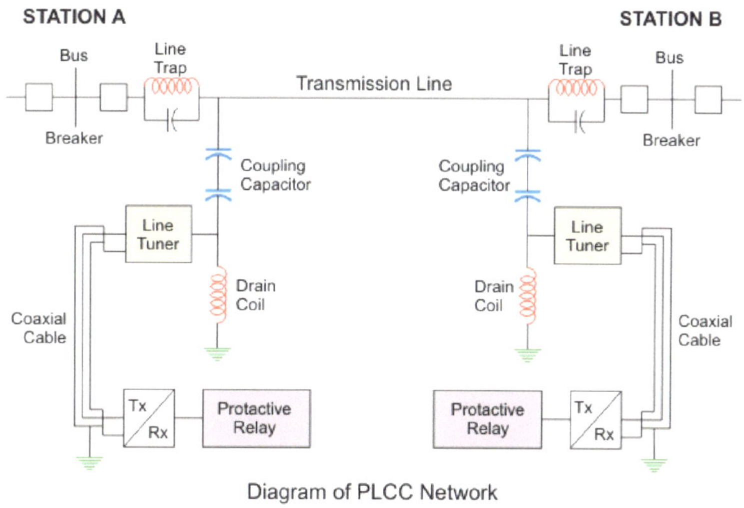

Figure 2.
Different parts of powerline communication can be optimized from end to end for more effective powerline communication [16].

can be useful for event detection [20], thus leading to lesser needs for having to install very expensive phasor measurement units (PMUs).

To improve on available methods of powerline impedance estimation, in [13], using an algorithm, the authors designed an adaptive inductor-capacitor-resistor-capacitor (LCRC) impedance matching circuit for improving the impedance matching problem in the PLC narrowband frequency region. Also, the authors in [17] measured impedance and attenuation of the PLC at the CENELEC bands in rural, urban, and industrial use cases, respectively. Results of the research are the production of a set of formulas that can be used to deduce impedances of the PLC in view of load variations on PLC networks. In [18], the authors produce a statistical model of PLC network impedance. Results of work discussed in [19] are a novel real-time impedance estimation method based on channel frequency response and machine learning variational mode decomposition (VMD) method. In [20], the authors propose a method by which powerline impedance can be estimated using device status detection algorithm and device individual energy and impedance signatures. In [21], the authors presented results of work in which the real-time estimation of powerline impedance is based on modal analysis theory, while the authors in [22] conducted a study on the design of a front-end optimal receiver impedance that maximizes signal-to-noise ratio (SNR) in broadband PLC.

One significant drawback of majority of existing PLC impedance estimation methods however is that they need dedicated equipment and the knowledge of the network topology. This is the problem that our approach in present work seeks to solve. We present a deterministic machine learning-based PLC impedance estimation method by which common PLC network data such as the PLC channel load transfer function, frequency, and phase can be used to estimate and predict PLC network impedance. A benefit of the deterministic AI impedance prediction approach adopted in our work is that data needed for impedance estimation and prediction is not excessively superfluous and such data can be easily stored in low-memory powerline network devices. In Section 2, we present a new set of results that shows the transfer function and attenuation profile of PLC in the narrowband frequency bands based on electrical loads connected to the powerline. In Section 3, we briefly discussed the random forest ensemble method, and we present results of how we used PLC network data to optimize results of PLC impedance prediction in the narrowband frequency bands. Section 4 details results and discussion and Section 5 presents conclusion of the chapter.

2. New results on powerline communication attenuation profile in the PLC narrowband frequency bands based on loads on the powerline

In literature, there exist several PLC models that are used to evaluate the behavior and performance of PLC networks. In Philip's echo model, the PLC transfer function is given in [14] as

$$H(f) = \sum_{i=1}^{N} p_i e^{-j2\pi f \tau_i} \tag{1}$$

In Eq. (1), N is the number of possible signal propagation paths, with each path in N delayed by time factor τ_i, while p_i is the product of transmission and reflection factors. Another popular model is the Zimmerman and Dostert model which accounts for PLC signal attenuation. The model is given by

$$H(f) = \sum_{i=1}^{N} g_i e^{-(a_0 + a_1 f^k) d_i} e^{-j2\pi f \frac{d_i}{v_p}} \tag{2}$$

Similar to Philip's echo model, g_i in Eq. (2) is the product of transmission and reflection. The path length for each path in N number of significant paths is d_i. Attenuation parameters can be obtained from measurements and they are k, a_0, and a_1. In Eq. (2), the term $\frac{d_i}{v_p}$ can also be represented as the path delay where v_p can be represented as

$$v_p = \frac{c_o}{\sqrt{\varepsilon_\tau}} \tag{3}$$

In Eq. (3), v_p is the phase velocity, $c_o = 3\,x\,10^8\ m/s$ represents the speed of light in a vacuum, while ε_τ is the dielectric constant. In narrowband PLC, few results exist that directly evaluate and explain the behavior of narrowband PLC networks. A recent result by the authors in [23] is given in Eq. (4).

$$H(f) = A \sum_{k=1}^{M} g_k(f) \exp\left(-(\alpha_0 + \alpha_1 f)\right) v_p \tau_k\, exp^{-j2\pi f \tau_k} \tag{4}$$

In Eq. (4), A is the constant coefficient for frequency response adjustment, and M is the number of significant paths. The weighting factor corresponding to each significant path is $g_k(f)$, while α_0 and α_1 are constant coefficients for powerline cable adjustment. However, in view of the importance, worldwide acceptability, and the need to better understand the narrowband PLC region (below 500 kHz) for powerline communication [23], this chapter presents new modeling results of the narrowband PLC region. The presented model is a novel result as it is accomplished by systematic addition of electrical loads for empirical evaluation of the PLC narrowband region. Our methodology is as shown in **Figure 3**. A de-embedded E5071C ENA vector network analyzer (VNA) is used to measure the attenuation profile of the low-voltage region, an indoor environment, when loads are added to the powerline segments between both ends of the VNA. In each measurement case, the

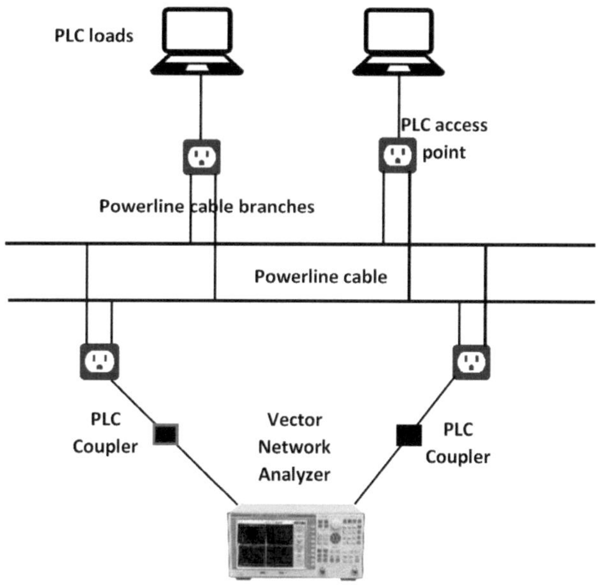

Figure 3.
Experimental setup for load-based attenuation profile measurement in the PLC narrowband communication band.

attenuation profile and frequency data are obtained from the VNA in Excel file sheet format, and for better visualization, the profile is plotted with Matlab. Electrical loads are added to the powerline in 500 watt increments. In the first instance, two 250 W-rated desktop computers were added to the powerline for a total of 500 W. In the second instance, a 500 W blender is added to the first two desktop computers for a total 1000 W.

Finally, a 520 W coffee maker is added to make the overall load approximately 1500 W. In each case, the attenuation profile of the powerline is measured with the aid of the de-embedded E5071C VNA. The indoor powerline cable used for this experiment is the 10 AWG Romex SIMpull CU NM-B cable. To examine the effect of distance, the cable distance is extended in increments of 100 m. Initially, a 150 m Romex indoor cable is used, and attenuation profile is measured using the VNA when 500 W load is connected to the 150 m cable located in between two ends of the VNA (**Figure 3**). The loads are subsequently increased to 1000 and 1500 W, respectively. The Romex cable length is increased to 250 and 350 m, respectively, and the network loads and measurements are repeated. Results of the attenuation profiles are shown in **Figures 4–6**, respectively. From **Figures 4** to **6**, effects of powerline length are noticeable as the VNA shows a profile that is increasingly attenuated as PLC channel length is increasing. Also, electrical loads on the channel have significant effect on the attenuation profile. The attenuation profile in **Figure 4** shows a channel that has more channel notches as more electrical loads are added to the network. When loads on the channel are only 500 W, the channel shows lesser number of notches than when loads on the channel increase to 1000 and to 1500 W, respectively. The more the loads, the more the number of notches. This indicates that when more electrical loads exist on the PLC channels, then data or signal sent on the channel will suffer increased attenuation than when less amounts of electrical loads exist on the network. Similar channel load effects are observed on the 250 m long and on the 350 m long PLC channels in **Figures 5** and **6**, respectively. However, the channel profile exhibits a characteristic similar to that described by the Zimmerman and Dostert PLC channel model. Thus, the

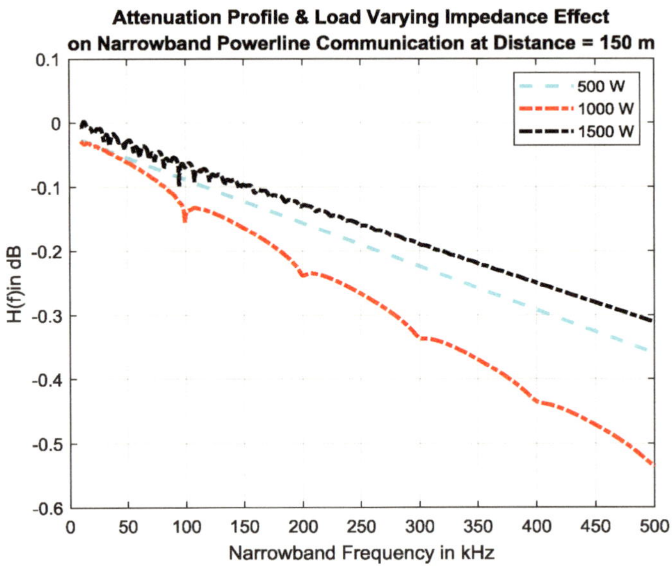

Figure 4.
Load-based attenuation profile for powerline communication at industrial indoor distance of 150 m.

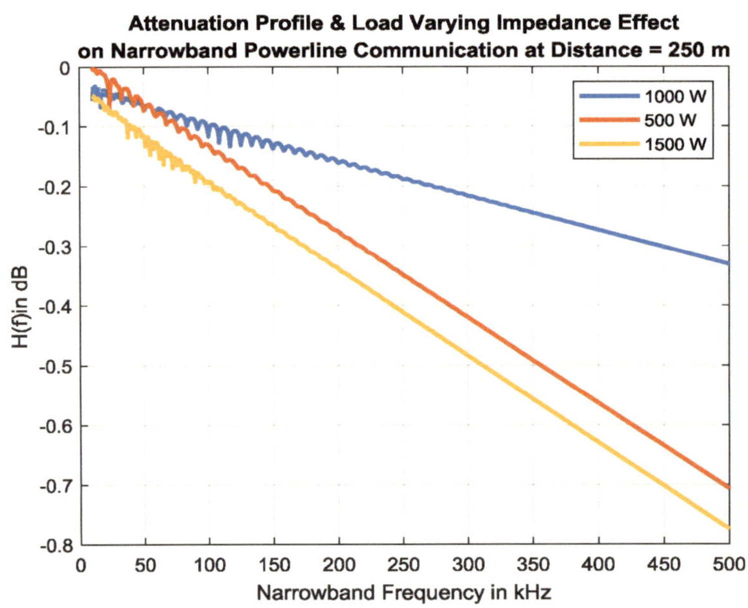

Figure 5.
Load-based attenuation profile for powerline communication at industrial indoor distance of 250 m.

Zimmerman and Dostert model is modified to show a narrowband channel model that considers the effect of PLC channel load. The resulting model which focuses primarily on the effect of electrical loads on the PLC channel at the PLC narrowband region is shown in Eq. (5), and it is simulated with Matlab and graphed in **Figure 7**. **Figure 7**, which is the derived model based on Eq. (5), is generally similar to the load-based PLC channel profile shown in **Figures 4** to **6**. In Eq. (5), μ is the channel load index where μ ε 1, 2, 3, ..., n. To replicate the channel profile of **Figure 7**, the load factor μ can be increased from 1 to n based on discrete channel load increments of 200 W. For the purpose of clarity, in Eq. (5), N is the number of significant paths, d_i is the path length of each significant path, v_p is the phase

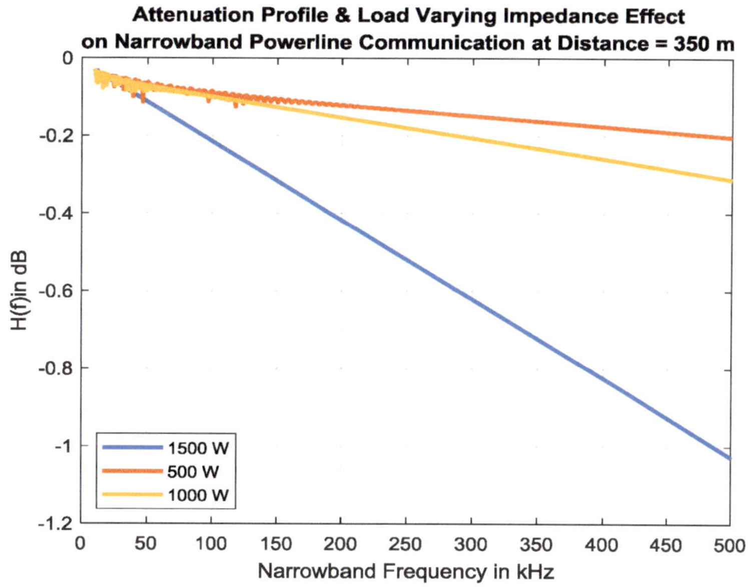

Figure 6.
Load-based attenuation profile for powerline communication at industrial indoor distance of 350 m.

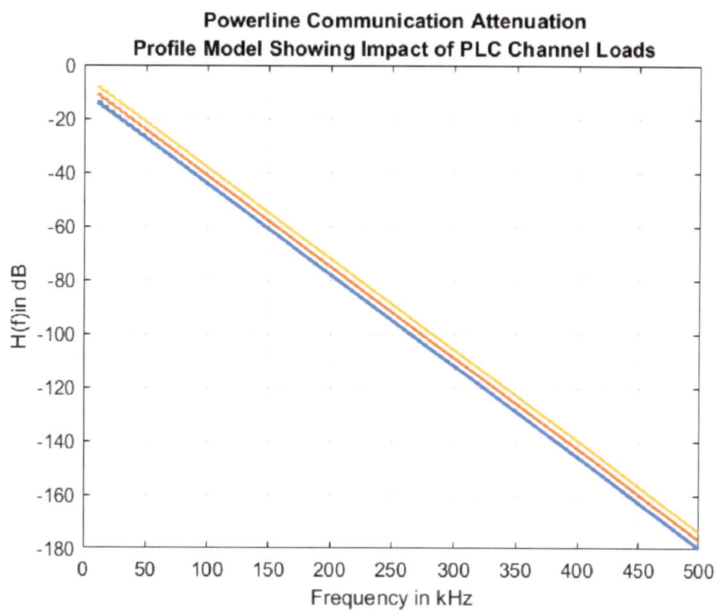

Figure 7.
Narrowband PLC model showing load-based attenuation profile.

velocity, and $\boldsymbol{g_i}$ is the weighting factor corresponding to each significant path. Constant coefficients of powerline cable adjustments are denoted with $\boldsymbol{a_0}$ and $\boldsymbol{a_1}$, respectively.

$$H(f) = -\mu \sum_{i=1}^{N} g_i e^{-\left(a_0 + a_1 f^k\right) d_i} e^{-j2\pi f \frac{d_i}{v_p}} \tag{5}$$

The precise and deterministic nature of the channel load index μ in Eq. (5) and the fact that the amount of PLC channel loads is directly related to the PLC channel impedance is exploited in this chapter to reduce the amount of data that can be used in machine learning ensemble algorithm to predict the PLC channel impedance. Our approach can thus be viewed as a deterministic data-optimization approach to PLC impedance prediction. In deterministic AI, data produced by systems whose behavior is governed by fundamental physical laws can utilize those laws for reducing data used in machine learning and other AI applications [24]. Deterministic AI methods have been successfully applied in large engineering systems such as altitude control of spaceships suffering from loss of vital parts [25]. It has also been applied for achieving better precision in AI algorithms [26] used for adaptive control of actuators [24, 27], in system identification [26], and in plant control [28], with results indicating that the deterministic AI method often leads to better precision in prediction performance and in reducing superfluous network data.

3. Machine learning ensemble regression method for PLC channel impedance estimation

PLC network impedance has significant effect on communication over powerline networks. The line impedance directly impacts the communication distance in an inverse relationship, i.e., the higher the line impedance, the lower the distance at which good communication can be achieved over the powerline. Also, if the powerline load impedance is lower than the PLC network transmitter impedance, then the load will provide an easier grounding pathway for the communication signal. The signal, thus, will get easily attenuated. Hence, due to the importance of impedance [29] to the success of communication over the powerline, it is essential that the impedance information of the PLC network is always available at the transmitter and PLC receiver ends [30, 31]. However, it is challenging to always predict the PLC network impedance in real time since electrical appliances are always being switched on and off, thus causing network impedance to vary always. In addition, VNA, PMUs, and other equipment useful for measuring PLC network impedance are always expensive, and thus, it is impossible to install such equipment at all possible nodes on the network for grid health monitoring. Hence, in this chapter, we have devised machine learning and deterministic data optimization-based approach by which PLC network impedance can be predicted using common PLC network load data. The machine learning approach adopted for this work is the use of random forest ensemble regression method.

In literature, different types of machine learning and artificial intelligence methods have been used for different types of engineering and large network problems [32–54]; however, the random forest ensemble regression method has been proven to be very useful since it is known to have high prediction accuracy, it is efficient on large datasets, and it also gives better predictive accuracy when there are cases on missing data [52–54].

Random forest is an ensemble classifier that consists of many decision trees and outputs the class that is the mode of the class's output by individual trees. Random forest works by training randomly selected subset of data from a large set of data on decision trees and then aggregating the results of each decision tree to form an ensemble result that often yields better prediction. In **Figure 8**, each decision tree is trained using a method called bootstrap aggregating.

At each split node and the resulting child nodes, another metric called the information gain which is the difference between the uncertainty of the starting node and the weighted impurity of the resulting two-child nodes is used to decide on which feature can be used to split the data. The combined use of the Gini index, information gain, bootstrap aggregation, and decision trees serves to make the

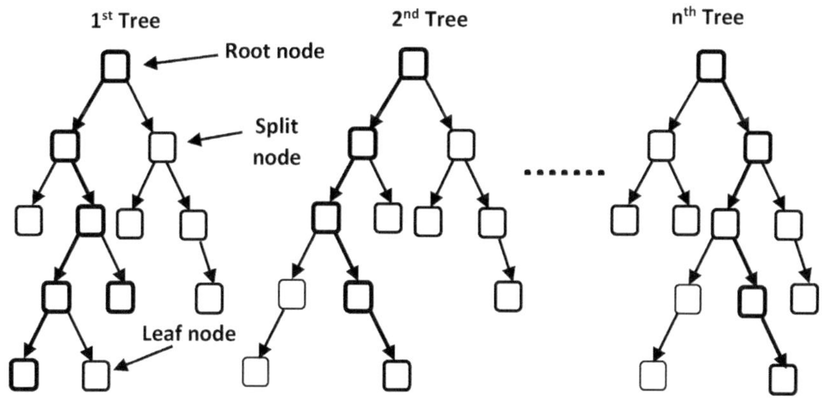

Figure 8.
Random forest ensemble method of tree selection and result aggregation.

random forest a valuable method for both classification- and regression-based predictions.

In our implementation of the random forest method for PLC impedance prediction, the de-embedded E5071C VNA is used to measure the network when different types and power ratings of electrical loads are plugged to the network of **Figure 3**. About 200, 400, 600, 800, and 1000 W loads of different ratings are separately plugged to the network, and PLC variables such as transfer function, frequency, phase, distance, and frequency data are obtained and used to predict PLC network impedance. Measurement data are obtained in Excel file format from the VNA, and random forest ensemble regression is used to predict PLC network impedance using those variables. Resulting Excel files are loaded onto an Ubuntu 18.04 Linux system. Python, including python libraries such as sklearn, pandas, and numpy, is used to import python-based random forest regression (ensemble-GradientBoostingRegressor)

Frequency (kHz)	Transfer function (1000 W loads)	Predicted impedance (Ω)
10	−0.041888548	2.683132621
10.01	−0.083776438	2.620954991
10.02	−0.125664329	2.558777556
10.03	−0.167552219	2.496600312
10.04	−0.209440109	2.434423254
10.05	−0.251327999	2.372246379
10.06	−0.293215889	2.310069682
10.07	−0.335103779	2.24789316
499.93	−0.502655337	19.13619916
499.94	−0.544543227	19.07860685
499.95	−0.586431116	19.00921205
499.96	−0.628319005	19.92970978
499.97	−0.670206895	19.84181646

Only two features are used in this instance.

Table 1.
Snapshot of data used to predict network impedance. Only data from frequency ranges 10–10.07 kHz and 499.93–499.97 kHz are shown.

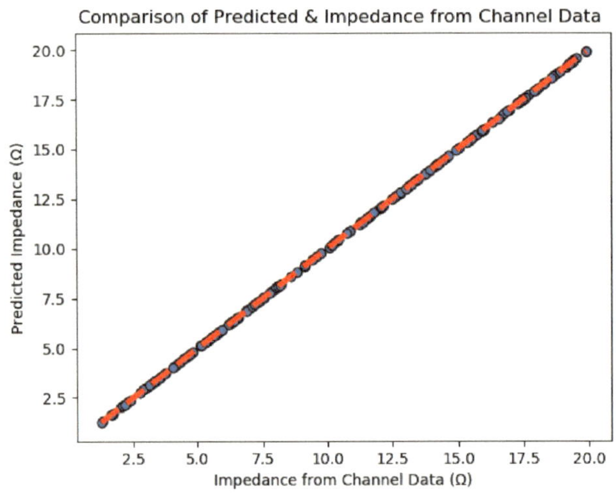

Figure 9.
Narrowband PLC impedance prediction using only three features showing effects of overfitting.

library to accomplish PLC impedance prediction. In each of the data set loaded onto the Linux system, the last column (to be predicted) by the ensemble random forest method is the PLC network impedance.

The random forest regressor parameters include splitting the training and test data in an 80:20 ratio, the number of estimators in each case is 500, and the maximum depth is 4. The learning rate of the network is 0.01. This rate is selected based on similar data rate selection in literature [32]. Since it is established in literature that random forest ensemble regression method works well for prediction efforts, our objectives include finding correct features of the PLC network that will yield the lowest possible MSE. Each data set exported from the de-embedded E5071C VNA to the Linux system contains 49,101 data points. Initially, only the frequency data and the transfer function of the 1000 W network load are used to predict PLC network impedance. A snapshot of the dataset and the predicted impedance yielded by the Linux system is shown in **Table 1**. A plot of the predicted impedance using only those two variables (frequency and 1000 W transfer function data) is shown in **Figure 9**.

4. Results and discussion

The MSE of using only two PLC network variables to accomplish impedance prediction is 0.005. As observed in **Figure 9** and from the MSE result, there is clearly an undesired effect of overfitting when only two features are used to predict the PLC network impedance. It can be seen that the fitted regression line (red) and the impedance prediction data (in blue) almost perfectly overlay each other. To improve on prediction accuracy, several PLC network parameters including transfer functions for 200, 400, 600, and 800 W, distance (150, 250, and 350 m), and phase data are measured and added to our prediction data. A snapshot of the new data used is shown in **Table 2**.

Results of using these data sets are shown from **Figures 10** to **17**. In **Figure 10**, it is observable that using 200, 400, 600, 800, and 1000 W transfer function data, frequency, phase, and 150 m distance data does not yield a very good impedance prediction result since the measured MSE is 59.59. In **Figure 11**, 250 m distance is added to the dataset that yielded result of **Figure 10**. It is also observed that the

DOI: http://dx.doi.org/10.5772/intechopen.91837

Frequency (kHz)	Tf. func (200 W)	Tf. func (400 W)	Tf. func (600 W)	Tf. func (800 W)	Tf. func (1000 W)	Tf func (1500 W)	Distance (m)	Phase (degree)	Predicted impedance
10	−0.278762778	−0.228976545	−0.467543787	−0.534524537	−0.354669876	−0.762554545	150	−0.7540	2.496600312
10.01	−0.245907689	−0.378620012	−0.290837890	−0.657890436	−0.876453095	−0.879698379	150	−0.8796	2.667887534
10	−0.278762778	−0.378400133	−0.287910770	−0.561996103	−0.678567899	−0.799721056	250	−2.8903	2.356813698
10.01	−0.300135667	−0.333501255	−0.315340097	−0.559899856	−0.668970778	−0.789987231	250	−2.7646	3.325678210
10	−0.278762778	−0.300198951	−0.315487632	−0.495908178	−0.712089758	−0.777180790	350	−3.1416	2.996754013
10.01	−0.278762778	−0.343590108	−0.456790799	−0.466320126	−0.787710967	−0.899870018	350	3.0159	3.132459810

Table 2.
Snapshot of data used to predict PLC network impedance. Several features are used in this instance.

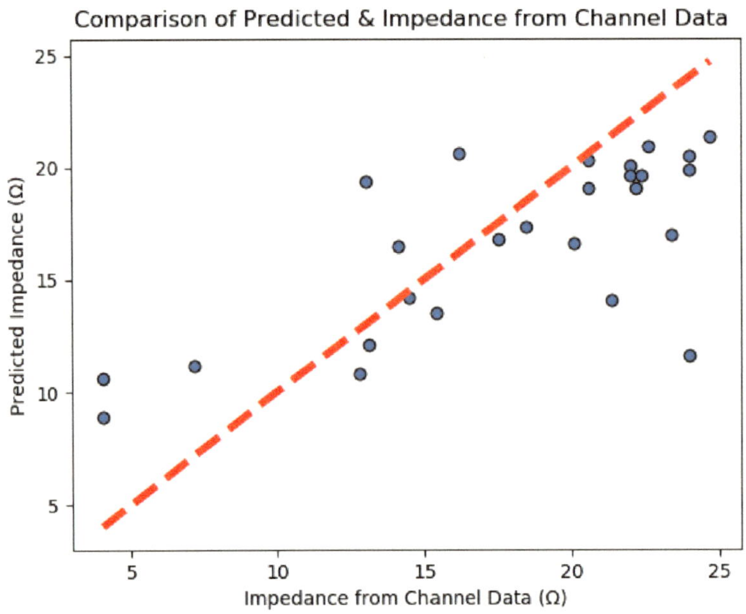

Figure 10.
Narrowband PLC impedance prediction using several features including 150 m distance data. Multicollinearity effect prevents optimized prediction; MSE = 56.59.

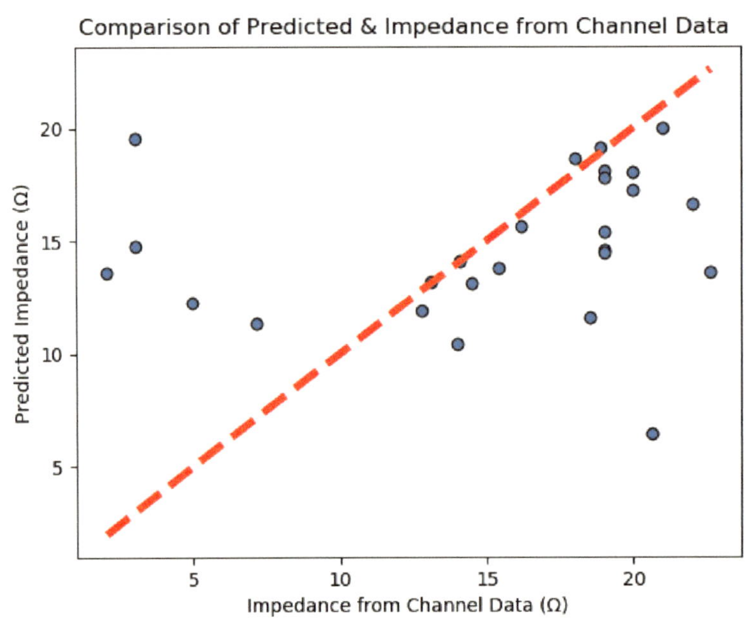

Figure 11.
Narrowband PLC impedance prediction using several features including 150 and 250 m distance data; MSE = 59.02.

prediction result in this instance is poor since MSE is 59.02. Likewise, when 350 m data is added (**Figure 12**), the MSE is 59.17, indicating poor performance by the ensemble regression method. Next, all the distance data were removed, leaving only 200, 400, 600, 800, and 100 W transfer function, phase, and frequency data. Impedance prediction result is shown in **Figure 13**, and the MSE is 37.82. It is also observed in **Figure 13** that the collective impedance result is approaching true values

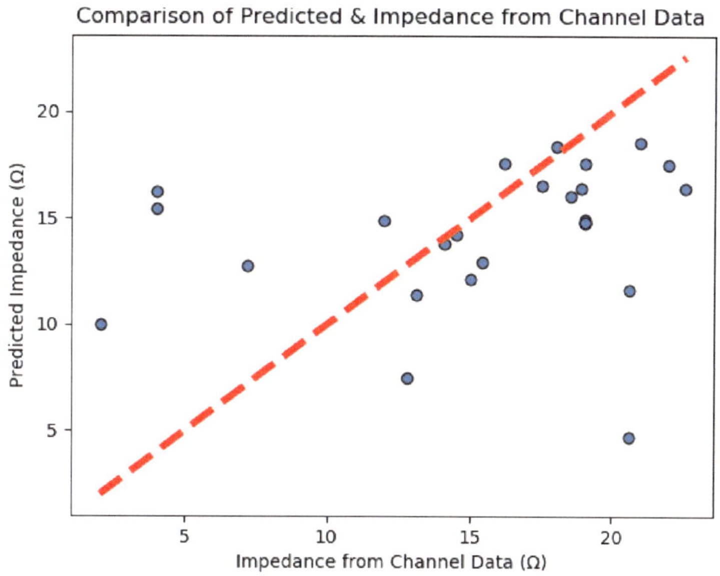

Figure 12.
Narrowband PLC impedance prediction using several features including 150, 250, and 350 m distance data. Multicollinearity effect prevents optimized prediction; MSE = 59.17.

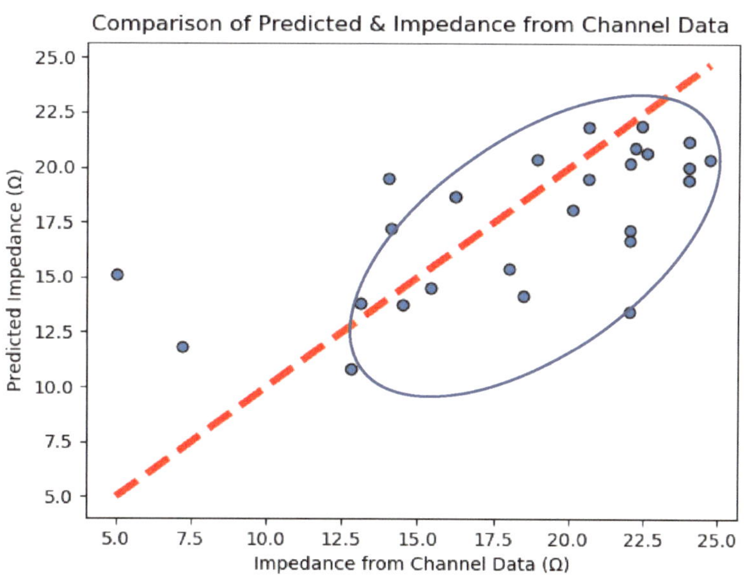

Figure 13.
Narrowband PLC impedance prediction with 200, 400, 600, 800, and 1000 W, frequency, and phase data. No distance data; MSE = 37.82.

of between 17 and 25 Ω for home PLC impedance [17] as shown by the inserted blue ring. Prior results from **Figures 10** to **12** do not yield such improved prediction.

To further optimize impedance prediction result using common PLC network data, only 200, 400, and 600 W, frequency, and phase data were used to predict impedance. The result of this is shown in **Figure 14**.

It is observable (using the inserted blue ring) that the impedance prediction is even better. The MSE for this result is 31.63. **Figure 15** shows the result of using only 200 and 400 W, phase, and frequency data. The MSE in this instance is only

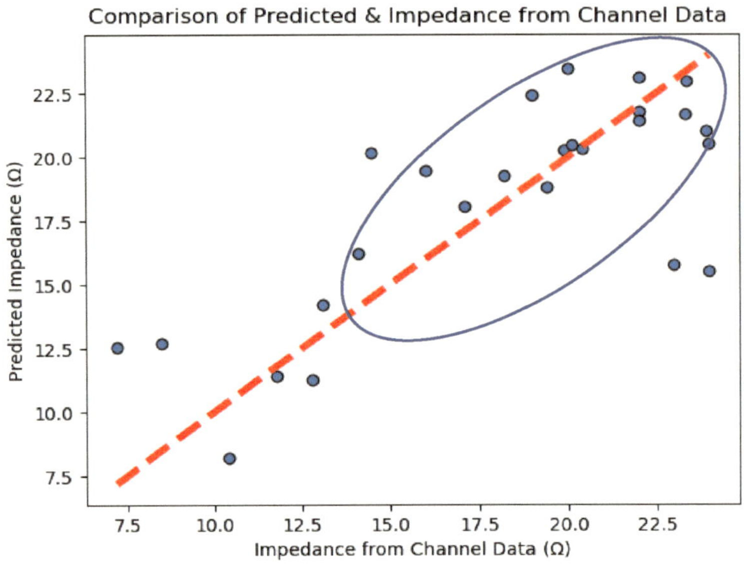

Figure 14.
Narrowband PLC impedance prediction with 200, 400, and 600 W, frequency, and phase data. No distance data; MSE = 31.63.

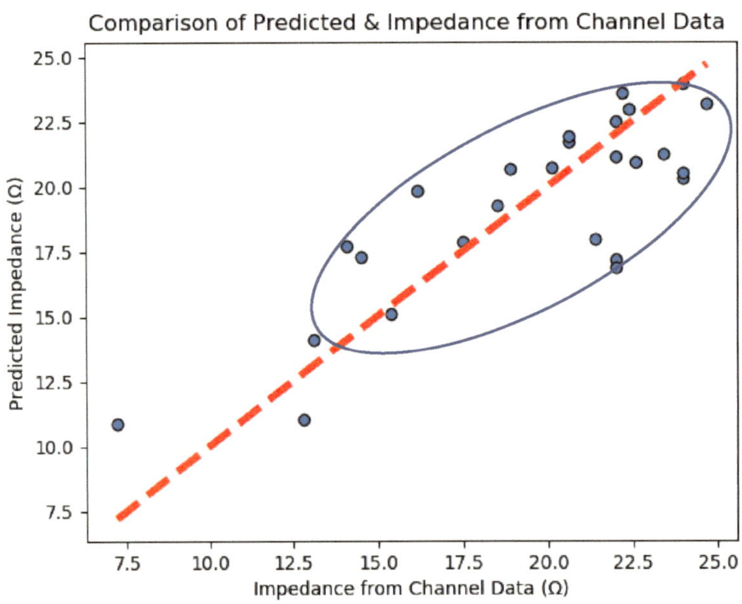

Figure 15.
Narrowband PLC impedance prediction using frequency, 200 and 400 W, and phase data; MSE = 17.02.

17.02. In **Figure 16**, only 400 W, frequency, and phase data were used for prediction, and the resulting MSE is 22.79. From the foregoing, it can be deduced that using two columns (200 and 400 W) of PLC network electrical load transfer function, frequency, and phase data works very well when random forest regression method is used for PLC network impedance prediction. To further test this deterministic hypothesis, a different set of 200 and 400 W load ratings are plugged into the PLC network, and the resulting impedance prediction shown in **Figure 17** yielded only an MSE of 17.12.

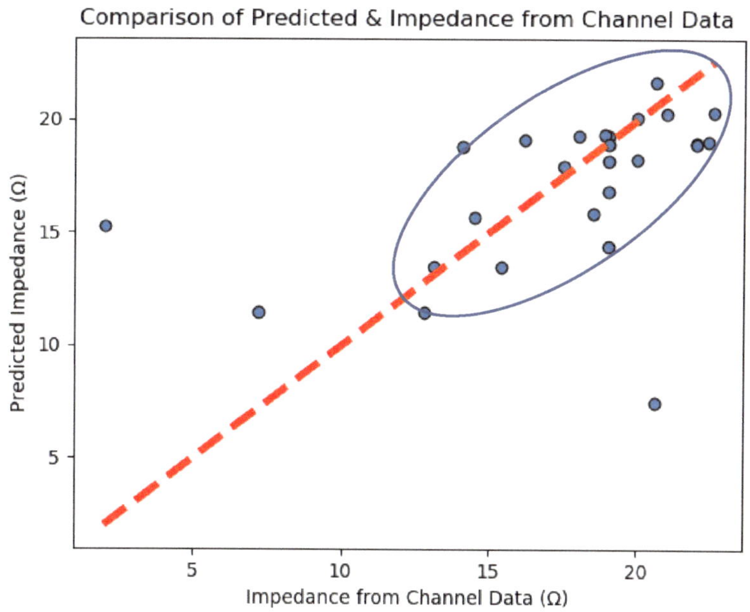

Figure 16.
Narrowband PLC impedance prediction using frequency and 400 W data only; MSE = 22.79.

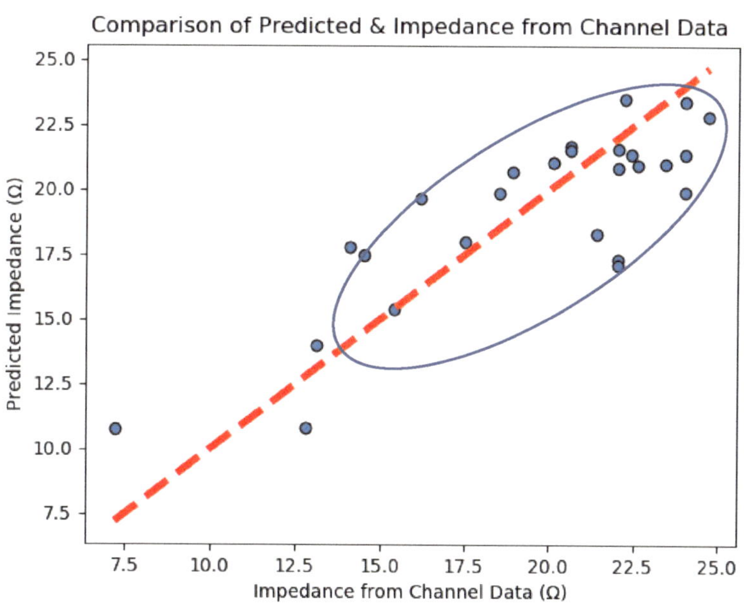

Figure 17.
Narrowband PLC impedance prediction using frequency, phase, and 200 and 400 W data; MSE = 17.12 (other sets of electrical loads).

5. Conclusion

In this chapter, a new set of attenuation profile result based on the load ratings of electrical devices existing on PLC network in the narrowband PLC frequency range has been obtained. The new result can be used to model the attenuation profile of the PLC network when the number and ratings of electrical loads on the network are considered. In addition, the random forest ensemble regression method is used to predict the PLC network impedance using commonly available PLC network data.

MSE result shows that using only four features including two columns of network load transfer functions, frequency, and PLC network phase data leads to optimized impedance prediction for the PLC network. Our result indicates that commonly available PLC network devices reinforced with deterministic data-optimization approach can be used for PLC impedance prediction. This is different from the state of the art, where very expensive devices are used for PLC network impedance measurement and prediction.

Acknowledgements

The authors wish to recognize the contributions of Schweitzer Engineering Laboratory (SEL), Pullman Washington, by donating research equipment that in part facilitated this research work.

Author details

Emmanuel Oyekanlu[1]* and Jia Uddin[2]

1 Physics Department, Drexel University, Philadelphia, Pennsylvania, USA

2 Computer Science and Engineering Department, BRAC University, Dhaka, Bangladesh

*Address all correspondence to: manuelbomi@yahoo.com; eao48@drexel.edu

References

[1] Ghasmpour A. Internet of things in smart grid: Architecture, applications, services, key technologies and challenges. MDPI Inventions. 2019. DOI: 10.3390/inventions 4010022

[2] Mahmood S, Salih A, and Khalil M. Broadband Services on Power Line Communication Systems: A Review; 2019 22nd International Conference on Control Systems and Computer Science (CSCS), Bucharest, Romania; 2019. pp. 465-470

[3] Dange H, Gondi V. Powerline communication based home automation and electricity distribution system. In: 2011 International Conference on Process Automation, Control and Computing, Coimbatore; 2011. pp. 1-6

[4] Stevan SL, Farias L, Barreto M, Leme M. Technical feasibility and performance analysis of G3-PLC standard for monitoring in industrial environment. IEEE Latin America Transactions. 2016;**14**(10):4241-4248. DOI: 10.1109/TLA.2016.7786300

[5] Farias L, Monteiro L, Leme M, Stevan SL. Empirical analysis of the communication in industrial environment based on G3-power line communication and influences from electrical grid. Electronics. 2018;7:194. DOI: 10.3390/electronics7090194

[6] Oyekanlu E. Powerline communication for the smart grid and internet of things – powerline narrowband frequency channel characterization based on TMS320C2000 C28x Digital Signal Processor; ProQuest, Drexel University, 2018

[7] Shekoni ON, Hasan AN, Shongwe T. Applications of artificial intelligence in powerline communications in terms of noise reduction: A review. Australian Journal of Electrical and Electronics Engineering. 2018;**15**(1–2):29-37. DOI: 10.1080/1448837X.2018.1496689

[8] Crăciunescu M, Chenaru O, Dobrescu R, Florea G, Mocanu Ş. IIoT gateway for edge Computing applications. In: Borangiu T, Trentesaux D, Leitão P, Giret Boggino A, Botti V, editors. Service Oriented, Holonic and Multi-Agent Manufacturing Systems for Industry of the Future. SOHOMA 2019. Studies in Computational Intelligence. Vol. 853. Cham: Springer; 2019

[9] Cristescu C, Dobrescu R, Chenaru O, and Florea G, DEW: A New Edge Computing Component for Distributed Dynamic Networks. In: 2019 22nd International Conference on Control Systems and Computer Science (CSCS), Bucharest, Romania; 2019. pp. 547-551

[10] Oyekanlu E. Fuzzy inference based stability optimization for IoT data Centers DC microgrids: Impact of constant power loads on smart grid communication over the Powerline. Journal of Energy – Energija. 2019;**68**(1)

[11] Huo Y, Prasad G, Atanackovic L, Lampe L, Leung V. Cable diagnostics with power line modems for smart grid monitoring. IEEE Access. 2019;**7**: 60206-60220. DOI: 10.1109/ACCESS.2019.2914580

[12] Yousuf MS, El-Shafei M. Power line communications: An overview - part I. Innovations in Information Technologies (IIT), Dubai. 2007;**2007**: 218-222. DOI: 10.1109/IIT.2007.4430363

[13] Chin PR, Wong A, Wong K, Barsoum N. Modelling of LCRC Adaptive Impedance Matching Circuit in Narrowband Power Line Communication, 2015 IEEE 11th International Conference on Power

Electronics and Drive Systems, Sydney, NSW; 2015. pp. 132-135

[14] Anatory J, Theethayi N. Broadband Power-Line Communication Systems Theory and Applications. Southampton, UK: WIT Press; 2010

[15] Oyekanlu E, Oladele P. Smart grid communication over DC powerline: Evaluation of powerline communication OFDM PAPR for new types of destabilizing electrical loads. In: IEEE 2018 First International Colloquium on Smart Grid Metrology (SmaGriMet), Split; 2018. pp. 1-7

[16] Powerline Carrier Communication [Internet]. 2018. Available from: https://www.electrical4u.com/power-line-carrier-communication/

[17] Cavdar H, Karadeniz E. Measurements of impedance and attenuation at CENELEC bands for power line communication systems. Sensors. 2008;**8**:8027-8036. DOI: 10.3390/s8128027

[18] Rasool B, Rasool A, Khan I. Impedance characterization of power line communication networks. Arabian Journal for Science and Engineering. 2014;**39**:6255-6267. DOI: 10.1007/s1339-014-1235-z

[19] Liang D, Guo H, Zheng T. Real-Time Impedance Estimation for Power Line Communication. In: Special Section on Advances in Power Line Communication and Its Applications, IEEE Access; 2019

[20] Pasdar AM, Cavdar IH, Sozer Y. Power-line impedance estimation at FCC band based on intelligent home appliances status detection algorithm through their individual energy and impedance signatures. IEEE Transactions on Power Delivery. 2014;**29**(3)

[21] Asti GA, Kurokawa S, Costa ECM, Pissolato J. Real-Time Estimation of Transmission Line Impedance Based on Modal Analysis Theory. 2011 IEEE Power and Energy Society General Meeting, MI, USA; 2011. pp. 1-7

[22] Antoniali M, Tonello AM, Versolatto F. A study on the optimal receiver impedance for SNR maximization in broadband PLC. Journal of Electrical and Computer Engineering. 2013. Article ID 635086. DOI: 10.1155/2013/635086

[23] Gassara H, Rouissi F, Ghazel A. Empirical modeling of the narrowband power line communication channel; IEEE 2016

[24] Baker K, Cooper M, Heidlauf P, Sands T. Autonomous trajectory generation for deterministic artificial intelligence. Electrical & Electronics Eng. 2018;**8**(3):59-68

[25] Lobo K, Lang J, Starks A, Sands T. Analysis of deterministic artificial intelligence for inertia modification and orbital disturbances. International Journal of Control Science and Engineering. 2018;**8**:53-62

[26] Sands T. Space system identification algorithms. Journal of Space Exploration. 2017;**6**(3):138

[27] Nakatami S, Sands T. Battale-damage tolerant automatic controls. Electrical and Electronics Engineering. 2018;**8**(1):10-23

[28] Sands T. Comparison and interpretation methods for predictive control of mechanics. Algorithms. 2019; **12**:232

[29] Shaver D, Su D, Popa D. Narrowband OFDM power line communication challenges, standardization, and semiconductor's role, 2013 IEEE Global Communications Conference (GLOBECOM), Atlanta, GA; 2013. pp. 2993-2997

[30] AN58825, Cypress Powerline Communication Debugging Tools; Cypress White Paper, April 2013

[31] Piante MD, Tonello AM. On Impedance Matching in a Power-Line Communication System. IEEE Transactions on Circuits and Systems II: Express Briefs. 2016;**63**(7)

[32] Uddin J, Kang M, Nguyen D, Kim J. Reliable fault classification of induction motors using texture feature extraction and a multiclass support vector machine. Mathematical Problems in Engineering. 2014;**2014**. Article ID: 814593, 9 p. DOI: 10.1155/2014/814593

[33] Oyekanlu E. Distributed osmotic computing approach to implementation of explainable predictive deep learning at industrial IoT network edges with real-time adaptive wavelet graphs. In: 2018 IEEE First International Conference on Artificial Intelligence and Knowledge Engineering (AIKE), Laguna Hills, CA; 2018. pp. 179-188

[34] Fallah S, Deo R, Shojafar M, Conti M, Shamshirband S. Computational intelligence approaches for energy load forecasting in smart energy management grids: State of the art, future challenges, and research directions. Energies. 2018;**11**:596. DOI: 10.3390/en11030596

[35] Androcec D, Vrcek N. Machine learning for the Internet of things security: A systematic review. In: The 13th International Conference on Software Technologies; 2018. pp. 563-570

[36] Shojafar M, Sookhak M. Internet of everything, networks, applications and computing systems (IoENACS). International Journal of Computers and Applications. 2020;**42**(3):213-215

[37] Uddin J, Islam R, Kim J. Texture feature extraction techniques for fault diagnosis of induction motors. Journal of Convergence. 2014;**5**:15-20

[38] Rawal BS. A proxy re-encryption-based webmail and file sharing system for collaboration in cloud computing environment. In: 2018 International Conference on Computational Techniques, Electronics and Mechanical Systems (CTEMS), Belgaum, India; 2018. pp. 213-218

[39] Mijac M, Androcec D, Picek R. Smart city services driven by IoT: A systematic review. Journal of Economic & Social Development. Sept., 2017;**4**(2):40-50

[40] Shojafar M, Cordeschi N, Amendola D, Baccarelli E. Energy-saving adaptive computing and traffic engineering for real-time-services data centers. In: Proceedings of the IEEE International Conference. Communications Workshop; 2015. pp. 1800-1806

[41] Oyekanlu E. Osmotic collaborative computing for machine learning and cybersecurity applications in industrial IoT networks and cyber physical systems with Gaussian mixture models. In: 2018 IEEE 4th International Conference on Collaboration and Internet Computing (CIC), Philadelphia, PA; 2018. pp. 326-335

[42] Androcec D. Systematic mapping study on osmotic computing. In: The 30th Central European Conference on Information & Intelligent Systems; 2019. pp. 79-84

[43] Javanmardi S, Shojafar M, Amendola D, Cordeschi N, Liu H, Abraham A. Hybrid Job Scheduling Algorithm for Cloud Computing Environment. In: Kömer P, Abraham A, Snášel V, editors. Proceedings of the Fifth International Conference on Innovations in Bio-Inspired Computing and Applications IBICA 2014. Advances

in Intelligent Systems and Computing, Vol. 303. Cham: Springer;

[44] Shojafar M, Pooranian Z, Sookhak M, Buyya R. Recent advances in cloud data centers towards fog data centers. Concurrency and Computation. 2019;**31**(8):e5164

[45] Islam R, Uddin J, Kim JM. Texture analysis based feature extraction using Gabor filter and SVD for reliable fault diagnosis of an induction motor. International Journal of Information Technology and Management. 2018;**17**: 20-32

[46] Rawal BS. Attack countermeasure tree (ACT) meets with the split-protocol. International Journal of Computer Networks & Communications (IJCNC). 2015;7(4)

[47] Androcek D. Overcoming Service-Level Interoperability Challenges of the IoT. In: Connected Environments for the Internet of Things. Springer; 2017. pp. 83-101

[48] Sodhro AH, Pirbhulal S, de Albuquerque VHC. Artificial intelligence-driven mechanism for edge Computing-based industrial applications. IEEE Transactions on Industrial Informatics. 2019;**15**(7): 4235-4243. DOI: 10.1109/TII.2019. 2902878

[49] Vijay A, Umadevi K. Explainable AI controlled architecture of D2D system for massive MIMO based 5G networks. International Journal of Scientific Research and Review. 2019;**07**(03): 33-40

[50] Tonello A, Letizia N, Righini D, Marcuzzi F. Machine learning tips and tricks for power line communication. In: Special Section on Advances in Power Line Communication and Its Applications, IEEE Access; 2019

[51] Oyekanlu E, Nelatury C, Fatade A, Alaba O, Abass O. Edge computing for industrial IoT and the smart grid: Channel capacity for M2M communication over the power line. In: 2017 IEEE 3rd International Conference on Electro-Technology for National Development, Owerri; 2017. pp. 1-11

[52] Valecha H, Varma A, Khare I, Sachdeva A, Goyal M. Prediction of consumer behavior using random forest algorithm. In: 2018 5th IEEE International Conference on Electrical, Electronics & Computer Engineering, Gorakhpur; 2018

[53] Kaur A, Malhotra R. Application of random forest in predicting fault-prone classes. In: 2008 IEEE International Conference on Advanced Computer Theory & Engineering; 2008

[54] Jaiswal J, Samikanu R. Application of random forest on feature subset selection and classification and regression. In: IEEE 2017 World Congress on Computing and Communication Technologies; 2017

Chapter 4

Application of Artificial Neural Networks for Accurate Prediction of Thermal and Rheological Properties of Nanofluids

Behzad Vaferi

Abstract

Nanofluids have recently been considered as one of the most popular working fluid in heat transfer and fluid mechanics. Accurate estimation of thermophysical properties of nanofluids is required for the investigation of their heat transfer performance. Thermal conductivity coefficient, convective heat transfer coefficient, and viscosity are some the most important thermophysical properties that directly influence on the application of nanofluids. The aim of the present chapter is to develop and validate artificial neural networks (ANNs) to estimate these thermophysical properties with acceptable accuracy. Some simple and easy measurable parameters including type of nanoparticle and base fluid, temperature and pressure, size and concentration of nanoparticles, etc. are used as independent variables of the ANN approaches. The predictive performance of the developed ANN approaches is validated with both experimental data and available empirical correlations. Various statistical indices including mean square errors (MSE), root mean square errors (RMSE), average absolute relative deviation percent (AARD%), and regression coefficient (R^2) are used for numerical evaluation of accuracy of the developed ANN models. Results confirm that the developed ANN models can be regarded as a practical tool for studying the behavior of those industrial applications, which have nanofluids as operating fluid.

Keywords: artificial neural networks, solid-liquid suspension, nanofluids, thermal property, rheological property

1. Introduction

Increasing price of fuels as well as hardening the environmental regulations/laws enforces the industrial processes to increase the efficiency of their consumed energy. Therefore, concentrations are focused on the technologies that improve the performance of heat transfer equipment. This improvement is often achieved by either enhancing the thermophysical characteristics of the traditional operating fluids or modifying the structure of heat exchangers [1–3]. Unfortunately, conventional heat transfer fluids (e.g. water, engine oil, and ethylene glycol) suffer from inherently low thermal properties and poor heat transfer characteristics [4, 5]. Conducting research for modifying poor thermophysical properties of the traditional fluids confirmed that adding solid particles to the base fluids can improve their heat transfer properties [6]. Since a solid metal has a larger thermal conductivity than a pure fluid, adding some of metallic solid particles in base fluids may improve their thermal behavior [7, 8]. Although, thermal conductivity of solid particle is typically an order-of-magnitude higher than the base fluid, adding micro-sized solid particles is not practically possible. The micro-sized solid particles that often simply settled down are responsible for some major problems including clogging the small passages, high pressure drop, and components erosion by abrasive action [9–12]. For solving these problems, most of the new studies have concentrated on synthesizing materials of nano-sized scale [9, 12]. Rapid progress of nanotechnology has motivated researchers to disperse various nanoscale particles (1–100 nm) in the operating fluids to form the new class of heat transfer fluid namely nanofluids [13–18]. The term of nanofluids was firstly proposed by Choi for addressing the homogeneous suspensions of nanoscale particles in base fluid [19]. Large relative surface area, higher heat conduction, excellent stability, and minimal clogging are the main advantages of nano-sized materials respect to micro-sized ones. It is possible to improve the thermophysical properties of the conventional fluids, and enhance their heat transfer ability by adding small amount of nano-sized solid particles [20]. It has been claimed that nanofluids are the best choice for the next generation of heat transfer fluids [5, 11].

Nanofluids have found high popularity due to their excellent ability in enhancement of heat transfer performances of various thermal systems during the recent years [16, 21, 22]. In spite of such potential benefits, nanofluid technology is still limited for commercial use as there are no proven standardized techniques for accurate prediction of important heat transfer characteristics of nanofluids [23, 24]. Availability of some accurate correlations/models for estimation of heat transfer characteristics of nanofluids is necessary during design, optimization, and control of those heat transfer devices that use these operating fluids. Therefore, in this chapter, great deals of efforts are made to correlate some thermophysical properties of nanofluids by artificial neural networks. In the next section, the procedure of working of artificial neural networks and four different types of ANN are briefly explained.

2. Artificial neural networks

Simulation of working procedures of the biological nervous system of the human brain is the basic idea for designing artificial neural networks [25]. Artificial neural network, as its name clearly implies is composed of some well-organized processing elements, namely neurons. Indeed, various types of these smart networks are constituted of a common processing unit namely artificial neuron or perceptron. The neuron has two regulating parameters that are often known as weight (w) and bias (b). The perceptrons receive their entry information from either other neurons or external source (x), and produces an output signal using Eq. (1).

$$out = f\left(\sum_{r=1}^{k} w_r x_r + b\right) \tag{1}$$

where *out* denotes the perceptron's output, and f is the activation function. ANN models often require different number of neurons in their layers for solving specific problems. Artificial neural networks can extract a function $g(\cdot) : R^{Ind} \rightarrow R^{Dep}$ by training on a dataset, where *Ind* and *Dep* indicate the number of dimensions for independent and dependent variables, respectively. Providing the ANN with a databank of independent variables $X = [Ind_1 \, Ind_2 \cdots Ind_n]^T$ and their related dependent variable(s), their parameters can be tuned by a proper backpropagation training algorithm. In this way, it is possible to simulate the behavior of even the most complicated nonlinear systems with an acceptable accuracy often smaller than AARD = 10% [26, 27]. Activation functions are responsible for providing the artificial neural networks with nonlinear behavior. Different types of ANN paradigm have found high popularity as a technique for parameter estimation, pattern detection, data clustering, text processing, fault discovery, and so on [28].

2.1 Types of ANN model

In this chapter, four different types of artificial neural networks include multilayer perceptron (MLP), cascade feedforward (CFF), radial basis function (RBF), and generalized regression (GR) neural networks that are used as artificial intelligent techniques for characterization of thermophysical properties of nanofluids. These types of ANN model are briefly illustrated in the following four subsections.

2.1.1 Multilayer perceptron neural networks

The MLP is the most well-known feedforward approach that often has one or more hidden layers between dependent and independent variables. This type of ANN methodologies is used in the supervised learning process for the adjustment of its parameters. The term feedforward implies that the entry signals can only move inside the neural network from input layer toward an output layer. The backward flow for signal is not allowed in the MLP neural networks. The multi-layer perceptron constitutes of several layers of nodes including one input layer, one or more hidden layer(s), and one output layer. This type of ANN models has found high-reputation because of its excellent performances for handling of both regression and classification problems [25–27].

2.1.2 Cascade feedforward neural networks

By conducting some modifications on the topology of the multi-layer perceptron networks, Fahlman and Lebiere designed a new class of ANN namely cascade feedforward neural network [29]. They do their modification by providing the CFF neural networks with synaptic connections for neuron of each layer with neurons of all subsequent layers [30]. It has been claimed that convergence rate of learning process of the CFB model is better than other ANN topologies [31].

2.1.3 Radial basis function neural networks

RBF neural network has been structured as a two-layer feedforward neural network model [32]. In the hidden and output layer of the RBF approach, Gaussian and linear transfer functions are always used, respectively [32]. The radial basis neural network that originally developed by Broomhead and Lowe in 1988, is a powerful tool for interpolation among data in multi-dimensional problems [33, 34].

2.1.4 Generalized regression neural networks

The GR neural network that was firstly developed in 1991 by Specht is often viewed as a special reformation of the RBF model [35]. The main benefit of the GR paradigm is that its parameters can be easily adjusted during training stage.

Parameters of the general regression neural network can be simply tuned by only one-pass training with the sufficient number of experimental data.

2.2 Training of artificial neural networks

The training process is a well-established procedure that tries to adjust parameters of the ANN model, i.e., biases and connection weights. During the learning process, the ANN model is provided with a sufficient number of experimental data containing both independent and dependent variables of the considered phenomena. Thereafter, an appropriate training algorithm is employed to adjust the parameters of ANN model in such a way that it could predict the actual targets with acceptable accuracy. The training stage begins with random values for the weights and biases of ANN model. Thereafter, the numerical signals of independent variable (s) are fed to the artificial network and are made to flow through it until they reach the output layer. Finally, the output layer is responsible for producing the output signal(s). A training algorithm is then applied to minimize the difference between the actual and calculated values for dependent variable(s) by regulating the parameters of the ANN model. This adjustment continues as far as the deviation between calculated and actual target values reaches the predefined tolerance. As soon as the training stage is completed, the weights and biases are adjusted and they are kept unchanged. In this stage, it is possible to employ the trained ANN approach for estimating the dependent variable(s) from new independent datasets.

2.3 Performance analyses of artificial neural networks

Several statistical accuracy indices including MSE, RMSE, AARD%, and R^2 have been applied to investigate accuracy of various ANN models. Values of MSE, RMSE, AARD%, and R^2 are mathematically calculated by Eq. (2) to Eq. (5), respectively.

$$MSE = \sum_{i=1}^{N} \frac{\left(D^{\exp.}(i) - D^{cal.}(i)\right)^2}{N} \tag{2}$$

$$RMSE = \left\{ \sum_{i=1}^{N} \frac{\left(D^{\exp.}(i) - D^{cal.}(i)\right)^2}{N} \right\}^{0.5} \tag{3}$$

$$AARD\% = \frac{100}{N} \sum_{i=1}^{N} \left(\left| \frac{D^{\exp.}(i) - D^{cal.}(i)}{D^{\exp.}(i)} \right| \right) \tag{4}$$

$$R^2 = \frac{\sum_{i=1}^{N}\left(D^{\exp.}(i) - \overline{\Delta D}\right)^2 - \sum_{i=1}^{N}\left(D^{\exp.}(i) - \Delta D^{cal.}(i)\right)^2}{\sum_{i=1}^{N}\left(D^{\exp.}(i) - \overline{\Delta D}\right)^2} \tag{5}$$

where D and N represent dependent variable and number of experimental data, respectively. $D_i^{\exp}$ is the experimental dependent variable, D_i^{cal} presents the value of ith predicted dependent variable by ANN model, and $\overline{\Delta D}$ is the average value of the experimental data points for dependent variable.

3. Characterization of properties of nanofluids by ANN approaches

In this section, different types on ANN are used for systematic estimation of thermophysical properties of nanofluids. The focus is concentrated on two thermal and a rheological property of nanofluids. Thermal conductivity coefficient, convective heat transfer coefficient, and viscosity of nanofluids tried to be modeled by ANN approaches. For each parameter, experimental data and procedure of developing ANN model are collected, and evaluation of performance of the developed model is presented.

3.1 Thermal conductivity coefficient

Thermal conductivity of homogeneous dispersion of solid particles in liquids has its own importance for dozen of decades [36]. Since the uniform suspensions of nano-sized solid particles in liquids have better thermal characteristics than their associated base liquids, they may be considered as operating fluids for heat transfer systems [7, 9, 37–41]. Maxwell [36] and Hamilton and Crosser [42] proposed some basic correlations for the calculation of thermal conductivity of the homogeneous suspensions from their particle dosage, thermal conductivity of base fluids as well as particles. Moreover, effects of shape and size of nanoparticle, chemistry of base fluids, temperature, and pH on the level of enhancement of thermal conductivity of pure base fluids have been deeply investigated [39, 43, 44]. Some researchers observed that thermal conductivity of nanofluids is dramatically increased by increasing temperature [39, 43–46]. Brownian motion of nanoparticles is often considered as a key mechanism to explain enhancement of thermal conductivity of uniform dispersion of nano-sized materials in different base fluids [39, 44]. It is a widely accepted theory that Brownian motion has a direct relation with the fluid temperature and it increases by increasing temperature. Indeed, particle motions increase by temperature and it results in increasing the thermal conductivity of nanofluid [39]. Enhancement of thermal conductivity of nanofluids by increasing the suspension temperature has been reported by different groups of researchers [45–48]. Increasing concentration of nanoparticles in base liquids that increase the possibility of collisions between fluid molecules and solid particles can also improve the thermal conductivity of nanofluids. Influence of shape and size of nanoparticle on thermal conductivity of nanofluids was comprehensively studied by different groups of researchers [7, 9, 37, 45, 48]. It is worthy to be noted that the thermal conductivity of nanofluid was reported, which may be lower than the base liquids under some specific circumstances [45, 48].

3.1.1 Experimental data

Available correlations in the literatures approve that the thermal conductivity ratio (TCR) of alumina-water nanofluid has relationship with nanoparticle size, concentration of nanoparticle in base liquids, and temperature of suspension [39, 45–58]. Therefore, these parameters are considered as independent variables for the estimation of TCR of alumina water-based nanofluid using MLP network. As reported in **Table 1**, 280 experimental datasets for TCR of alumina-water nanofluids are collected from various literatures [39, 45–58]. The collected experimental data covers the fluid temperature ranging from 1 to 133.8°C, alumina nanoparticle size of 8–283 nm, volume fraction from 0.0013 to 0.16, and TCR values ranging from 0.99 to 1.2902.

There exists a well-known role of thumb that states the multi-layer perceptron neural networks with a single hidden layer can precisely learn a behavior of any multi-variable function with a desired tolerance [22]. Therefore, in this section, a MLP network is structured with only one hidden layer to predict thermal conductivity ratio of the alumina-water nanofluid. Number of hidden neurons has been selected using trial and error procedure on minimizing both MSE and AARD%, and maximizing R^2 values for training as well as testing datasets. **Table 2** reports

Temperature range (°C)	Nanoparticle volume fraction	Nanoparticle diameter (nm)	Thermal conductivity ratio	N*	References
21–51	0.01–0.04	38.4	1.02–1.242	12	[39]
21–71	0.01–0.04	11–150	1.01–1.2902	34	[45]
27.5–34.7	0.02–0.1	36	1.077–1.1513	22	[46]
21–60	0.01	80–150	1.033–1.106	10	[47]
10–50	0.0013–0.0052	20–100	1.004–1.147	36	[48]
20–40	0.031–0.09	36	1.157–1.259	30	[49]
1–40	0.01–0.04	30	0.99–1.219	15	[50]
10–60	0.05	40	1.096–1.128	6	[51]
10–50	0.03–0.16	20	1.06–1.214	12	[52]
15–60	0.01–0.08	120	1.025–1.257	30	[53]
20–60	0.03–0.13	30–80	1.041–1.257	24	[54]
23.5–27.4	0.0186–0.04	8–283	1.0214–1.185	21	[55]
24–133.8	0.01–0.04	12	0.99–1.228	24	[56]
35.5	0.0033–0.03	36	1.015–1.096	5	[57]
20	0.005–0.06	43	1.063–1.28	4	[58]

**Number of experimental data.*

Table 1.
Physical and operating conditions of various experimental datasets.

numerical values for the observed MSE and AARD% between calculated TCRs and their associated experimental data. It should be mentioned that the only difference between these MLP models is the number of hidden neurons. For reducing the effect of random selection of weights and biases on the final results, all of the MLP models are trained and tested 10 different times, and only the best obtained results for each topology is reported in **Table 2**. Indeed, in this section, we checked 200 MLP paradigms to find the best one.

3.1.2 Development of ANN model

It can be simply understood from **Table 2** that predictive performance of the MLP for the training subset is improved by increasing the number of hidden neurons. The AARD% for MLP model having 1–20 hidden neurons continuously decreases from 4.24 to 0.91%. But, performance of the MLP approach for estimation of the testing dataset only improves up to 14 hidden neurons, and thereafter no impressive progress is observed. It can be concluded that increasing the hidden neurons more than 14 only enlarges the MLP networks and has no positive effect on improving the accuracy [59]. Therefore, by considering the reported results in **Table 2**, a MLP approach with single hidden layer having 14 neurons (the bold row) is selected as the best structure for estimation of thermal conductivity ration of alumina-water nanofluid. This optimal MLP model is capable to estimate the testing dataset by MSE and AARD% of 6.3×10^{-4} and 1.75%, respectively.

This optimal MLP paradigm provides excellent R^2 values between the predicted and the actual values of TCR for both training and testing dataset. The calculated values of R^2 for the MLP models with 1–20 hidden neurons are depicted in **Figure 1**.

Number of hidden neuron*	AARD%		MSE	
	Training	Testing	Training	Testing
1	4.24	4.42	0.004542	0.004210
2	3.86	3.48	0.003877	0.003723
3	3.48	4.06	0.003397	0.004666
4	3.04	3.51	0.002563	0.003569
5	2.94	2.97	0.002171	0.001974
6	2.41	3.06	0.001696	0.002183
7	1.81	2.97	0.000736	0.002246
8	2.39	3.22	0.001295	0.002848
9	1.75	2.79	0.000681	0.003002
10	1.66	1.83	0.000687	0.001031
11	1.78	1.92	0.000781	0.000741
12	1.37	2.43	0.000429	0.001689
13	1.14	2.64	0.000345	0.002499
14	**1.23**	**1.75**	**0.000330**	**0.000630**
15	1.11	1.94	0.000303	0.001152
16	1.02	2.14	0.000273	0.00139
17	1.14	2.76	0.000343	0.002737
18	1.07	2.67	0.000354	0.003447
19	1.28	2.45	0.000484	0.002184
20	0.91	2.16	0.000201	0.001754

**The best obtained results among 10 various trained network per each topology.*
The bold values indicate the best obtained results for the considered AI models.

Table 2.
Evaluation of the best topology of the MLP model.

The values of observed AARD% and MSE by MLP models with different numbers of hidden neurons for the overall dataset (training + test) are shown in **Figure 2**.

To simulate behavior of a given system by the MLP neural network, a relatively huge amount of experimental data is required. **Figure 3** depicts variation of observed mean square errors (between MLP predictions and actual data of TCR of alumina-water nanofluids) as function of the number of epoch. As mentioned earlier, the procedure of adjustment of weights and biases of the MLP model is done by an optimization technique namely training algorithm. It is obvious that the optimization technique tries to minimize the observed MSE by an iteration procedure. In **Figure 3**, the term of epoch shows the number of interactions that the training algorithm has tried to tune the MLP parameter using the given procedure in Section 2.2. It can be seen from **Figure 1** that by increasing the number of iterations (i.e. epoch), weights and biases of the MLP model converge to their optimized values, and therefore, the observed MSE continuously decreases. After 800 iterations, the training algorithm enforces the MSE to converge 3.3×10^{-4}. Since this level of MSE between predicted and actual values of TCR is relatively small value, it can be said that the training was successful.

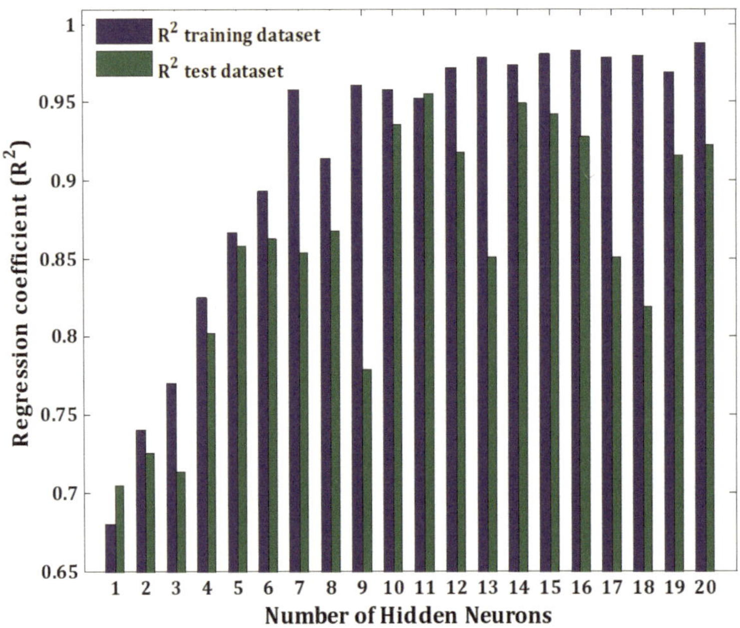

Figure 1.
R^2 values of the proposed model for training and testing subsets.

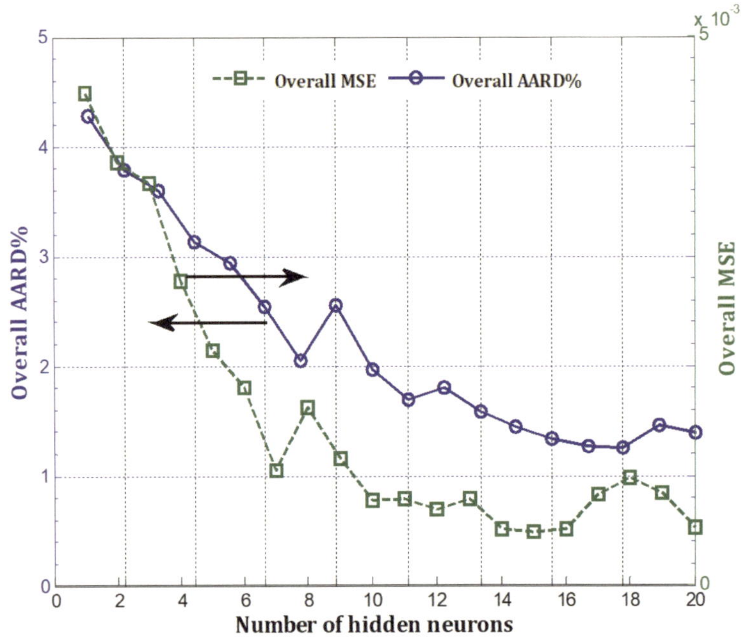

Figure 2.
Overall AARD% and MSE of various ANN models over training and testing subsets.

3.1.3 ANN model evaluation

A databank with 228 experimental datasets for TCR of water-alumina nanofluids has been collected from different literatures [39, 45–58]. These datasets have been used to design and validate the accuracy performances of different MLP networks as well as to find the best topology of the MLP model. Moreover, 57 experimental

TCR data-points, which were not utilized in the training process have been used to check the predictive accuracy of the proposed MLP paradigm.

In this part, performance of the proposed MLP approach tried to be evaluated by plotting the predicted values of TCRs as function of their associated experimental values for both testing and training subsets. **Figure 4** confirms an excellent performance and remarkable accuracy of the optimal MLP model for the estimation of experimental values of TCR of water-alumina nanofluids for overall databank. The most exact prediction (calculated TCRs = experimental data) is shown by a solid dashed 45° line. A relatively large R^2 = 0.971875 that observed for predicting all the experimental TCRs justifies that there is an excellent agreement between the predications of MLP model and the actual experimental data.

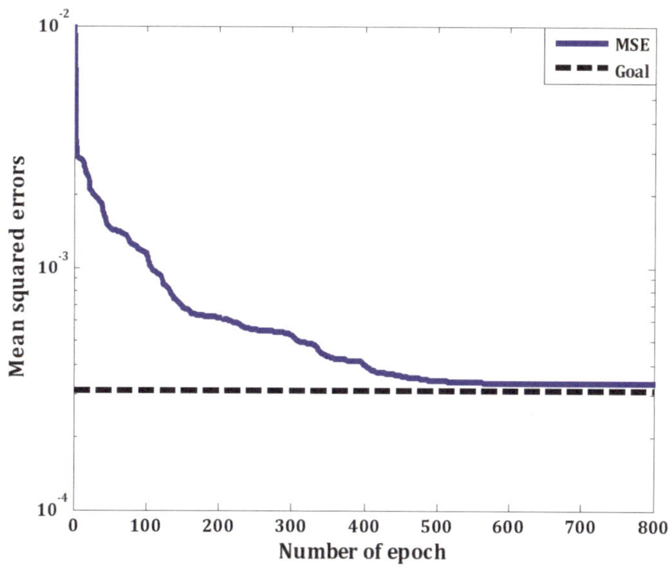

Figure 3.
Variations of the mean squared errors with epoch during MLP training.

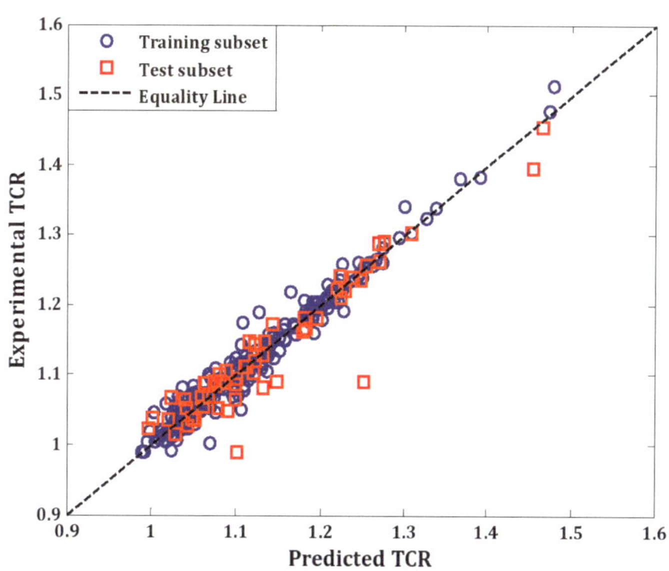

Figure 4.
Predicted thermal conductivity ratio vs. measured ones for the overall dataset.

Table 3 summarizes an accuracy of the optimal MLP model with the six well-known empirical correlations for prediction of experimental data reported by Das et al. [39, 45, 47, 49, 60–62]. This table shows that the proposed MLP model presents the best overall AARD of 0.866% for the considered experimental data. The proposed model by Chon et al. [45] provides an AARD = 1.331% that is the best results among the considered correlations.

Table 4 reports results of estimation of experimental TCR data reported by Chandrasekar et al. [57] using our smart model as well as various empirical correlations [45, 47, 49, 60–62]. It can be simply seen that our proposed MLP model predicts the experimental data with the smallest deviation (AARD = 0.117%). The proposed correlations by Yu and Choi [60] and Xie et al. [61] that provide relatively similar results (AARD = 0.39%) are the best empirical correlations.

3.2 Convective heat transfer coefficient

It is obvious that a convective heat transfer coefficient (HTC) of nanofluids depends on concentration of the dispersed nanoparticles, their shape and size, flow structure, thermal conductivity and heat capacity of both nanoparticles and base liquid, and viscosity of nanofluid. Generally, addition of nanoparticles to the base liquid improves its thermal conductivity. Increasing an amount of energy transfer by the liquid leads to a higher temperature gradient between tube wall and bulk of nanofluid. It is a reason that is often highlighted for explanation is an increasing rate of convection heat transfer between nanofluid and tube wall [63].

Volume fraction of Al_2O_3	The considered intelligent approach and empirical correlations							
	Chonet al. [45]	Murshedet al. [47]	Mintsaet al. [49]	Yu and Choi [60]	Xieet al. [61]	Nanet al. [62]	MLP model	Actual TCR [39]
0.01	1.09	1.08	1.02	1.03	1.03	1.03	1.10	1.111
0.02	1.15	1.16	1.04	1.07	1.07	1.06	1.14	1.141
0.03	1.20	1.25	1.05	1.10	1.10	1.09	1.16	1.170
0.04	1.24	1.34	1.07	1.14	1.14	1.12	1.26	1.241
AARD%	1.331	4.818	10.270	6.909	6.909	7.744	0.866	—

Table 3.
Comparison among accuracy of various approaches for the prediction of experimental TCRs measured by Das et al. [39] (T = 51°C, Dp = 38.4 nm).

Volume fraction of Al_2O_3	The considered intelligent approach and empirical correlations							
	Chonet al. [45]	Murshedet al. [47]	Mintsaet al. [49]	Yu and Choi [60]	Xieet al. [61]	Nanet al. [62]	MLP model	Actual TCR [57]
0.003	1.0136	1.0253	1.0058	1.0117	1.0118	1.0097	1.0145	1.015
0.0075	1.0220	1.0594	1.0136	1.0230	1.0231	1.0214	1.0306	1.031
0.010	1.0331	1.0818	1.0175	1.0341	1.0343	1.0292	1.0316	1.032
0.020	1.0545	1.1646	1.0351	1.0672	1.0673	1.0584	1.0750	1.074
0.030	1.0760	1.2523	1.0516	1.1023	1.1025	1.0896	1.0920	1.096
AARD%	0.587	3.406	1.524	0.388	0.386	0.635	0.117	—

Table 4.
Comparisons of the predictive accuracy of different smart and empirical correlations over experimental TCR measured by Chandrasekar et al. [57] (T = 35.5 °C, Dp = 36 nm).

The objective of this part of chapter is to design a smart approach based on artificial neural networks for accurate estimation of convective HTC of different nanofluids flowing inside circular tubes. The great deals of effort are made to predict the HTC of nanofluids from the easily measurable characteristics of a system. Correlation matrix analysis approves that size of nanoparticles, their molecular weight (Mw) and volume concentration fraction (V_f), critical pressure and temperature of the base fluids (Pc and Tc), their acentric factor (ω), Reynolds number (Re), and the wall condition are the most important factors that influence on the convective HTC of nanofluids. It should be mentioned that we consider two different conditions for tube wall including uniform heat flux and constant temperature. From practical point of view, these two conditions are often encountered in various industrial applications.

The major part of the current section is dedicated to find the best ANN type as well as its topology for the considered task. Indeed, the ANN type with the smallest size that could provide the most accurate results for estimation of HTC of nanofluids is considered as the best topology. After evaluating the most accurate ANN type and its topology, we tried to compare its prediction results with available empirical correlations in different literatures.

3.2.1 Experimental databank

For the convective HTCs, 346 experimental data which covered the Reynolds number 600–8.9 $\times$ 10^4 and nanoparticle size of 20–100 nm are collected from different literatures [64–68]. The considered physical properties and their ranges as well as minimum-maximum values of convective HTCs of the collected experimental data, which collected from various literatures are presented in **Table 5**. These experimental data are used for developing ANN models and validating their predictive capabilities.

3.2.2 Designing an ANN model

All the experimental datasets have been randomly allocated to two different subsets namely train and test subsets. These two subsets have different application

Nanofluid	Nanoparticle size (nm)	Heat flux (W/m^2)	Temperature, Range (K)	Vf, Range (%v)	Re	*h* (W/m^2 K)	*N**	Reference
Al_2O_3/Water	45	8842	—	0.25–1.5	600–2200	600–2000	58	[64]
Water	—	8842	—	—	900–2100	500–800	6	[64]
Al_2O_3/EG-W	45	218,000	—	2–10	3000–15,000	8000–19,000	57	[65]
SiO_2/EG-W	20, 50, 100	218,000	—	4, 2	3000–15,000	6000–19,000	37	[65]
CuO/EG-W	29	218,000	—	4	3000–12,000	8000–18,000	10	[65]
EG-W	—	218,000	—	—	4000–17,000	5000–16,000	11	[65]
Al_2O_3/Water	40	—	20–60	0.1–2	3000–18,000	2000–13,000	76	[66]
Water	—	—	20–60	—	3000–18,000	2000–11,000	17	[66]
Fe_3O_4/Water	36	12,489	—	0.02–0.6	3000–22,000	2000–49,000	51	[67]
Water	—	12,489	—	—	3000–22,000	900–8000	13	[67]
EG-W	—	500,000	—	—	10,000–89,000	7000–38,000	10	[68]

**Number of experimental data.*

Table 5.
Physical and operational conditions of various datasets.

in the development of ANN model. Indeed, the training datasets have been used for adjusting weights and biases of the ANN approach as well as selecting its best structure. On the other hand, the predictive performance of this trained ANN model is often validated by the testing subsets. Since the testing datasets are not used during training stage and the ANN model did not see them previously, they could be considered as a reliable benchmark for evaluation/validation performance of the model in the unknown situations.

Various ANN types including RBF, MLP, CFB, and GR neural network are checked and the best one is selected based on its predictive capabilities. The optimal size of ANN approach (number of hidden neurons) is the smallest network, which can predict both train and test subsets within an acceptable error.

In this section, an iterative constructive method is used for determination of an optimal numbers of hidden neurons. Iterative constructive method increases the number of neurons in hidden layer gradually as long as a testing error be fixed or begins to rise. Values of observed AARD% for estimation of both testing and overall experimental data for 20 different MLP models that have 1–20 neurons in their hidden layer are presented in **Figure 5**. It can be simply understood from **Figure 5** that the testing errors are decreased by increasing the number of hidden neurons up to 10. Thereafter, no significant reduction in AARD% can be seen. Accordingly, the single hidden layer MLP approach having 10 hidden neurons is selected as the best structure for estimation of convective HTC of six different nanofluids and five considered pure liquids.

Values of the R^2 and MSE between experimental convective HTC and those HTC values predicted by various MLP networks are presented in **Figures 6** and 7, respectively. It can be seen from these figures, the 10 hidden neurons that present the largest value for R^2 as well as the smallest value for MSE over huge experimental databank can be regarded as the optimum value. It is worthy to be mentioned that vertical axis of **Figure 6** is in logarithmic scale to magnify increasing trend of MSE after 10 hidden neurons. The observed MSE for estimation of the testing datasets decreases by increasing the number of hidden neurons up to 10. After that no notable improvement in expense of enlarging the MLP model can be found. It can

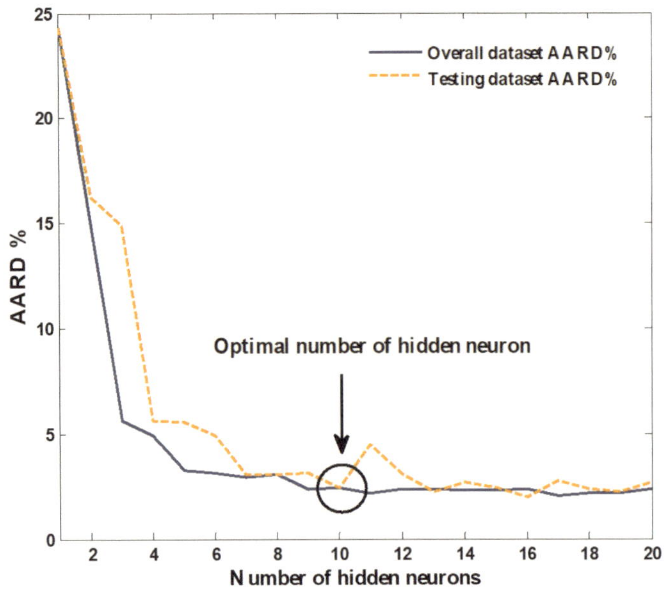

Figure 5.
AARD% of various MLP topologies for testing and overall subsets.

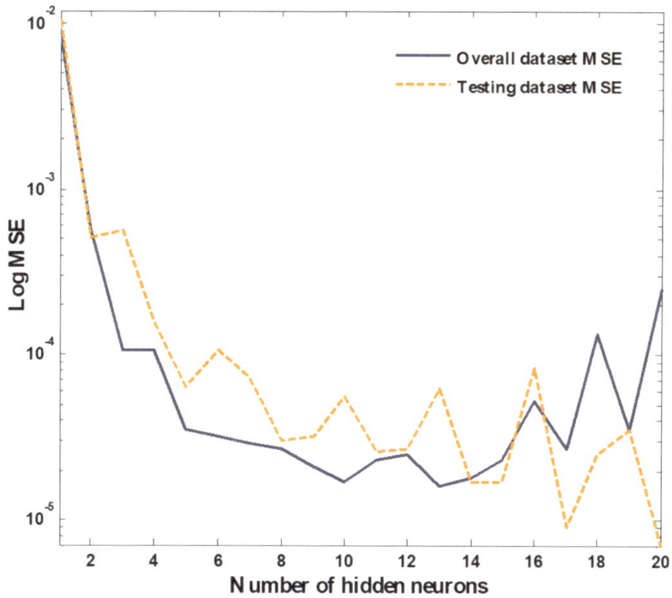

Figure 6.
MSE logarithm of various ANN topologies for testing and overall sets.

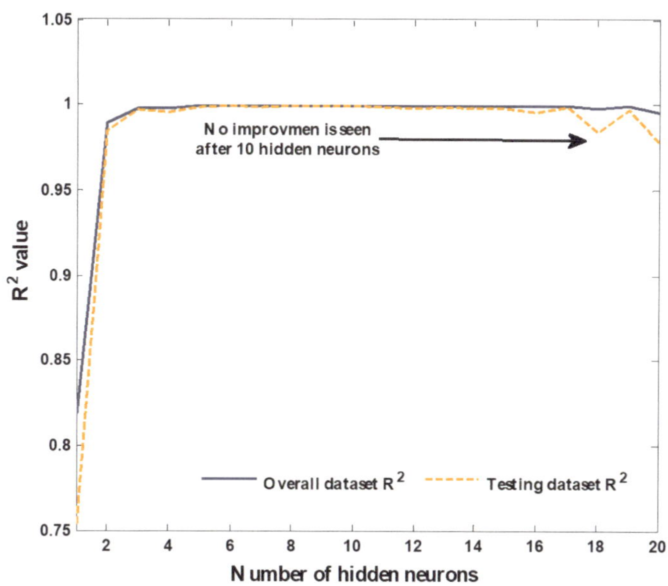

Figure 7.
Associated R^2 values of ANN topologies for testing and overall sets.

be said that using more than 10 hidden neurons for the MLP models not only increase the size of the model but it has no positive effect on reducing the magnitude of the errors.

Here, we tried to do some comparisons between predictive performance of the optimum MLP model with other available feedforward neural networks, i.e., radial basis, cascade feedforward, and generalized regression neural networks. **Table 6** summarizes the result of four smart models for simulation of the behavior of convective HTC of different pure fluids and nanofluids. It should be mentioned that all of these four intelligent models, i.e., MLP, RBF, GR, and CFF neural networks

ANN model		Accuracy indices		
		MSE	AARD (%)	R^2
Multi-layer perceptron neural network	Train subset	0.000016	2.63	0.999692
	Test subset	0.000019	2.36	0.999512
	Whole databank	0.000017	2.41	0.999664
Cascade feedforward neural network	Train subset	0.002319	2.67	0.999774
	Test subset	0.013574	2.41	0.999156
	Whole databank	0.004628	2.46	0.999596
Radial basis function neural network	Train subset	0.002413	3.54	0.999767
	Test subset	0.023266	2.88	0.998812
	Whole databank	0.006692	3.01	0.999439
Generalized regression neural network	Train subset	3.194334	12.82	0.639363
	Test subset	6.687986	15.05	0.386423
	Whole databank	3.911239	14.59	0.579964

Table 6.
Comparison of performances of different ANN models.

have single hidden layer with 10 neurons. The multi-layer perceptron, cascade feedforward, radial basis function, and generalized regression approach shows AARDs of 2.41, 2.46, 3.01, and 14.59% for prediction of whole experimental databank, respectively. It is clear that the MLP model presents the smallest error (AARD% = 2.63) for training subset while the worst results for estimation of this dataset (AARD% = 12.82) was presented by the GR model. It is widely accepted that a GR approach in which hidden neurons equals with the number of training data-points can provide the best accuracy for estimation of any continuous function. The worst result that is provided by the GR neural network in this study may be associated with the discontinuity in the experimental data of convective HTC or/ and the number of 10 hidden neurons that is very low than its theoretical threshold. Comparison among the predictive performances of these four ANN paradigms reveals that the MLP approach simply outperforms other ANN model for predicting the experimental values of convective HTC of both pure fluids and nanofluids. Therefore, a single hidden layer MLP model with 10 neurons that present the best performance for estimation of the convective HTC is considered as the best neural network model.

Figure 8 depicts change of the MSE for training dataset for the best MLP model. It is obvious that the MSE reaches relatively small value of 1.6×10^{-5} after 1000 iterations. Consequently, it can be claimed that the learning procedure of the MLP model was successful and this trained model can be used for more analyses.

3.2.3 Evaluation of the performance of developed MLP model

Figure 9 illustrates the plot of training (square symbols) and testing groups (spheres symbols) for experimental data of convective HTC as function of predicted values by the best MLP model. The most exact predictions, i.e., (predictions = experimental) is depicted by the dashed 45° line. The relatively slight deviations from the dashed line justify that MLP predictions are properly mapped on their associated experimental data.

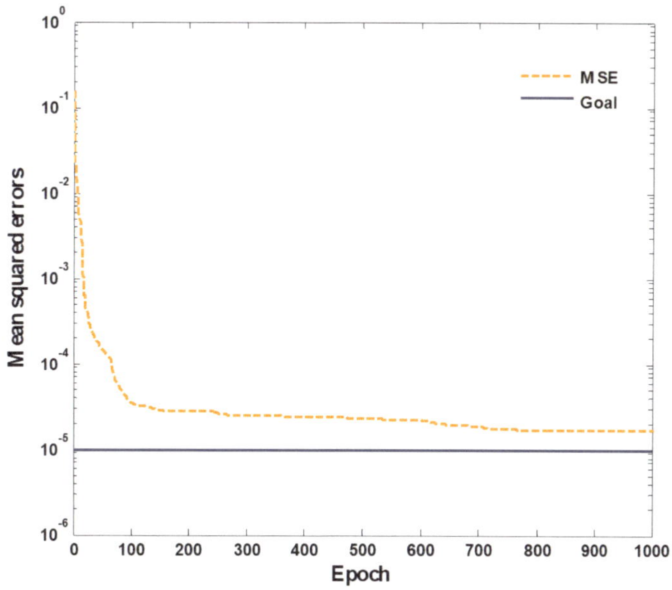

Figure 8.
MSE variation versus epoch for optimal MLP model predicting heat transfer coefficient, solid line represents goal while dashed line is training.

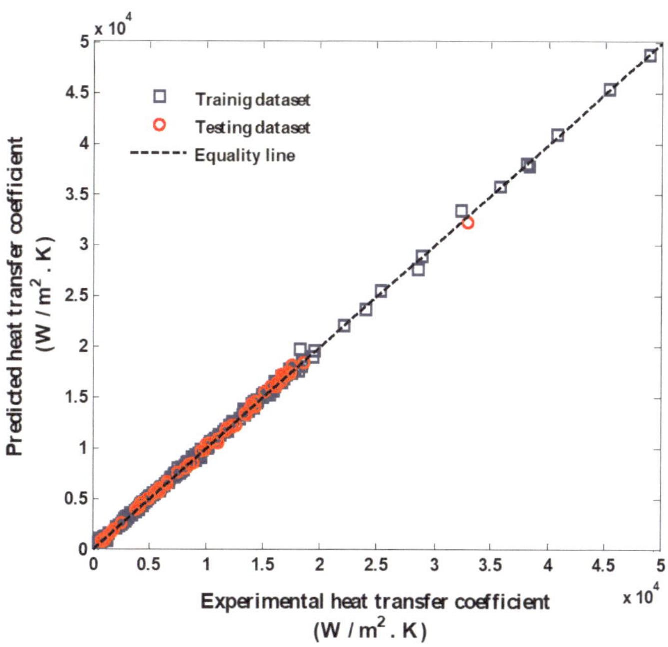

Figure 9.
Schematic presentation of the proposed optimal MLP network capability in estimating the experimental heat transfer coefficient over training + testing datasets.

Our developed MLP model with optimum configuration shows regression coefficient of 0.999692 for the prediction of training dataset of convective HTCs. It also presented the MSE and AARD of 1.6×10^{-5} and 2.63% for training group, respectively. Moreover, it can predict the testing dataset with impressing $R^2 = 0.999512$, AARD = 2.365%, and MSE = 1.9×10^{-5}.

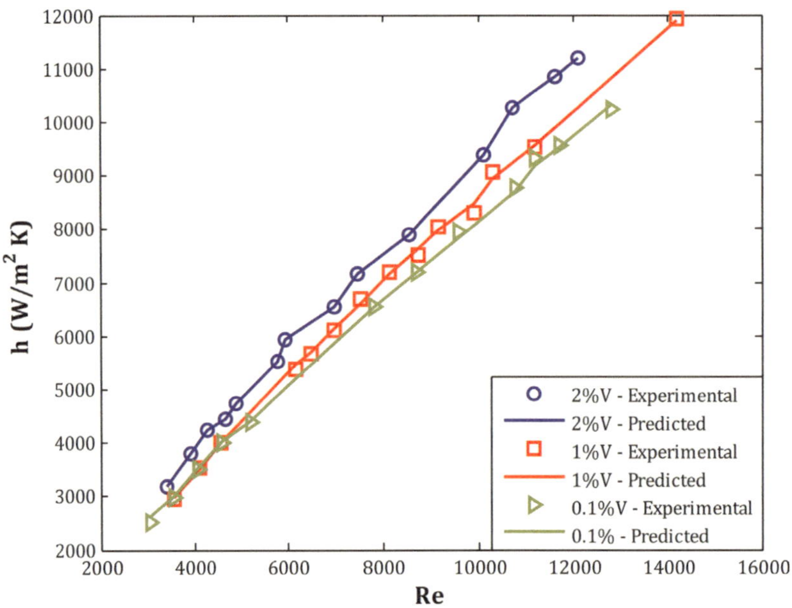

Figure 10.
Effect of particle volumetric concentration on the convective heat transfer coefficient, closed circles represent experimental data and solid lines are the results of MLP model.

The effect of particle volumetric concentration on the convective heat transfer coefficient of Al_2O_3 nanofluid flowing through a circular tube is investigated in **Figure 10**. It is obvious that the convective HTC increases by increasing the nanoparticle concentration in base fluid. Moreover, the level of this increase for higher Reynolds number (higher velocity) is more substantial. This behavior may be explained by more turbulence movement of nanoparticles in higher Reynolds number. High concentration of nanoparticles in base fluids is a factor that is responsible for increasing the interface between fluid and particles and enhancement of heat transfer rate.

Result of another analysis that is performed to investigate an effect of type of nanoparticles including Al_2O_3, CuO, and SiO_2 on HTC of water-based nanofluids is shown in **Figure 11**. It can be simply understood that the convective HTC of water-based nanofluids is remarkably higher than the pure water. Chaotic movement of nanoparticles as well as higher thermal conductivity of nanofluids may be responsible for higher heat transfer rate of nanofluids than the pure base fluids. A significant difference between convective HTC of the considered nanoparticles can also be seen in **Figure 11**. A possible reason for this difference may be the difference in thermophysical properties of nanoparticles. Since the metallic particles (CuO and Al_2O_3) have higher density, higher thermal conductivity in comparison with non-metallic particles (SiO_2), a higher heat transfer coefficients are provided in the presence of metallic particles.

3.3 Viscosity

Viscosity is one of the most important properties of fluids/nanofluids that directly influences on their heat transfer applications and flow behavior. Accurate and reliable estimation of viscosity is required for calculation of convection HTC, Prandtl, and Reynolds numbers, amount of pressure drop, and theoretical power of pump.

3.3.1 Experimental databank

Both empirical correlations [57, 69–77] and published literature data [24, 78–88] approved that the dynamic viscosity of nanofluids is essentially dependent on chemistry of base liquid, characteristics of nanoparticle, and ranges of operating conditions. Considering the corresponding state theory, the base fluids are tried to be introduced based on their critical temperature, critical pressure, and acentric factor [89]. Numerical values of these fundamental parameters for different base liquids are reported in **Table** 7. It is worthy to be noted that critical temperature, critical pressure, and acentric factor for mixtures of water-ethylene glycol are obtained using the Kay's mixing rule [90].

Temperature is likely the most important operating condition that could change the viscosity of both pure fluids and nanofluids. For incorporation, the effect of

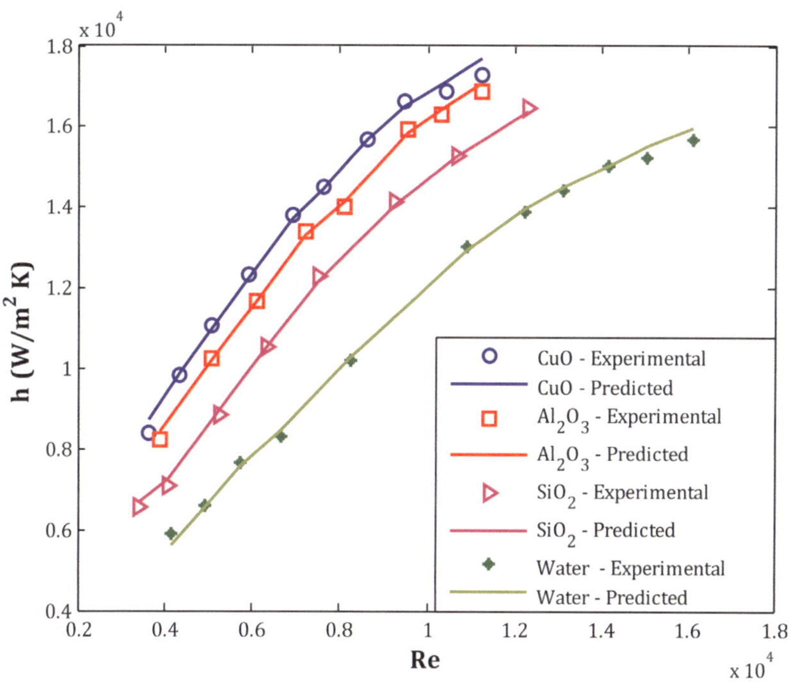

Figure 11.
Effect of particle type on the heat transfer coefficient, closed circles represent experimental data and solid lines are the results of MLP model.

Liquid	Pc (MPa)	Tc (K)	Acentric factor
Water	22.06	647.1	0.343
Propylene Glycol (PG)	6.04	626	1.102
EG/water (60/40)	17.71	669.1	0.387
EG/Water (45/55)	19.31	661	0.371
EG/Water (40/60)	19.73	658.9	0.366
Ethylene glycol (EG)	7.71	719.7	0.487

Table 7.
Acentric factor and critical properties of the pure base liquids.

Liquid	Dp (nm)	Vp (%)	Temperature (K)	Viscosity (mPa.s)	No. of data	Reference
Water	47	1–9.4	294–343	0.43–4.91	81	[80]
Water	13	1.34–2.78	293–345	0.63–2.49	14	[81]
Water	30	0.01–0.3	294–312	0.66–1.00	114	[82]
Water	33	1–2	293–313	0.65–1.09	10	[83]
Ethylene glycol (EG)	8–43	0.5–6.6	283–323	7.51–81.51	96	[78]
Ethylene glycol (EG)	10	1–5	298–328	8.14–37.28	21	[79]
Propylene glycol (PG)	27–50	0.5–3	303–333	7.9–38.6	36	[85]
EG/water (20/80)	36	0–1.5	273–333	0.59–4.6	89	[84]
EG/water (40/60)	36	0–1.5	273–333	0.96–13.64	90	[84]
EG/water(45/55)	30	0–2	283–333	1.54–11.08	33	[24]
EG/water(60/40)	36	0–1.5	273–333	1.5–35.35	90	[84]
Overall ranges	8–50	0–9.4	273–345	0.43–81.51	674	[24, 78–85]

Table 8.
Brief description of collected experimental datasets for dynamic viscosity of alumina-based nanofluids.

nanoparticles, their diameter, and volumetric concentration (Vp) in liquid are also regarded as independent factors. A brief description of experimental databank including independent and dependent variable(s), their associated ranges, and number of collected datasets from different literatures are presented in **Table 8** [24, 78–85].

Table 8 states that our experimental databank for viscosity of different base fluids - alumina nanoparticle has 674 data-points. The databank includes seven different base liquids in temperature range of 273–345 K. These base liquids may have up to 9.4 volume percent of alumina nanoparticle with diameter of 8 to 50 nm. The dynamic viscosity of the considered nanofluids varies from 0.43 to 81.51 mPa.

3.3.2 ANN model development

Similar to two previous modelings, the best structure of MLP model is selected through trial and error analyses. The results of this trial and error procedure on the number of hidden neurons for the MLP network were reported in **Table 9**. Different MLP models having 1 to 15 hidden neurons were developed, trained, tested, and their performances were evaluated. The smallest number of hidden neurons that provides an acceptable accuracy is often selected as an optimum structure.

Table 9 clearly shows that performance of the MLP model got better by increasing the number of hidden neuron up to 14. After that, a relatively worse result is obtained for testing subset even by spending higher computational time and effort. Thus, a two-layer MLP approach constituting of 14 hidden neurons (the bold rows) was selected as the best topology for prediction of dynamic viscosity of dispersion of alumina nanoparticles in different base fluids. It is obvious that this MLP model predicted whole of the experimental data-points with R^2 of 0.99947, MSE of 0.1442, AARD of 4.13%, and RMSE of 0.3797.

It is common to compare the predictive performance of various types of ANN and find the best one in terms of some statistical indices. **Table 10** summarizes the

Number of hidden neurons	Database	Sensitivity accuracy analyses			
		AARD%	MSE	R^2	RMSE
2	Training	24.62	3.4708	0.98488	1.8630
	Testing	27.07	6.5978	0.99033	2.5686
	Overall	24.99	3.9394	0.98562	1.9848
4	Training	17.02	1.5977	0.99414	1.2640
	Testing	17.79	1.5941	0.99402	1.2626
	Overall	17.14	1.5972	0.99409	1.2638
6	Training	12.94	0.5584	0.99795	0.7473
	Testing	15.09	0.7587	0.99726	0.8710
	Overall	13.26	0.5884	0.99783	0.7671
8	Training	8.80	0.3267	0.99876	0.5715
	Testing	10.79	1.0471	0.99723	1.0233
	Overall	9.10	0.4346	0.99841	0.6593
9	Training	8.20	0.1343	0.99946	0.3665
	Testing	9.64	0.2289	0.99961	0.4784
	Overall	8.41	0.1485	0.99946	0.3853
10	Training	6.55	0.1183	0.99956	0.3440
	Testing	7.81	0.1864	0.99940	0.4318
	Overall	6.74	0.1285	0.99953	0.3585
11	Training	6.53	0.1263	0.99956	0.3554
	Testing	8.19	1.7631	0.99352	1.3278
	Overall	6.78	0.3716	0.99866	0.6096
	Training	5.63	0.0906	0.99968	0.3011
12	Testing	6.04	0.2209	0.99891	0.4700
	Overall	5.69	0.1102	0.99959	0.3319
13	Training	4.38	0.0859	0.99969	0.2931
	Testing	6.30	0.3259	0.99869	0.5709
	Overall	4.67	0.1219	0.99955	0.3491
14	**Training**	**4.11**	**0.1025**	**0.99962**	**0.3202**
	Testing	**4.22**	**0.3804**	**0.99867**	**0.6167**
	Overall	**4.13**	**0.1442**	**0.99947**	**0.3797**
15	Training	4.72	0.0799	0.99971	0.2827
	Testing	5.91	0.3091	0.99861	0.5560
	Overall	4.90	0.1143	0.99958	0.3381

The bold values indicate the best obtained results for the considered AI models.

Table 9.
Trial and error procedure for finding the best structure for MLPNN model.

obtained results by the best topology of the CFF, MLP, RBF, and least square support vector machines (LS-SVM) models for training, testing, and overall datasets in term of AARD%, MSE, R^2, and RMSE.

Focusing on reported results in **Table 10** clearly confirms that the MLP neural network provides the best predictive performance for prediction of dynamic viscosity of different Al_2O_3-based nanofluids. Since, it outperforms other

AI model	Dataset	AARD%	MSE	R^2	RMSE
MLP	**Training stage**	**4.11**	**0.1025**	**0.99962**	**0.3202**
	Testing stage	**4.22**	**0.3804**	**0.99867**	**0.6167**
	Overall data	**4.13**	**0.1442**	**0.99947**	**0.3797**
CFF	Training stage	4.13	0.0989	0.99965	0.3144
	Testing stage	4.74	0.1850	0.99911	0.4302
	Overall data	4.22	0.1118	0.99959	0.3343
LS-SVM	Training stage	6.33	0.0791	0.99971	0.2812
	Testing stage	10.27	2.5489	0.99073	1.5965
	Overall data	6.92	0.4492	0.99834	0.6702
RBF	Training stage	57.91	5.599	0.9759	2.366
	Testing stage	50.58	14.425	0.9753	3.798
	Overall data	56.81	6.922	0.9745	2.631

The bold values indicate the best obtained results for the considered AI models.

Table 10.
Comparison among the capabilities of different AI approaches in prediction of viscosity of nanofluids.

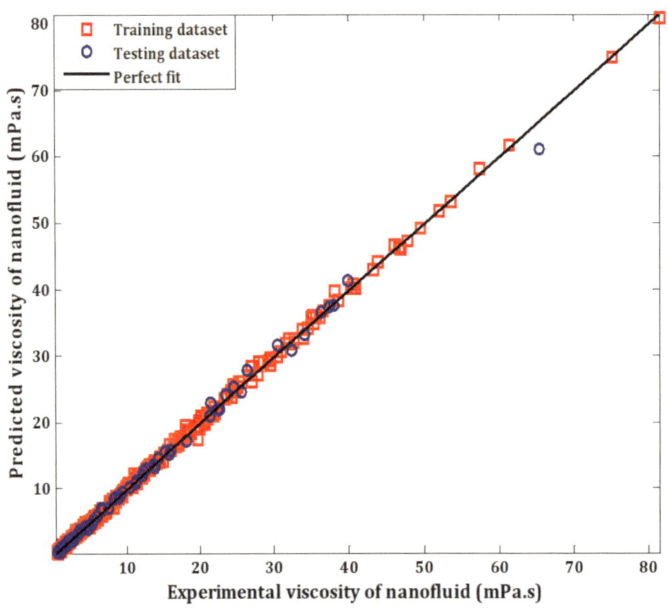

Figure 12.
Performance of the best AI model for estimation of viscosity of alumina-based nanofluids.

considered AI approaches; it therefore can be regarded as the best AI approach for considered task.

3.3.3 Evaluation the ANN model performances

Plot of estimated viscosity for different nanofluids by the optimum MLP network with respect to their associated experimental data for training and testing datasets are depicted in **Figure 12**. Aggregation of the symbols for training as well as testing subsets around the 45° solid line approves that the developed MLP model is a

Experimental data	Einstein [69]	Brinkman [70]	Frankel and Acrivos [71]	Nguyen et al. [72]	Batchelor [73]	Maiga et al. [74]	Thomas and Muthukumar [75]	Rea et al. [76]	Chandrasekar et al. [57]	Heyhat et al. [77]
Ethylene glycol [78]	24.20	23.98	94.03	27.84	23.90	11.56	23.96	54.46	27.80	34.40
Ethylene glycol [79]	39.37	39.15	82.83	42.93	39.06	26.59	39.13	38.38	42.90	24.95
Water [80]	33.80	33.17	180.63	39.36	32.97	11.92	33.12	383.73	39.31	168.62
Water [81]	44.63	44.53	165.32	47.17	44.48	37.11	44.52	11.04	47.14	16.15
Water [82]	2.97	2.97	173.55	3.23	2.97	2.45	2.97	1.26	3.23	1.32
Water [83]	7.24	7.18	337.49	8.73	7.16	5.80	7.18	34.77	8.70	29.54
EG/water (20/80) [84]	10.18	10.16	286.76	11.61	10.15	7.08	10.16	6.66	11.60	5.35
EG/water (40/60) [84]	27.91	27.91	252.39	28.17	27.91	27.68	27.91	31.24	28.16	30.32
EG/water(45/55) [24]	35.87	35.84	147.00	36.90	35.83	33.14	35.84	24.17	36.89	25.70
EG/water(60/40) [84]	38.94	38.93	120.06	39.72	38.92	37.10	38.93	31.12	39.72	32.01
Propylene glycol [85]	15.90	15.74	273.78	19.51	15.68	7.06	15.73	37.10	19.48	29.47
Overall AARD%	24.20	23.02	180.25	25.14	22.97	16.76	23.01	68.40	25.12	38.80

Table 11.
Provided AARD% for prediction of experimental datasets by different empirical correlations.

Experimental data	MLP	CFF	LS-SVM	Correlation*	RBF
Ethylene glycol [78]	1.94	1.67	2.28	11.56	7.56
Ethylene glycol [79]	3.61	3.53	2.72	24.95	12.34
Water [80]	2.82	4.58	4.59	11.92	170.58
Water [81]	7.65	5.93	15.68	11.04	100.90
Water [82]	2.59	1.19	8.94	1.26	28.11
Water [83]	29.02	11.26	35.64	5.8	53.48
EG/water (20/80) [84]	5.96	6.30	11.71	5.35	84.15
EG/water (40/60) [84]	4.53	6.12	8.16	27.68	62.74
EG/water (45/55) [24]	5.42	5.43	7.10	24.17	35.03
EG/water (60/40) [84]	4.75	6.63	4.29	31.12	38.29
Propylene glycol [85]	1.56	0.90	0.33	7.06	16.70
Overall AARD%	4.13	4.24	6.92	14.50	56.81

**The best obtained result among all of the considered empirical correlations.*

Table 12.
Provided AARD% for prediction of experimental datasets by different methodologies.

practical tool for accurate estimation of the dynamic viscosity of different Al_2O_3-based nanofluids in wide ranges of operating conditions.

In this section, some analyses are performed to compare predictive accuracy of the proposed AI model with 10 well-known empirical correlations in literature [57, 69–77]. The obtained AARD% values by the considered empirical correlations for prediction of dynamic viscosity of nanofluids are reported in **Table 11**. It is obvious that the proposed model by Maiga et al. [74] is the most accurate empirical correlation, while the model developed by Frankel and Acrivos [71] presents the worst results. The earlier one has an AARD of 16.76%, while the later shows the AARD of 180.25%.

The obtained values for AARD by various AI models and the best obtained results by the considered empirical correlations are summarized in **Table 12**. It can be easily understood that the best results among 10 empirical correlations only outperforms the RBF model and predictive performance of other AI models is more better than the empirical correlations.

4. Conclusions

Nanofluids are new and high-tech class of operating fluids that recently found high popularity in the field of heat transfer equipment. In spite of both practical and potential application of nanofluids, three developed no accurate correlations for estimation of thermophysical properties of nanofluids in wide ranges of conditions. In this chapter, the focus was concentrated on estimation of conduction heat transfer coefficient, convective HTC, and viscosity of different nanofluids by four different artificial neural networks. MLP, RBF, CFF, and GR are the types of ANN methodology that are employed for these estimations. The best structures of ANN models are determined, their predictive performances are compared and the best one is presented. Some statistical error indices including MSE, RMSE, AARD%, and R^2 are used for evaluation of the accuracy of the ANN models. Results confirm that

ANN models capable of accurate estimation of thermophysical properties of nanofluids and show better performances than the available empirical correlations.

Acronyms and abbreviations

ANN	artificial neural network
MSE	mean square errors
RMSE	root mean square errors
AARD%	average absolute relative deviation percent
MLP	multilayer perceptron
CFF	cascade feedforward
RBF	radial basis function
GR	generalized regression
TCR	thermal conductivity ratio
HTC	heat transfer coefficient
EG	ethylene glycol
PG	propylene glycol
LS-SVM	least square support vector machines

Appendices and nomenclature

R^2	regression coefficient
w	weight
b	bias
out	perceptron's output
f	activation function
Ind	number of dimensions of independent variable
Dep	number of dimensions of dependent variable
N	number of experimental data
D	value of dependent variable
Exp	experimental data
Cal	calculated values
Dp	diameter of nanoparticle
T	temperature
Mw	molecular weight
Vf	volume fraction of nanoparticle
ω	acentric factor
Pc	critical pressure of base fluids
Tc	critical temperature of base fluids
Re	Reynolds number
h	convective heat transfer coefficient
Vp	volume percent of nanoparticle

Author details

Behzad Vaferi
Department of Chemical Engineering, Shiraz Branch, Islamic Azad University, Shiraz, Iran

*Address all correspondence to: behzad.vaferi@gmail.com

References

[1] Ghanem A, Habchi C, Lemenand T, Della Valle D, Peerhossaini H. Energy efficiency in process industry–high-efficiency vortex (HEV) multifunctional heat exchanger. Renewable Energy. 2013;**56**:96-104

[2] Marques C, Kelly KW. Fabrication and performance of a pin fin micro heat exchanger. Journal of Heat Transfer. 2004;**126**:434-444

[3] Huminic G, Huminic A. Application of nanofluids in heat exchangers: A review. Renewable and Sustainable Energy Reviews. 2012;**16**:5625-5638

[4] Mondragón R, Segarra C, Martínez-Cuenca R, Juliá JE, Jarque JC. Experimental characterization and modeling of thermophysical properties of nanofluids at high temperature conditions for heat transfer applications. Powder Technology. 2013;**249**:516-529

[5] Xiao B, Yang Y, Chen L. Developing a novel form of thermal conductivity of nanofluids with Brownian motion effect by means of fractal geometry. Powder Technology. 2013;**239**:409-414

[6] Salimi-Yasar H, Heris SZ, Shanbedi M, Amiri A, Kameli A. Experimental investigation of thermal properties of cutting fluid using soluble oil-based TiO_2 nanofluid. Powder Technology. 2017;**310**:213-220

[7] Wang X, Xu X, Choi SUS. Thermal conductivity of nanoparticle-fluid mixture. Journal of Thermophysics and Heat Transfer. 1999;**13**:474-480

[8] Hwang Y, Lee JK, Jeong YM, Cheong SI, Ahn YC, Kim SH. Production and dispersion stability of nanoparticles in nanofluids. Powder Technology. 2008;**186**:145-153

[9] Lee S, Choi SS, Li SA, Eastman JA. Measuring thermal conductivity of fluids containing oxide nanoparticles. Journal of Heat Transfer. 1999;**121**: 280-289

[10] Trisaksri V, Wongwises S. Critical review of heat transfer characteristics of nanofluids. Renewable and Sustainable Energy Reviews. 2007;**11**:512-523

[11] Sharma P, Baek IH, Cho T, Park S, Lee KB. Enhancement of thermal conductivity of ethylene glycol based silver nanofluids. Powder Technology. 2011;**208**:7-19

[12] Saeedinia M, Akhavan-Behabadi MA, Nasr M. Experimental study on heat transfer and pressure drop of nanofluid flow in a horizontal coiled wire inserted tube under constant heat flux. Experimental Thermal and Fluid Science. 2012;**36**:158-168

[13] Choi SUS. Enhancing thermal conductivity of fluids with nanoparticles. In: Siginer DA, Wang HP, editors. Developments and Applications of Non-Newtonian Flows. Vol. 66. New York: ASME; 1995. pp. 99-105

[14] Sundar LS, Sharma KV, Naik MT, Singh MK. Empirical and theoretical correlations on viscosity of nanofluids: A review. Renewable and Sustainable Energy Reviews. 2013;**25**: 670-686

[15] Chiam HW, Azmi WH, Usri NA, Mamat R, Adam NM. Thermal conductivity and viscosity of Al_2O_3 nanofluids for different based ratio of water and ethylene glycol mixture. Experimental Thermal and Fluid Science. 2017;**81**:420-429

[16] Ariana MA, Vaferi B, Karimi G. Prediction of thermal conductivity of alumina water-based nanofluid by artificial neural networks. Powder Technology. 2015;**278**:1-10

[17] Yang L, Du K, Zhang X. A theoretical investigation of thermal conductivity of nanofluids with particles in cylindrical shape by anisotropy analysis. Powder Technology. 2017;**314**:328-338

[18] Yang L, Xu J, Du K, Zhang X. Recent developments on viscosity and thermal conductivity of nanofluids. Powder Technology. 2017;**317**:348-369

[19] Choi SUS. Enhancing thermal conductivity of fluids with nanoparticles. In: Proceedings of the ASME International Mechanical Engineering Congress and Exposition, San Francisco. 1995. pp. 99-105

[20] Goshayeshi HR, Safaei MR, Goodarzi M, Dahari M. Particle size and type effects on heat transfer enhancement of Ferro-nanofluids in a pulsating heat pipe. Powder Technology. 2016;**301**:1218-1226

[21] Duangthongsuk W, Wongwises S. An experimental study on the heat transfer performance and pressure drop of TiO_2-water nanofluids flowing under a turbulent flow regime. International Journal of Heat and Mass Transfer. 2010;**53**:334-344

[22] Nguyen CT, Roy G, Gauthier C, Galanis N. Heat transfer enhancement using Al_2O_3–water nanofluid for an electronic liquid cooling system. Applied Thermal Engineering. 2007;**27** (8–9):1501-1506

[23] Mallick SS, Mishra A, Kundan L. An investigation into modelling thermal conductivity for alumina–water nanofluids. Powder Technology. 2013; **233**:234-244

[24] Yu W, Xie H, Li Y, Chen L, Wang Q. Experimental investigation on the heat transfer properties of Al_2O_3 nanofluids using the mixture of ethylene glycol and water as base fluid. Powder Technology. 2012;**230**:14-19

[25] Gurney K. Neural networks for perceptual processing: From simulation tools to theories. Philosophical Transactions of the Royal Society B. 2007;**362**(1479):339-353

[26] Ghaffarian N, Eslamloueyan R, Vaferi B. Model identification for gas condensate reservoirs by using ANN method based on well test data. Journal of Petroleum Science and Engineering. 2014;**123**:20-29

[27] Vaferi B, Eslamloueyan R, Ghaffarian N. Hydrocarbon reservoir model detection from pressure transient data using coupled artificial neural network-wavelet transform approach. Applied Soft Computing. 2016;**47**:63-75

[28] Demuth HB, Beale MH, De Jess O, Hagan M. Neural Network Design. Oklahoma: Martin Hagan; 2014

[29] Fahlman S, Lebiere C. The cascade-correlation learning architecture. In: Touretzky D, editor. Advances in Neural Information Processing Systems 2. San Mateo: Denver, CO. Morgan Kaufmann Publishers; 1990:524-532

[30] Lashkarbolooki M, Vaferi B, Shariati A, Hezave AZ. Investigating vapor-liquid equilibria of binary mixtures containing supercritical or near-critical carbon dioxide and a cyclic compound using cascade neural network. Fluid Phase Equilibria. 2013; **343**:24-29

[31] Cheng G, Zhou J, Zhang XJ, Zhang ZJ. A daily load forecasting method based on cascaded back propagation and radial basis function neural networks. Power System Technology. 2009;**33**:101-105

[32] Chen S, Cowan CFN, Grant PM. Orthogonal least squares learning algorithm for radial basis function networks. IEEE Transactions on Neural Networks. 1991;**2**:302-309

[33] Broomhead DS, Lowe D. Multivariable functional interpolation and adaptive networks. Complex Systems. 1988;**2**:321-355

[34] Zhao N, Wen X, Yang J, Li S, Wang Z. Modeling and prediction of viscosity of water-based nanofluids by radial basis function neural networks. Powder Technology. 2015;**281**:173-183

[35] Specht DF. A general regression neural network. IEEE Transactions on Neural Networks. 1991;**2**:568-578

[36] Maxwell JC. A Treatise on Electricity and Magnetism. London: Oxford University Press; 1873

[37] Xie H, Wang J, Xi T, Liu Y, Ai F, Wu Q. Thermal conductivity enhancement of suspensions containing nanosized alumina particles. Journal of Applied Physics. 2002;**91**:4568-4572

[38] Kahani M, Zeinali Heris S, Mousavi SM. Comparative study between metal oxide nanopowders on thermal characteristics of nanofluid flow through helical coils. Powder Technology. 2013;**246**:82-92

[39] Das SK, Putra N, Thiesen P, Roetzel W. Temperature dependence of thermal conductivity enhancement for Nanofluids. Journal of Heat Transfer. 2003;**125**:567-574

[40] Yoo DH, Hong KS, Yang HS. Study of thermal conductivity of nanofluids for the application of heat transfer fluids. Thermochimica Acta. 2007;**455**: 66-69

[41] Hatami M, Sheikholeslami M, Ganji DD. Laminar flow and heat transfer of nanofluid between contracting and rotating disks by least square method. Powder Technology. 2014;**253**:769-779

[42] Hamilton RL, Crosser OK. Thermal conductivity of heterogeneous two component systems. Industrial & Engineering Chemistry Fundamentals. 1962;**1**:187-191

[43] Masuda H, Ebata A, Teramae K, Hishinuma N. Alteration of thermal conductivity and viscosity of liquid by dispersing ultra-fine particles dispersion of Al_2O_3, SiO_2 and TiO_2 ultra-fine particles. Netsu Bussei. 1993;**7**:227-233

[44] Murshed SMS, Leong KC, Yang C. Enhanced thermal conductivity of TiO_2-water based nanofluids. International Journal of Thermal Sciences. 2005;**44**: 367-373

[45] Chon CH, Kihm KD, Lee SP, Choi SUS. Empirical correlation finding the role of temperature and particle size for nanofluid (Al_2O_3) thermal conductivity enhancement. Applied Physics Letters. 2005;**87**:153107-1-153107-3

[46] Li CH, Peterson GP. Experimental investigation of temperature and volume fraction variations on the effective thermal conductivity of nanoparticle suspensions (nanofluids). Journal of Applied Physics. 2006;**99**: 084314-1-084314-8

[47] Murshed SMS, Leong KC, Yang C. Investigations of thermal conductivity and viscosity of nanofluids. International Journal of Thermal Sciences. 2008;**47**:560-568

[48] Teng TP, Hung YH, Teng TC, Mo HE, Hsu HG. The effect of alumina/water nanofluid particle size on thermal conductivity. Applied Thermal Engineering. 2010;**30**:2213-2218

[49] Mintsa HA, Roy G, Nguyen CT, Doucet D. New temperature dependent thermal conductivity data for water-based nanofluids. International Journal of Thermal Sciences. 2009;**48**:363-371

[50] Longo GA, Zilio C. Experimental measurement of thermophysical

properties of oxide–water nano-fluids down to ice-point. Experimental Thermal and Fluid Science. 2011;**35**: 1313-1324

[51] Timofeeva EV, Gavrilov AN, McCloskey JM, Tolmachev YV, Sprunt S, Lopatina LM, et al. Thermal conductivity and particle agglomeration in alumina nanofluids: Experiment and theory. Physical Review E. 2007;**76**: 061203-1-061203-16

[52] Zhang X, Gu H, Fujii M. Effective thermal conductivity and thermal diffusivity of nanofluids containing spherical and cylindrical nanoparticles. Experimental Thermal and Fluid Science. 2007;**31**: 593-599

[53] Yiamsawasd T, Dalkilic AS, Wongwises S. Measurement of the thermal conductivity of titania and alumina nanofluids. Thermochimica Acta. 2012;**545**:48-56

[54] Buschmann MH. Thermal conductivity and heat transfer of ceramic nanofluids. International Journal of Thermal Sciences. 2012;**62**: 19-28

[55] Beck M, Yuan Y, Warrier P, Teja A. The effect of particle size on the thermal conductivity of alumina nanofluids. Journal of Nanoparticle Research. 2009; **11**:1129-1136

[56] Beck M, Yuan Y, Warrier P, Teja A. The thermal conductivity of alumina nanofluids in water, ethylene glycol, and ethylene glycol + water mixtures. Journal of Nanoparticle Research. 2010; **12**:1469-1477

[57] Chandrasekar M, Suresh S, Chandra Bose A. Experimental investigations and theoretical determination of thermal conductivity and viscosity of Al_2O_3/ water nanofluid. Experimental Thermal and Fluid Science. 2010;**34**: 210-216

[58] Li CH, Peterson GP. The effect of particle size on the effective thermal conductivity of Al_2O_3-water nanofluids. Journal of Applied Physics. 2007;**101**: 044312-1-044312-5

[59] Canakci A, Ozsahin S, Varol T. Modeling the influence of a process control agent on the properties of metal matrix composite powders using artificial neural networks. Powder Technology. 2012;**228**:26-35

[60] Yu W, Choi SUS. The role of interfacial layers in the enhanced thermal conductivity of Nanofluids: A renovated Maxwell model. Journal of Nanoparticle Research. 2003;**5**: 167-171

[61] Xie H, Fujii M, Zhang X. Effect of interfacial nanolayer on the effective thermal conductivity of nanoparticle-fluid mixture. International Journal of Heat and Mass Transfer. 2005;**48**: 2926-2932

[62] Nan CW, Birringer R, Clarke DR, Gleiter H. Effective thermal conductivity of particulate composites with interfacial thermal resistance. Journal of Applied Physics. 1997;**81**: 6692-6699

[63] Xuana Y, Roetzel W. Conceptions for heat transfer correlation of nanofluids. International Journal of Heat and Mass Transfer. 2000;**43**: 3701-3707

[64] Anoop KB, Sundararajan T, Das SK. Effect of particle size on the convective heat transfer in nanofluid in the developing region. International Journal of Heat and Mass Transfer. 2009;**52**: 2189-2195

[65] Vajjha RS, Das DK, Kulkarni DP. Development of new correlations for convective heat transfer and friction factor in turbulent regime for nanofluids. International Journal of Heat and Mass Transfer. 2010;**53**:4607-4618

[66] Heyhat MM, Kowsary F, Rashidi AM, Alem Varzane Esfehani S, Amrollahi A. Experimental investigation of turbulent flow and convective heat transfer characteristics of alumina water nanofluids in fully developed flow regime. International Communications in Heat and Mass Transfer. 2012;**39**:1272-1278

[67] SyamSundar L, Naik MT, Sharma KV, Singh MK, Siva Reddy TC. Experimental investigation of forced convection heat transfer and friction factor in a tube with Fe_3O_4 magnetic nanofluid. Experimental Thermal and Fluid Science. 2012;**37**:65-71

[68] Bayat J, Nikseresht AH. Thermal performance and pressure drop analysis of nanofluids in turbulent forced convective flows. International Journal of Thermal Sciences. 2012;**60**:236-243

[69] Einstein A. Eine neue bestimmung der moleküldimensionen. Annalen der Physik. 1906;**324**:289-306

[70] Brinkman HC. The viscosity of concentrated suspensions and solution. The Journal of Chemical Physics. 1952;**20**:571-581

[71] Frankel NA, Acrivos A. On the viscosity of a concentrate suspension of solid spheres. Chemical Engineering Science. 1967;**22**:847-853

[72] Nguyen CT, Desgranges F, Galanis N, Roy G, Maré T, Boucher S, et al. Viscosity data for Al_2O_3 - water nanofluid - hysteresis: Is heat transfer enhancement using nanofluids reliable? International Journal of Thermal Sciences. 2008;**47**:103-111

[73] Batchelor GK. The effect of Brownian motion on the bulk stress in a suspension of spherical particles. Journal of Fluid Mechanics. 1977;**83**:97-117

[74] Maiga SEB, Nguyen CT, Galanis N, Roy G. Heat transfer behaviours of nanofluids in a uniformly heated tube. Superlattices and Microstructures. 2004;**35**:543-557

[75] Thomas CU, Muthukumar M. Three-body hydrodynamic effects on viscosity of suspensions of spheres. The Journal of Chemical Physics. 1991;**94**:5180-5189

[76] Rea U, McKrell T, Hu LW, Buongiorno J. Laminar convective heat transfer and viscous pressure loss of alumina-water and zirconia-water nanofluids. International Journal of Heat and Mass Transfer. 2009;**52**:2042-2048

[77] Heyhat MM, Kowsary F, Rashidi AM, Memenpour MH, Amrollahi A, Momenpour MH. Experimental investigation of laminar convective heat transfer and pressure drop of water-based Al_2O_3 nanofluids in fully developed flow regime. Experimental Thermal and Fluid Science. 2013;**44**:483-489

[78] Pastoriza-Gallego MJ, Lugo L, Legido JL, Piñeiro MM. Thermal conductivity and viscosity measurements of ethylene glycol-based Al_2O_3 nanofluids. Nanoscale Research Letters. 2011;**6**:1-11

[79] Hachey MA, Nguyen CT, Galanis N, Popa CV. Experimental investigation of Al_2O_3 nanofluids thermal properties and rheology - effects of transient and steady-state heat exposure. International Journal of Thermal Sciences. 2014;**76**:155-167

[80] Nguyen CT, Desgranges F, Roy G, Galanis N, Mare T, Boucher S, et al. Temperature and particle-size dependent viscosity data for water-based nanofluids – Hysteresis phenomenon. International Journal of Heat and Fluid Flow. 2007;**28**:1492-1506

[81] Pak BC, Cho YI. Hydrodynamic and heat transfer study of dispersed fluids

with submicron metallic oxide particles. Experimental Heat Transfer. 1998;**11**: 151-170

[82] Lee JH. Effective viscosities and thermal conductivities of aqueous nanofluids containing low volume concentrations of Al_2O_3 nanoparticles. International Journal of Heat and Fluid Flow. 2008;**51**:2651-2656

[83] Ho CJ, Wei LC, Li ZW. An experimental investigation of forced convective cooling performance of a microchannel heat sink with Al_2O_3/water nanofluid. Applied Thermal Engineering. 2010;**30**:96-103

[84] Syam Sundar L, Venkata Ramana E, Singh MK, Sousa ACM. Thermal conductivity and viscosity of stabilized ethylene glycol and water mixture Al_2O_3 nanofluids for heat transfer applications: An experimental study. International Communications in Heat and Mass. 2014;**56**:86-95

[85] Prasher R, Song D, Wang J, Phelan P. Measurements of nanofluid viscosity and its implications for thermal applications. Applied Physics Letters. 2006;**89**:133108-133101

[86] Yang L, Yuhan H. Toward TiO_2 Nanofluids-part 1: Preparation and properties. Nanoscale Research Letters. 2017;**12**:417

[87] Yang L, Yuhan H. Toward TiO_2 Nanofluids—Part 2: Applications and challenges. Nanoscale Research Letters. 2017;**12**:446

[88] Yang L, Jiang W, Chen X, Du K. Dynamic characteristics of an environment-friendly refrigerant: Ammonia-water based TiO_2 nanofluids. International Journal of Refrigeration. 2017;**82**:366-380

[89] Carruth GF, Kobayashi R. Extension to low reduced temperatures of three-parameter corresponding states: Vapor pressures, enthalpies and entropies of vaporization, and liquid fugacity coefficients. Industrial and Engineering Chemistry Fundamentals. 1972;**11**: 509-517

[90] Poling BE, Prausnitz JM, O'connell JP. The Properties of Gases and Liquids. New York: Mcgraw-Hill; 2001

Chapter 5

The Technique of Automated Design of Technological Objects with the Application of Artificial Intelligence Elements

Tatyana Zubkova and Marina Tokareva

Abstract

The chapter describes the methodology of using artificial intelligence methods to build an integrated environment for computer-aided design components of technological objects based on their classification, integration and configuration. It describes the formation of CAD based on the object-oriented approach, methods of configuring the integrated environment and the organization of single information space. The configuration of the system components and the methodology for organizing the interaction of CAD components, obtaining the final CAD architecture, focused on solving the problem, is shown. The application of the Mamdani method for the formal description of project operations and the use of genetic algorithms to optimize the operational parameters of the process and the design of the technological machine are described.

Keywords: technological machines, CAD, object-oriented approach, information system, configuration of components, integration of components, creation of a single information space, fuzzy inference algorithms, genetic algorithm

1. Introduction

Technological machines have a fairly wide range of applications in all areas of person's production activity. Designing them, it is necessary to take into account the properties of the material being processed, the requirements for the technological process, the quality of the finished product, as well as the geometric and design features of the machine itself. Market competition forces manufacturers to improve and create new technologies to increase the range of their products. Therefore, production must be flexible, with the ability to re-adjust to different types of raw materials, product configurations, productivity, etc., depending on the current market needs.

The design of sophisticated technological machines is currently focused on the use of computer-aided design (CAD) systems to solve a wide range of engineering problems: strength calculation, dynamics, kinematics, heat transfer, acoustics, durability, etc., modeling of technological processes of manufacturing and product assembly. This is achieved by combining modern hardware and software, the parameters and characteristics of which are selected with maximum consideration for the features of the tasks of the design process.

The purpose of the work is to show the methodology of computer-aided design of technological objects using intelligent methods. The volume of design and engineering work, the proposed approaches, allows to increase the productivity of design engineers. The use of artificial intelligence methods is particularly relevant when there are no well-developed methods of designing or creating a fundamentally new and demanding creative work.

2. Statement of the problem of CAD formation based on an object-oriented approach

An adequate information system (IS) is necessary for designing technological objects.

A feature of solving the problems of designing technological objects is the presence of specialized subsystems. The need for a narrow specialization of the components of the applied area is justified by the following factors:

- ease of component data abstraction for the users and for other software components;
- the possibility of parallel development of components of a specific task;
- modification and replacement of the component with an alternative one, if the equipment or the target platform has changed, without changing the other components.

The requirements presented can be achieved by applying object-oriented decomposition. Based on this decomposition for the designed CAD components, the technological requirements may be as follows:

- components must have certain software interfaces for interaction;
- for the implementation of components it is necessary to use the principles of object-oriented design and programming;
- component functions must solve certain tasks [1–4].

The object-oriented approach allows us to consider the CAD system as an independent system S, the properties of which are inherited from the components included in its composition. The system S has a finite number of characteristics $F = \{F_i\}, i = \overline{1, n}$, where n is the number of properties. Let it be m possible ways of forming the system S. In the $k -$ y $(k \in m)$ method of formation $S_k = \{R_p\}, p = \overline{1, P_k}$, where P_k is the number of subsystems in the $S\,k -$ y decomposition method, each CAD resource (component) is characterized by a set of properties $F = \{F_{P_k}\}, k = \overline{1, K}$, each of which has an individual numerical measure. The set of properties of all resources R_k in $k -$ y the first decomposition $F_k = \cup_{p=1}^{P_k} \{F_{P_k}\}$. Interacting with each other, resources generate many system processes $Z_k = \{Z_{kj}\}, j = \overline{1, J}$, where J is the number of processes.

The optimal organization of CAD is the selection and distribution of resources $r \in R_k$ between project tasks Z_k according to a given decomposition scheme k to ensure the extreme values of the system properties $extr(F_k)$ necessary to perform the required operations. At the same time, the time t_k to solve each of the project tasks Z_k while ensuring $extr(F_k)$ should be minimized (**Figure 1**).

Formalization of the selected conditions is represented as a system (1).

$$\begin{cases} \sum_{j=1}^{J} Q_j\left(\bigcup_{p=1}^{P_j}\{F_{jp}\}\right) \rightarrow \max; \\ \sum_{j=1}^{J} t_j\left(\bigcup_{p=1}^{P_j}\{F_{jp}\}\right) \rightarrow \min. \end{cases}, \qquad (1)$$

where Q_j is the selection function of system properties, under which the quality characteristics for each design task are maximized; t_j is the selection function of system properties, which minimizes time for each project task; F—finite set of characteristics; P—number of subsystems; J—number of processes.

System (1) contains two particular criteria with different directions of optimization (for qualitative characteristics, maximization, for temporal characteristics, minimization).

To determine the target function we use the additive criterion. The objective function is formed by adding the normalized values of the partial criteria and in the case of the application of the additive criterion will take the form:

$$\sum_{j=1}^{J}\left(c_j \frac{Q_j(F_j)}{Q^0{}_j} - v_j \frac{t_j(F_j)}{t^0{}_j}\right) \rightarrow \max, \qquad (2)$$

where F_j is the property of the alternative subsystem for solving the j-y design problem (controlled parameter), and $F_j \in \cup_{p=1}^{P_j}\{F_{jp}\}$, $Q^0{}_j$, $t^0{}_j$—j-y normalizing divider for quality and time characteristics, respectively; c_j v_j—weights of the j-y particular criterion.

When searching for the values of the objective function, the qualitative characteristics have a higher priority; if the values of the qualitative indicators are equal (the presence of the required properties) of the program components, the choice is made according to the time characteristics. Thus, the values of the weighting factors must meet the condition $\frac{c_j}{v_j} \rightarrow \infty$.

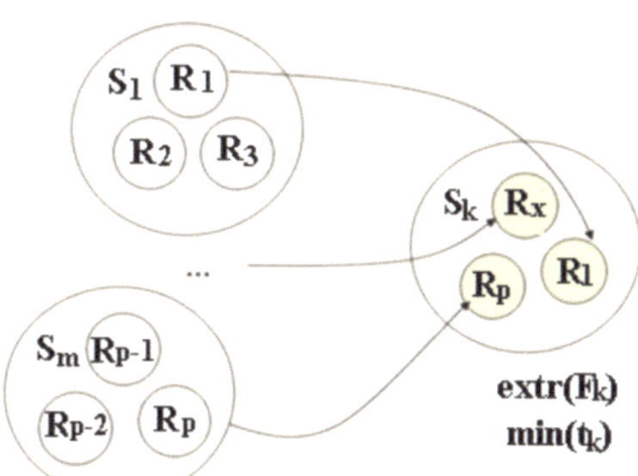

Figure 1.
Organization and distribution of resources between project tasks.

The controlled parameters are the properties of the system (F) and the totality of the components (R) that provide these properties:

$$U = \begin{cases} F, \\ R. \end{cases} \quad (3)$$

In real conditions, the choice of the values of the controlled variables, most often, is imposed by the limitations associated with the available resources, power and other features. Functional limitations establish certain dependencies between the controlled parameters, which cannot be violated under the terms of ensuring the performance or efficiency of the technical system [1, 5].

The development of an integrated environment by adding new software modules that automate individual functional and managerial procedures makes it necessary to create a methodology for managing the configuration of an integrated environment.

3. Components of the methodology for configuring the integrated environment and the organization of a single information space

In relation to the problem area of development, the following components of the methodology are highlighted (**Figure 2**):

- single realizable environment;
- classification of system components;
- integration interfaces;
- integration principles of components;
- configuration of system components.

Classification of system components form a generalized representation of groups and subgroups of components of a software system (PS).

A single executable environment is a software environment where components function and interact with each other.

Integration interfaces are software interfaces that provide interaction between software systems of a single executable environment and implemented components.

Component integration principles—a set of rules necessary for the interaction of two or more components. Since complex CAD consists of components that perform

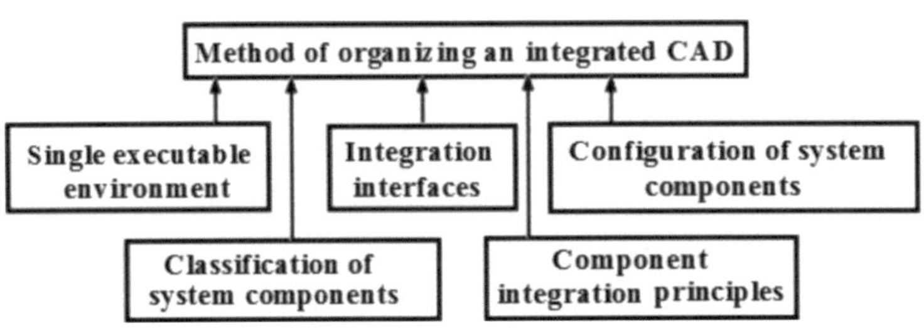

Figure 2.
Components of integrated CAD.

synthesizing, analyzing, evaluating, converting functions, it is necessary to consider various principles of the organization of interaction between subsystems.

Configuration of system components is a change in the set of software components depending on the design tasks to be solved [6, 7].

The use of various automated systems (AS) by independent developers in the product life cycle processes raises the problem of the information compatibility of these systems, which limits the possibility of using the same data and sharing it. This necessitates the presentation of data in the form of a single structured information model that is accessible to all specialists in the design process. The common information space (UIS) allows:

- accept and store the product design electronically;
- keep track of the current state of the product;
- organize a quick view of all models and documents;
- to ensure the rapid exchange of information between users of the integrated environment;
- to ensure information consistency and exchange between all subsystems of CAD.

These requirements for the UIS can be fulfilled if the synthesizing, constructive and analyzing design processes in the CAD system are automated. And also, if the project information enters the information space automatically and is available to all users of the system in accordance with the existing access rights.

In most cases, the integration of various CAD subsystems is carried out using API (application programming interface) interfaces (**Figure 3**) and CAD (computer aided design), CAE (computer aided engineering) systems.

The disadvantages of organizing this interaction are:

- narrow specialization of the developed integration interface designed to solve the interaction problem only for certain subsystems;
- dependence of the functioning of the system on changes in the API;
- the need to develop additional integration when introducing new CAD and CAE systems;
- lack of free access to API software products.

Thus, the integration option, based only on the API, allows you to create the core of the enterprise UIS, but in this case the system is limited from changes in API functions to changes in the level of replacement of subsystems.

A fundamental solution to the problems considered is the introduction of CALS-technologies. CALS (continuous acquisition and lifecycle support—continuous information support for supplies and product life cycle) is a modern approach to the

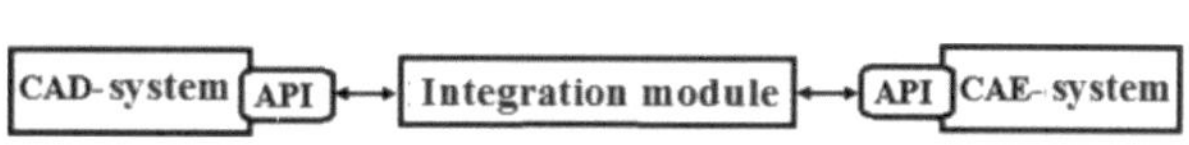

Figure 3.
Interaction scheme of CAD-system and PS through API.

design and manufacture of high-tech and knowledge-intensive products, which consists in using computer technology and modern information technologies at all stages of the product life cycle. The main CALS tool is SDE (shared data environment).

The CALS approach is to free the user from dependence on the manufacturer of the software being used. The basis of the approach is a single information space in accordance with the international standard for data presentation. The main standard is ISO 10303 STEP (standard for exchange of product model data), based on the express language. There are also standards IGES (international graphical exchange format) and DXF (drawing interchange format), which are currently one of the main data storage formats for some CAD-systems. As an alternative language for the exchange of geometric and technical data about the product can be used XML markup language. For CALS, of interest are the subsets of product definition exchange (PDX) and 3D XML dedicated to data exchange in CAD.

Due to the considered features, the general organization of interaction between the CAD subsystems looks like that shown in **Figure 4**. The use of CALS technologies can significantly reduce the scope of design work, since the descriptions of machines and systems, many components of equipment that were previously designed, will be stored in the PS database in unified format.

The solution of the integration task is to integrate ready-made software solutions using interfaces into a single system of modules. The connecting element is a special module designed for the transmission and transformation of data. Formed a single executable environment provides a functional basis for the introduction of various components into the system [8–10].

The interaction of integration components with external CAD systems (CAD and CAE systems) and modules of the PS being developed is presented in **Figure 5**.

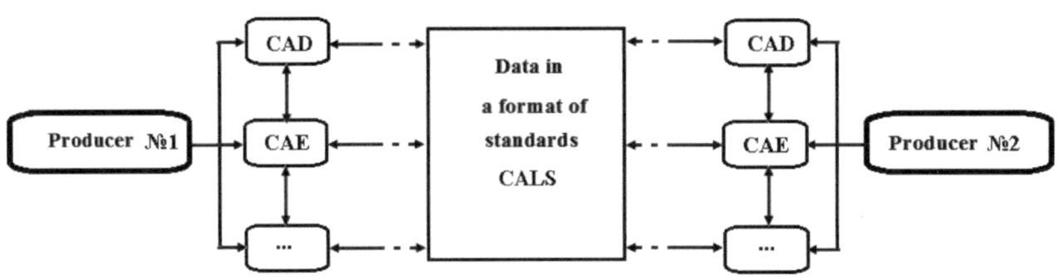

Figure 4.
CALS technology.

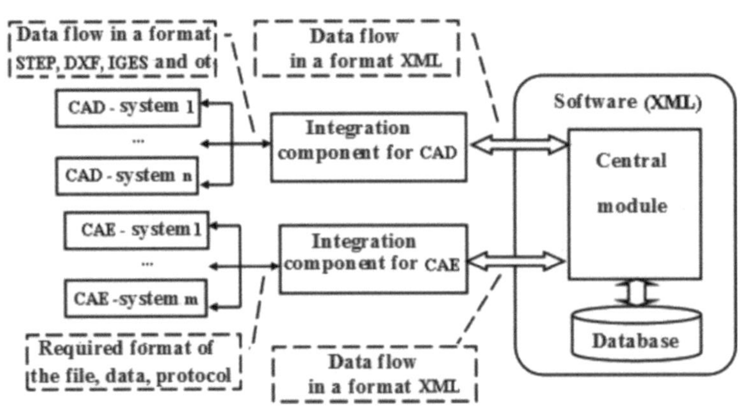

Figure 5.
The interaction of systems in the integrating complex.

CALS standards have been chosen as the format for exchanging design data. Thus, according to the presented scheme, geometric models presented in STEP, DXF, IGES formats can be used as imported (exported) design information. The format of data exchange between the internal components of the software core (PS) is the product model, represented in the XML markup language. The use of a similar organization of the internal representation of the central module will allow to include in the product model, in addition to the design parameters, also the parameters of the technological process, the rheology of the material, temperature characteristics in different parts of the machine and other characteristics necessary for analyzing the designed structure and its identification in the system.

The interaction of external components of the integrated environment is provided by:

- using exchange files;
- unidirectional or bidirectional software interfaces;
- using database tables (DB).

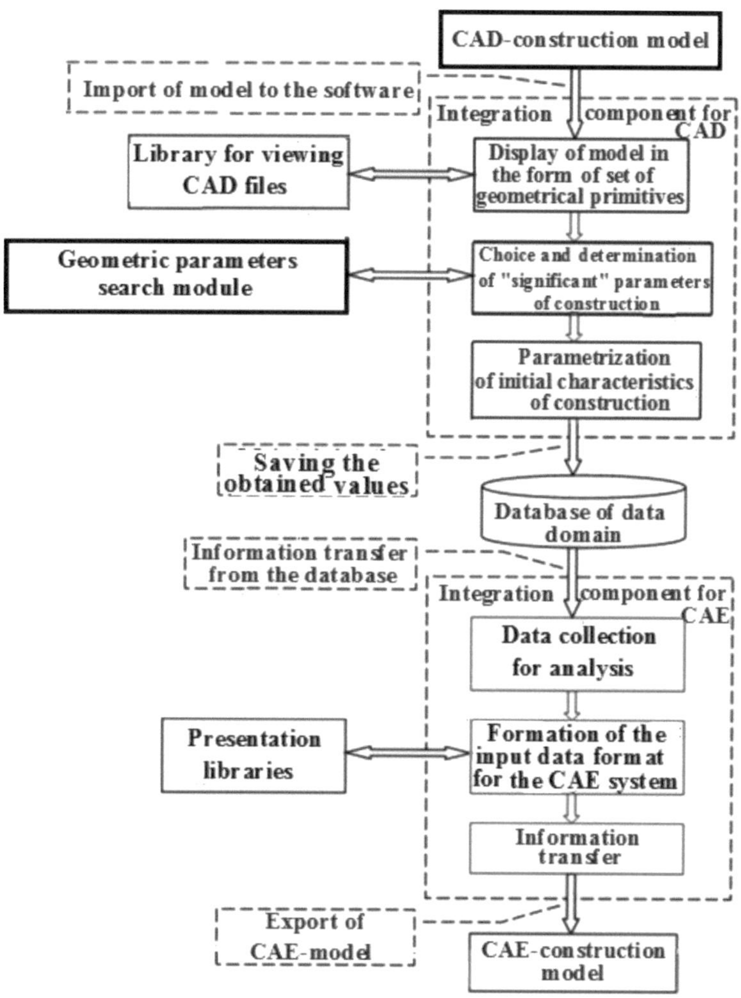

Figure 6.
Methods of organizing the interaction of CAD and CAE-systems.

The use of the software interface provided by the manufacturers restricts the functionality of the system, its extensibility and scale. Thus, exchange files are selected as the main method of interaction between external CAD components. The connection between the components of the central module is organized by building a database of the subject area.

CAD systems for design and CAE systems for analysis interact poorly with each other, despite their wide distribution. CAD and CAE models use different types of geometric models, and there is no common unified model that contains information for design and analysis.

As a solution to these problems, a variant of CAD-CAE bidirectional integration is proposed. Then the system will allow the CAD system to automatically generate models for analysis, and the CAE system will automatically modify the geometry of the parts and carry out a new analysis. The transformation process will be repeated until the specified criterion is reached.

Based on this approach, a method was developed for obtaining the required CAE model from an imported structural drawing (**Figure 6**).

The technique is implemented by a sequence of steps performed in the integration components. Each of the integration stages is implemented as a separate functional unit.

According to the CAD/CAE-integrated approach, the implementation of the inverse transform from the CAE model to the geometric representation of the structure is also required. In this case, the technique will be similar to that shown in **Figure 6**. At the same time, the functional blocks will also be located in the integration components, which will significantly reduce the complexity of implementing the interaction between the CAD and CAE subsystems.

Based on the bi-directionality and versatility of this technique, it is possible to track product adjustments at each of the design stages. This will automatically modify the CAD/CAE model in accordance with the changes made.

4. Configuring system components and methods of organizing the interaction of CAD components

In CAD, models are presented in the form of problem-solving algorithms, and then in the form of software. Technological objects, divided into private sub-models, are divided into simpler individual aspects of the object's functioning (that is, they are decomposed into particular models). Each individual model is represented by some mathematical transformation (**Figure 7**).

Figure 7—$Z = \{z_i, i = 1, \ldots, k\}$ is a set of output parameters of the model; *V*—operator (model) of the transformation (*V*—function of the input variables); A vector $X = \{x_i, i = 1..n\}$ is a set of external parameters coming from a model of a more general system; A vector $Y = \{y_i, i = 1, ..m\}$ is a set of input controlled

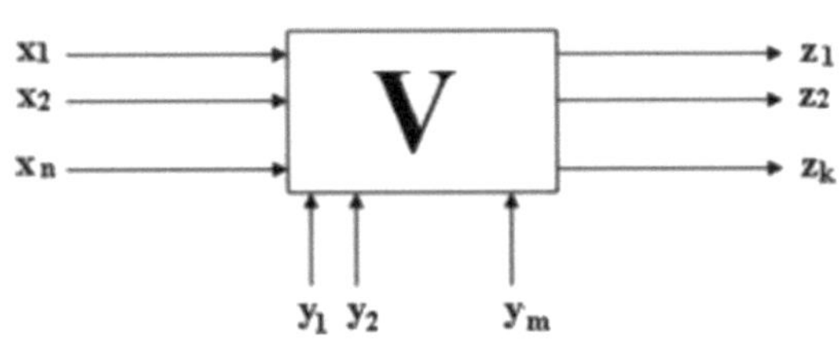

Figure 7.
Mathematical transformation.

parameters of the model that the designer can operate on during the design process. Controlled input parameters can vary within specified limits, i.e., so-called parametric constraints are imposed on them: $y_i^н \leq y_i \leq y_i^в, i = 1..m,$ where $y_i^н$ and $y_i^в$ are lower and upper limits.

With regard to the technological machine, the requirements for the technological process, which affect the kinematic parameters, the structural parameters of the mechanism and the geometrical parameters of the interaction space, act as the rheological properties of the material being processed as input parameters of the mathematical model (MM). All this affects the internal characteristics of the system, which determines the scale, efficiency of the process and the quality of products.

Building techniques and methodological principles for the operation of complex systems simplifies and streamlines the process of developing CAD software, and presents a sequence of operations in the form of a logic diagram. This methodology represents an approach to the design and development of CAD, based on the interaction of software solutions available on the market in the field of automation and its own software design algorithms.

Figure 8 shows the sequence of steps in the proposed method of functioning CAD systems.

In the *first step* of the implementation of the methodology, tasks (including new ones) and a set of components for their implementation are determined based on the initial design requirements. The choice of a set of components is implemented according to their classification by functionality. *Next* is the organization of the interaction, configuration, and the formation and exchange of data. Thus, the final set of components will allow you to find solutions to all the tasks, or to determine the set of tasks that cannot be solved with the existing set of subsystems.

After performing the first step, we obtain a specific set of components and an approximate system architecture. Each component performs a specific task at a certain level of logical implementation.

In the *second step*, a single executable environment is formed.

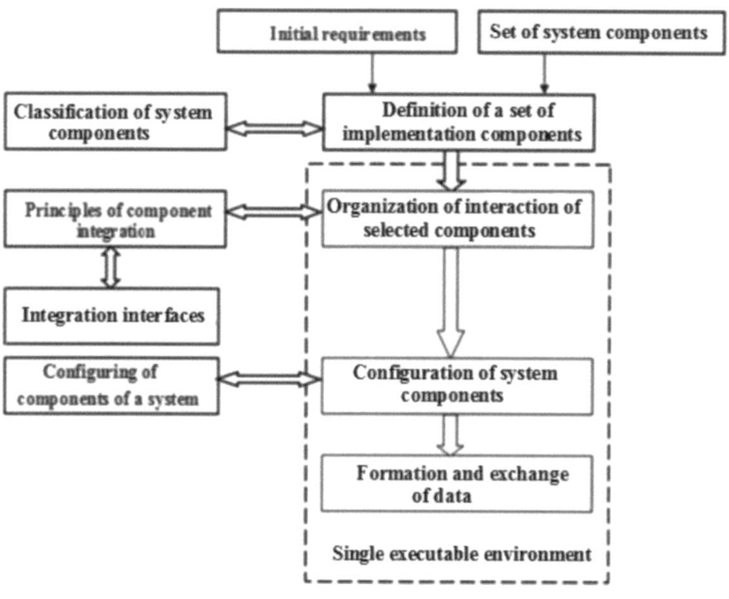

Figure 8.
Technique of functioning of CAD.

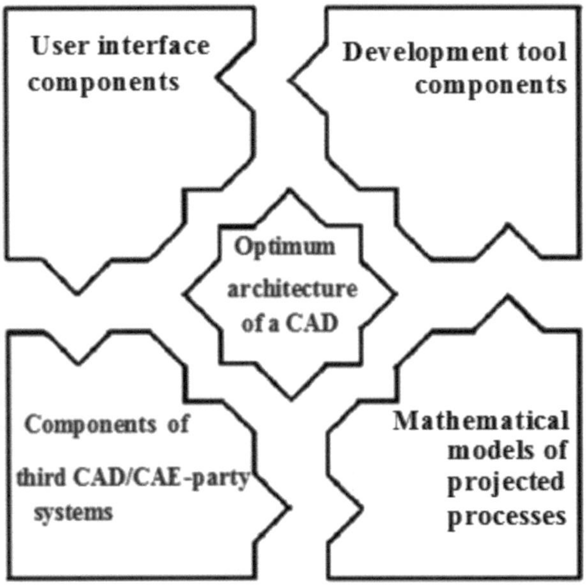

Figure 9.
Configuring CAD components.

The *first stage* of formation is the realization of interaction between the selected components. The interaction is carried out in accordance with the principles based on the use of integration and implementation interfaces and a connecting component. The interfaces required for the operation of each component are determined.

The *second stage* is the configuration of the selected components. This stage involves the selection among alternative algorithms that involve solving the same tasks, the most adapted for the design of a particular product (initial system requirements) [11, 12].

Further, in the *third stage* of the second step, the source data is modified to exchange them between the selected components. An example would be a change in the geometric design in the product model required for analysis.

The result of the *second step* is a formed single executable system environment, which has mechanisms for implementing external PSs and for ensuring their interaction with the components of the entire system. This is the final architecture of CAD, focused on solving the problem (**Figure 9**).

5. Formal description of project operations

Supporting the choice of the right MM configuration among many alternatives is similar to the task of building CAD systems, which consists in allocating resources R_k between design tasks Z_k in such a way as to ensure optimal values of system properties $extr(F_k)$ in the system S_k (**Figure 1**).

To apply each of the alternative mathematical models, it is required to check the ability of its functioning in a given configuration of the system. The graph of component configuration is supplemented with transition events (U_k) and is represented as a Petri net for the system S_k method of decomposition (**Figure 10**) [13].

As conditions for the transition (U) to a specific MM, we will use verification of the required set of initial data, including constructive (U_K), geometric (U_G), kinematic (U_P) and rheological (U_R) parameters.

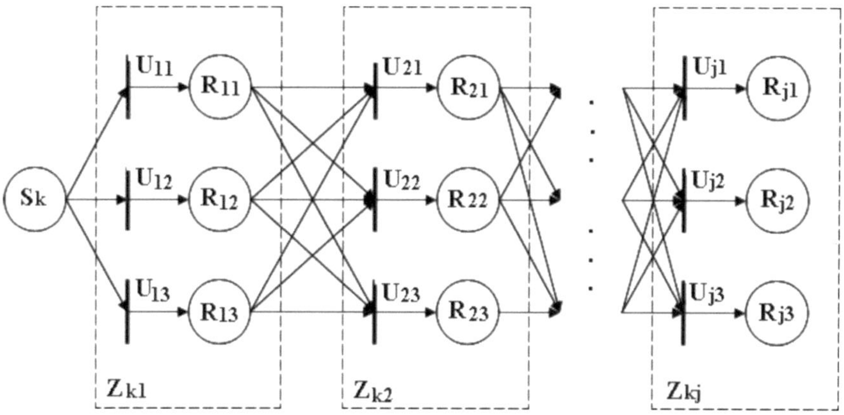

Figure 10.
MM component configuration graph.

Thus, the system S_k must solve many design problems $Z_k = \{Z_{kj}\}, j = \overline{1, J}, J$ is the number of tasks. To solve each project problem there is a set of alternative resources (components) $R_j = \{R_{jy}\}, y = \overline{1, Y}$, Y—the number of resources intended for solving the problem. Each resource R_{jy} is characterized by a set of properties $F_{jy} = \{F_{jyl}\}, l = \overline{1, L}, L$ is a set of properties of the j resource. The performance of each of the properties of the resource is limited by the condition of transition to the specified resource $U_j = \{U_{jy}\}, y = \overline{1, Y}$.

The task of optimal configuration of MM is to allocate resources $r \in R_j$ between project tasks Z_k in such a way as to provide extreme values of system properties, as well as to support the ability to use each of the selected resources $extr(F_k) \wedge M_j(U_j, R_j, Z_k, S_k)$ (where M_j is the function of checking transition U_j to a resource R_j to solve the problem Z_k in the system S_k).

Thus, the objective function of building CAD (2) is relevant for the configuration of MM. At the same time, the system of control parameters will not change its composition (3), the system of restrictions, which is characterized by design tasks, design features of the product, technological requirements of production will be complemented by transition conditions (U):

$$C = \begin{cases} Z, \; where \; Z \in \{Z_S, \; Z_A, \; Z_E, \; Z_C, \; Z_V, \; Z_D\}, \\ K, \; where \; K \subseteq \{ \; K_I, \; K_Z, \; K_S, \; K_F, \; K_{FI}, \; K_O, \; K_P, \; K_{FS}\}, \\ T, \; where \; T \subseteq \{ \; T_n, \; T_\mu, \; T_\sigma, \; T_t\}, \\ U, \; where \; U \subseteq \{ \; U_K, \; U_G, \; U_P, \; U_R\}. \end{cases}$$

But it is impossible to apply optimization tasks to the described subject domain based on graph theory, since there is no complete information about the relationships between the components:

- management;
- according to information;
- by placement;
- by effects.

Decision making in most cases consists in generating possible alternative solutions, evaluating them and choosing the best option. When choosing an option, one has to take into account a large number of uncertain and contradictory factors. Uncertainty is an integral part of decision-making processes [14–16].

To do this, use systems based on "soft" calculations, which include:

- probabilistic calculations and fuzzy logic;
- neurocomputing—training, adaptation, classification, system modeling and identification;
- genetic computation—synthesis, tuning, and optimization using systematic random search and evolution.

Fuzzy inference algorithms mainly differ in the type of rules used, logical operations, and the type of dephasing method. There are models of Mamdani, Sugeno, Larsen, Tsukamoto.

The Mamdani method is the most common method of inference in fuzzy systems. It uses the minimax composition of fuzzy sets. This method includes the following sequence of actions in relation to the task of reconfiguring MM:

1. Formation of the rule base. The rules are as follows: If <condition 1> and <condition 2> ... and <condition *n*>, then <output>. The conditions indicate the compliance of the input parameters X_i ($i \in [1, \ldots, n]$) to the requirements. Based on the input parameters, as well as the estimated opinion, <condition> takes a value in the interval [0 ... 1]. "Inference" corresponds to the choice of using the component for which the rule is made.

2. Fuzzifikation of input variables. This stage is called reduction to illegibility. The input contains the generated rule base and the input data array $A = \{a_1, \ldots, a_m\}$, where m is the number of input variables. The purpose of this stage is to obtain truth values for all sub-conditions from the rule base. For each of the sub-conditions, there is a value $b_i = \lambda_i(a_j)$, where λ is the membership function, which associates the specific values of the degree of truth with all values of the input variables; j = 1,..., m; i = 1,..., k, where k is the total number of sub-conditions in the rule base. Thus, a set of values is obtained b_i.

3. Aggregation of sub-conditions. The purpose of this stage is to determine the degree of truth of the conditions for each rule of the fuzzy inference system: $c_i = \min\{b_i\}$.

4. Activation of sub-conclusions. At this stage there is a transition from the conditions to the sub-conclusions. For each subconclusions is the degree of truth $d_i = c_i \cdot F_i$, where $i = 1, \ldots, q$, q—the total number of subconclusions in the rule base, F—weights, meaning the degree of confidence in the truth of the subconclusions. Then, again, i for each subconclusion, the set is compared D_i with the new membership function. Its value is determined as a minimum from d_i and the values of the component membership function from the sub-clauses. This method is called min-activation, which is formally written as follows: $\lambda_i^{'}(x) = \min\{d_i, \lambda_i(x)\}$.

5. Accumulation of conclusions. The purpose of this stage is to obtain a fuzzy set (or their union) for each of the output variables. It is executed as follows: i

output variable is associated with the union of the sets $E_i = \cup D_j$. Where j—numbers of sub-conclusions in which the output i variable participates $i = 1..s$. The union of two fuzzy sets is the third fuzzy set with the following membership function: $\lambda_i'(x) = \max\{\lambda_1(x), \lambda_2(x)\}$, where $\lambda_1(x)$, $\lambda_2(x)$ are the membership functions of the joined sets.

6. Defusing output variables. The purpose of defuzzification is to obtain a quantitative value (crisp value) for each of the output linguistic variables. The i output variable and the related set are considered. Then, using the defuzzification method, the total quantitative value of the output variable is found $E_i(i = 1..s)$. In this algorithm implementation, the center of gravity method is used, in which the value of the i output variable is calculated using the formula:

$$y_i = \frac{\int_{Min}^{Max} x \cdot \lambda_i(x)dx}{\int_{Min}^{Max} \lambda_i(x)dx},$$

where $\lambda_i(x)$—membership function of the corresponding fuzzy set E_i; *Min* and *Max*—boundaries of the universe of fuzzy variables; y_i—result of defuzzification.

The advantage of the method is the ability to take into account the unlimited number of various conditions and make the rules of various forms. The accuracy of the results depends on the size of the knowledge base.

Thus, based on the result of the defuzzification stage for a specific rule, one can judge about the need to use a specific MM.

6. Optimization of process parameters and technological machine design

On the basis of the decomposition of the technological process and its mathematical model, a reverse action can be carried out—the compositional design of the technological object. The method of composite design allows to achieve the optimal design solution [7].

As a rule, when searching for the optimal combination of design parameters of a technological machine, it is necessary to control its thermal and mechanical tension, also the intensity of interaction of the material with the working parts of the pressing mechanism and other control factors that limit the area of optimal search and are limitations. In view of the presence of constraints on design optimization, without the possibility of simplification and omission, it reduces the current type of optimization to the problem of conditional multiparameter optimization.

Among the methods of conditional multiparameter optimization, there are three approaches. The first is based on the distribution of criteria by importance and their consistent optimization with allowance for the tolerance. The purpose of the second approach is to single out the main criterion and translate the rest into restrictions. The third approach is the convolution of a vector criterion into one generalized criterion. However, this method is very inconvenient, since to find all effective points (Pareto sets), it is required to change the coefficients of the parameterized function of the global criterion. The second drawback is the need to repeat the algorithm several times (the number of iterations is equal to the power of the Pareto set) to obtain the entire set of effective points.

Thus, the considered classical methods have drawbacks when solving multicriteria optimization problems. It seems more promising to use an evolutionary approach to speed up the process of obtaining Pareto-optimal points, thanks to the ability of genetic algorithms (GA) to find a solution even when the algorithm is executed once.

GA do not guarantee that a global solution will be found, however, they are good for finding a "good enough" problem solution "fast enough." Even where existing techniques work well, improvements can be achieved by combining them with GA.

The genetic algorithm works with a certain objective function $Q(u_1, \ u_2, \ldots, \ u_n)$ and as a result finds either its maximum or minimum (depending on the task). It does not require finding the derivative of the function Q and other calculations, since the genetic algorithm considers the objective function as a block (a set of some actions, operations and calculations), which at the input receives a certain set of values $u_1, \ u_2, \ldots, \ u_n, u_1, \ u_2, \ldots, \ u_n$ and the output gives the result, directly dependent on them.

The GA, which includes the ability to set various selection criteria, will allow to take into account the boundary conditions necessary for the successful course of the technological process.

It should be noted that the use of classical (exact) mathematical optimization methods is not always appropriate, because The simulation model is not an absolute copy of the real system (there is a certain degree of accuracy), while the use of exact methods requires significant computational costs, which is critical in many cases. Therefore, as a search engine optimization algorithm, it is more expedient to use a method that does not necessarily guarantee the achievement of an exact optimum, but finds solutions that are close to optimal, and at the same time ensures fast search convergence of the algorithm.

The work of a genetic algorithm is an iterative process that continues until a specified number of generations or some other stopping criterion is fulfilled. A generalized block diagram of the work of the GA is shown in **Figure 11**.

Of particular importance is the creation of the initial population. The rate of convergence of the method and the place of the local maximum depend on the choice of the initial data. Often this choice is made randomly, but it is rational to use the results obtained earlier, which are contained in the database.

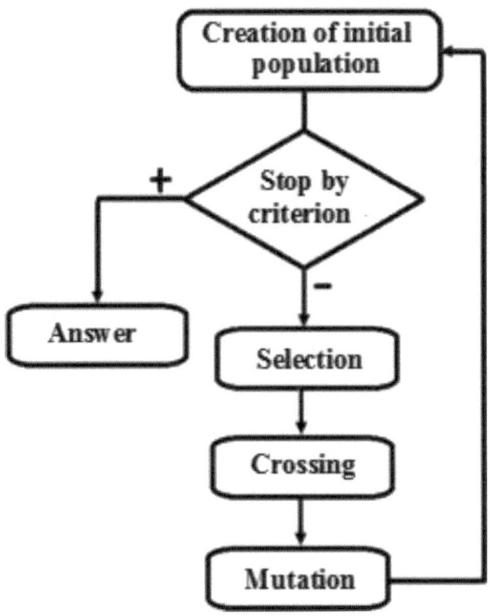

Figure 11.
Generic genetic algorithm scheme.

As a method of selecting values from a set of results, taking into account the criteria and objectives of optimization imposed on them, we will use the Mamdani method (Section 4), based on "soft" calculations.

It uses a minimax composition of fuzzy sets:

$$MF = \max(\min(A_{ik}(x_k)))$$

where x_k—input variables (extruder design parameters D_1, $s_ш$, $p_ш$, $h_ш$, L); A_{ik}—given fuzzy sets with membership functions of input variables to the required parameters.

At each iteration of the GA, selection, single-point crossover and mutation are implemented.

At the selection stage, the "fitness" of each structure is evaluated. The selection is made by assigning each structure a probability equal to the ratio of its adaptability to the total adaptability of the population:

$$P_S(i) = \frac{f(i)}{\sum_{j=1}^{N} f(j)},$$

where $i = 1, \ldots, N$; N—number of estimated machine designs; $f(i)$—compliance with the requirements i—construction.

In genetic algorithms, a crossover operator (crossover) is responsible for transferring descendants of parents to descendants. In the simplest case, the crossover in the genetic algorithm is implemented as shown in **Figure 12**.

Since in this case the information about the construction is presented in the form of a set of real numbers, therefore, a type of genetic algorithm is used, which is called continuous GA or a genetic algorithm with real coding.

A continuous GA crossing operator generates one or more descendants from two parent sets. As a matter of fact, it is required to get new vectors from two vectors of real numbers according to some laws. Most of these algorithms generate new vectors in the neighborhood of parent pairs.

In this case, an extended line crossover is considered (**Figure 13**), which can formally be represented as a formula:

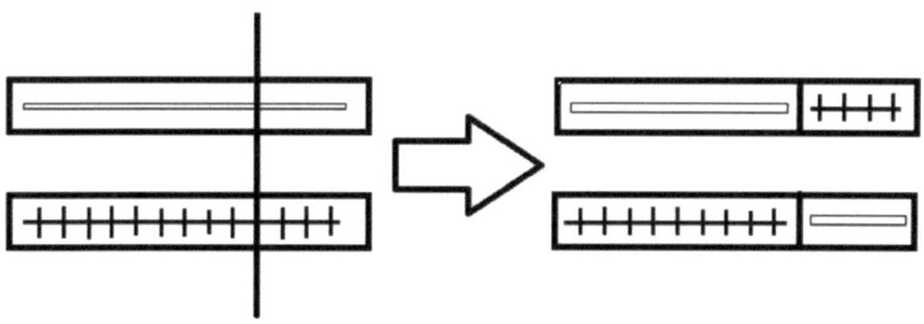

Figure 12.
Concept of crossing over.

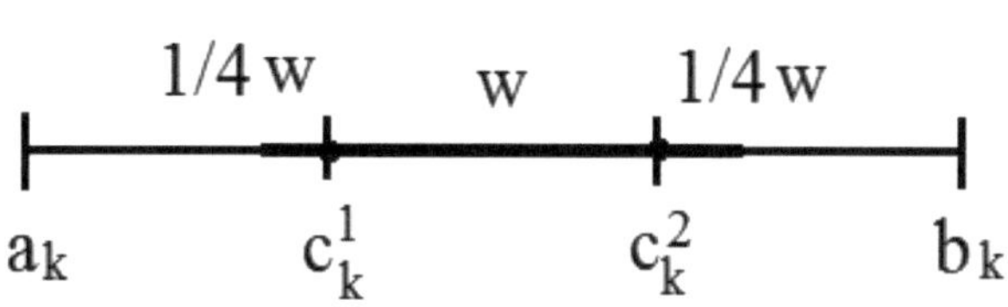

Figure 13.
Line crossover.

$$h_k = c_k^1 + w \times \left(c_k^2 - c_k^1\right)$$

where h_k–k—construction parameter; $H = (h_1, ..., h_n)$, $k = \overline{1, n}$; n—number of parameters; c_k^m–k—parent element $C^m = \left(h_1^m, ..., h_n^m\right)$, $k = \overline{1, n}$, $m = \overline{1, 2}$; w—random number of interval $[-0, 25;\ 1, 25]$.

A mutation is a random change in one or more positions in a set of characteristics, designed to maintain diversity and to protect against premature convergence.

The mutation element will be defined as follows:

$$x_k = a_k + (b_k - a_k) \times u,$$

where x_k–k—construction parameter $X = (x_1, ..., x_n)$, $k = \overline{1, n}$ determined on interval $[a_k;\ b_k][a_k;\ b_k]$; u—random number of interval $[0;\ 1][0;\ 1]$.

Crossing procedures, mutations, assessment of fitness, the choice of the best solution are repeated in the cycle until the stop criterion works. The fulfillment of a certain condition is used as such a criterion. The essence of the condition is as follows: if the difference between the best solutions at the moment and at the previous iteration is insignificant (less than a certain set ε), or the maximum number of iterations is completed (the number of iterations performed is more than a certain set n), the algorithm stops its work. The last best solution found is the optimal set of parameters.

This method has several disadvantages—it is convergence to a local optimum, lack of accuracy of the results.

Therefore, if it is necessary to optimize a specific parameter when changing only one indicator and the invariance of others, then it is more rational to use exact methods of multidimensional optimization (the coordinatewise descent method, the Hook-Jeeves method, etc.).

The advantage of applying this modification of the genetic algorithm is the scalability of the optimization problem. Using this method, it is possible to optimize a different set of parameters, as well as to establish all possible optimization conditions, both for a single resulting indicator and for several. The method does not require significant computational costs, which are necessary for the implementation of exact methods, and which are often impossible in complex systems. GA provides fast search convergence of the algorithm. The results of the method satisfy the conditions of the technological process, as obtained by simulation.

As a solution to the identified deficiencies, it is possible to combine the presented method with accurate methods of multidimensional optimization.

7. Conclusion

The implementation of the developed methodology has several advantages for developers and end users:

- costs are reduced for the development of user interface and application applications (for example, control program editors, network connection configurators, etc.);
- it is possible to determine the required set of components, and the tasks they implement, in the early stages of designing applied software;
- reduced time of release of the new system, due to the possibility of issuing a lightweight (preliminary) version with a subsequent increase in functionality.

The developed technique with the use of artificial intelligence methods of building an integrated environment allows organizing the interaction of CAD components based on their classification, integration and configuration.

Author details

Tatyana Zubkova* and Marina Tokareva
Orenburg State University, Orenburg, Russia

*Address all correspondence to: bars87@mail.ru

References

[1] Mustyukov NA, Zubkova TM. Application of the genetic algorithm for carrying out parametrical synthesis of construction of an extruder. 2013;**4**:114-118. the ITMO Scientific and technical bulletin St.Petersburg State University

[2] Korobeynikov AG, Fedosovsky ME, Zharinov IO, Shukalov AV, Gurjanov AV. Development of conceptual modeling method to solve the tasks of computeraided design of difficult technical complexes on the basis of category theory. International Journal of Applied Engineering Research. 2017;**12** (6):1114-1122

[3] Gorbunov AA, Pripadchev AD, Bykova IS, Elagin VV. Simulation modelling for computer aided design of secondary aerodynamic wing surfaces. Advances in Systems Science and Applications. 2015;**15**(4):346-358

[4] Gorokhov Yu V, Timofeev VN, Belyaev SV, Kirko VI, Avdulov AA, Konstantinov IL, et al. Conform installation structural elements design methods. Journal of Engineering and Applied Sciences. 2017;**12**(9):2917-2922

[5] Zubkova TM. Development of methodology of mathematical modeling of technological objects. 2002;**2**:209-213. Messenger of the Orenburg state university

[6] Zubkova TM. Automated design of the extrusion equipment using intellectual systems. Intelligence. Innovations. Investments. 2017;**8**:51-55

[7] Kirillov NP. Description of the method of combined conceptual modeling of technical systems. Tr. SPIIRAS. 2013;**31**:223-235

[8] Zubkova TM, Mustyukov NA, Tokareva MA. Creation of architecture of a CAD of one-screw extruders using elements of artificial intelligence. 2016; **4**:176-182

[9] Vasiliev PV, Kuzenyi VV. Improving the effectiveness of scenario development in the intellectual-modeling environment. Tr. SPIIRAN. 2011;**19**:288-297

[10] Shishigin DS. To the choice of integration technology for application software with CAD. Proceedings of SPIIRAS. 2016;**4**(47):211-224

[11] Zubkova TM. Automated industrial design based on artificial intelligence. Russian Engineering Research. 2018; **38**(5):394-398

[12] Zubkova TM, Tokareva MA, Sultanov NZ. Creation of system of computer-aided design for technological objects. Journal of Physics: Conference Series. 2018;**1015**:052031. DOI:10.1088/1742-6596/1015/5/052031. Techniques and technologies of the automated mechanical engineering.

[13] Zubkova TM, Mustyukov NA, Kolobov AN. Reconfiguring of a CAD for design of one-screw extruders on the basis of model of an indistinct output of Mamdani. 2013;**1**:176-181. the Messenger of regional public institution

[14] Troitsky AK. Two-level multiple face detection algorithm based on local feature search and structure recognition methods. International Journal of Applied Engineering Research. 2016; **11**(6):4640-4647

[15] Kobersy IS, Shkurkin DV, Zatonskiy AV, Volodina JI, Safyanova TV. Moving objects control under uncertainty. ARPN Journal of Engineering and Applied Sciences. 2016; **11**(5):2830-2834

[16] Molodtsov DA. Soft probability of large deviations. Advances in Systems Science and Applications. 2013;**13**(1): 53-67

Section 2

Deterministic Approaches

Chapter 6

Deterministic Approaches to Transient Trajectory Generation

Matthew A. Cooper

Abstract

This chapter studies a deterministic approach to transient trajectory generation and control as applied to the forced Van der Pol oscillatory system. This type of system tends towards a strongly nonlinear system, which can be considered chaotic. A classical tuning method, targeted exponential weighting, and isolated trajectory fractionalization trajectory generation methods are examined. Illustrating the given deterministic approach via the Van der Pol system highlights the potentially iterative nature of deterministic methods, and that traditional optimal linear time-invariant control techniques are unable to perform as desired whereas even an idealized nonlinear feedforward control significantly outperforms at the steady-state. It will be shown that utilizing a-priori knowledge of the system dynamics will enable the isolated trajectory fractionalization method to minimize the nonlinear transient effects due to miss-modeled or unmodeled plant dynamics, and that this benefit can be coupled with the targeted exponential weighting approach for greatly decreased trajectory tracking error on the order of a 92% reduction of the objective cost function in the presented case study based on the forced Van der Pol system.

Keywords: Van der Pol, trajectory generation, path planning, nonlinear transients, control systems, nonlinear dynamic system, aerospace engineering, non-stochastic, deterministic, autonomy, intelligent systems, feedforward, dynamic inversion, disturbance modeling, phase portrait tuning

1. Introduction

Transient trajectory generation research is an interesting area, and often finds itself in a highly nonlinear environment. Similar to trajectory optimization problems [1–9], the goal of designing transient trajectories is to reach the desired steady-state trajectory more quickly while simultaneously minimizing and unwanted micro-transients along the way. Micro-transients can be considered as a subcategory of transient trajectories. Transient trajectories are smaller trajectories that connect two steady-state trajectories and can be quite volatile and full of nonlinear micro transients that may push the system towards instability. Section 1 will introduce the reader to basic control theory, and the Van der Pol oscillator which will be used to illustrate transient trajectory generation approaches. Section 2 will describe a classical tuning method, targeted exponential weighting, and isolated trajectory fractionalization trajectory generation methods and present the corresponding results of each method. Section 3 will finish off the chapter by summarizing the results in table format.

1.1 Basic control theory

An introduction to control theory will be conducted to set the understanding baseline in common controls. This refresher will start with state-space nomenclature and then quickly step through the most common feedback control, feedforward control, observers, and adaptive designs. This will be the ground work that is used to later illustrate to the trajectory generation techniques and the inherent complexity in nonlinear dynamical systems such as the Van der Pol oscillator. Any dynamical system can be represented in state-space matrix form [10] to provide a solution formed as shown in Eq. (1):

$$\begin{cases} \dot{\mathbf{x}} = \mathbf{A}\mathbf{x} + \mathbf{B}\mathbf{u} \\ \mathbf{y} = \mathbf{C}\mathbf{x} + \mathbf{D}\mathbf{u} \end{cases}, \tag{1}$$

where A is a matrix representing the system states (also referred to as the plant). B is an input matrix, C is the output matrix, and D is the feedback/feedforward control input matrix. A symbolic representation of a feedback control loop is illustrated in **Figure 1**.

The input to **Figure 1** is nominally a desired position (output) from a user which may be converted to a usable command in the generate trajectory block. For the initial output the input will be fed directly to the plant for a resulting position. If this is not the desired position, then the feedback controller will calculate that error between the desired and resulting position and produced an appropriately weighted control signal to adjust the input. This will happen cyclically until the error approaches zero, and is typically referred to as a zero-seeking negative-feedback approach [10]. A common way to represent the interaction between the input and output of a system is as a transfer function [11], and is usually presented in the Laplacian domain as shown as H in Eq. (2). Also known as the S-domain, this can be an easier format to mathematically manipulate the system variables primarily due to the fact that the system blocks interact in a convolutional way in the time-domain whereas in the S-domain one can just perform multiplication and achieve equivalent results [11].

$$H(s) = \frac{A(s)}{1 + D(s)A(s)} \tag{2}$$

A very common way to implement a feedback controller is through the use of a proportional-integral-derivative (PID) controller [11] as shown in **Figure 2**.

The PID controller is the staple of many feedback control systems [11], and can be formulated such that it is a zero-seeking architecture by calculating the difference between the measured output of the system and the desired output as shown in **Figure 2** and Eq. (4). The error signal is then fed into the proportional, integral, and derivative blocks, and summed together to provide an additional control input to the plant. The proportional block assigns a constant gain (K_p) to the error signal, the

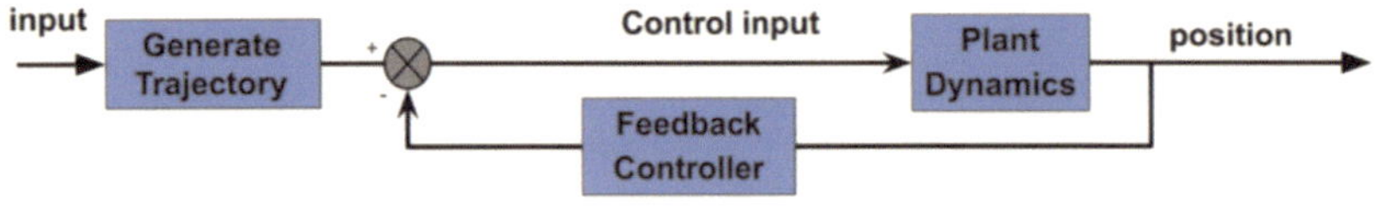

Figure 1.
Generic feedback control schematic.

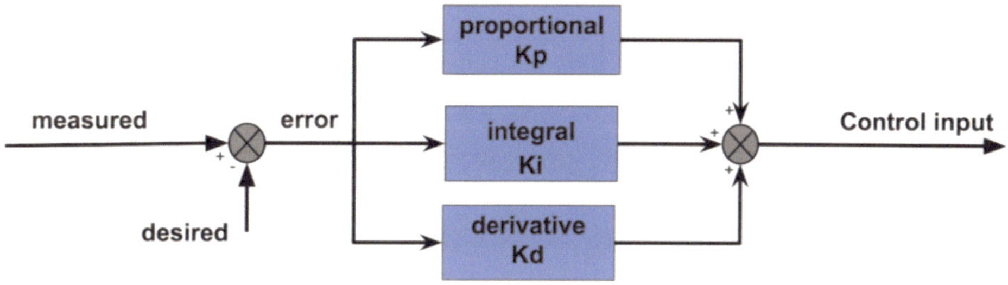

Figure 2.
Generalized PID feedback controller.

integral block calculates the integral of the error signal and applies a different gain (K_i). There are many different ways and variations of implementing a PID controller such as sometimes only utilizing one or two components as shown in Eq. (3) as a typical PI controller example.

$$u = (\tilde{q} - q)(K_p + \frac{K_i}{s}), \tag{3}$$

where q is the desired position and $\hat{q}$ is the measured position and the error is defined as:

$$e = \hat{q} - q \tag{4}$$

The third and final component of the PID feedback controller is the derivative block which calculated the derivative of the error signal and assigns a corresponding gain (K_d) to it. If all three components are summed together as shown in **Figure 2**, it will result in Eq. (5) for the time-domain solution, and Eq. 6 for the S-domain. Eqs. (5) and (6) illustrate both the time-domain equation and the S-domain equation for ease of comparison.

$$u(t) = K_p e(t) + K_i \int e(\tau)\mathrm{d}\tau + K_d \frac{\mathrm{d}\ e(t)}{\mathrm{d}t} \tag{5}$$

$$u(S) = e\left(K_p + \frac{K_i}{S} + K_d S)\right) \tag{6}$$

Another common feedback control method extends into the realm of optimal control [1, 2] which is focused primarily at looking at control as a cost minimization problem. A linear quadratic regulator (LQR) is one way to treat a feedback control system as an optimal control problem [1]. One variation based in the continuous time-domain treats the problem with a focus on the infinite steady-state, the infinite-horizon continuous-time LQR. The cost function of this type of solution is identified in Eq. (7).

$$J = \int_0^\infty \left(x^T Q x + u^T R u + 2x^T N u\right) dt, \tag{7}$$

where Q is the state cost matrix, R is the input cost matrix, and N is the final state cost matrix with a feedback control law of:

$$u = -Kx \tag{8}$$

where:

$$K = R^{-1}(B^T P + N^T), \tag{9}$$

and P is found by solving the continuous time Riccati equation [11]:

$$A^T P + PA - (PB + N)R^{-1}(B^T P + N^T) + Q = 0 \tag{10}$$

For a linear system, with a linear response, an appropriately chosen cost function, J, can achieve optimal feedback control parameters and find the feedback control parameters that minimize the control cost J.

When full-state feedback is not present in a system, i.e. the outputs cannot be fully known, the control system will either need to be designed without the need for the missing information or those states will need to be estimated based on the sensed outputs as seen in **Figure 3**. In this case an estimator is also referred to as a state observer. A state observer's role is to estimate the internal states of a given system based on the current inputs and outputs. For a more thorough discussion the reader is referred to [10].

An example of taking the general formulation above and applying it to a specific system is illustrated in **Figure 4** for a spacecraft, more specifically a satellite. Here the system dynamics will also include control moment gyros, and other physical restraints/limitations of a real-world plant [12–20]. Additionally, the control variables here are in angle, angular rate, and angular acceleration in order to apply the correct torque on the motors to affect the desired outcome.

The key takeaway here is that the high-level depiction of the system identified in **Figure 4** is not very different from the general case, only that the details within the blocks encompass many more physical variables.

1.2 The Van der Pol oscillator

Balthasar van der Pol (1889–1959) was a Dutch physicist who became interested in the differential equations of coupled electrical systems, which formed into

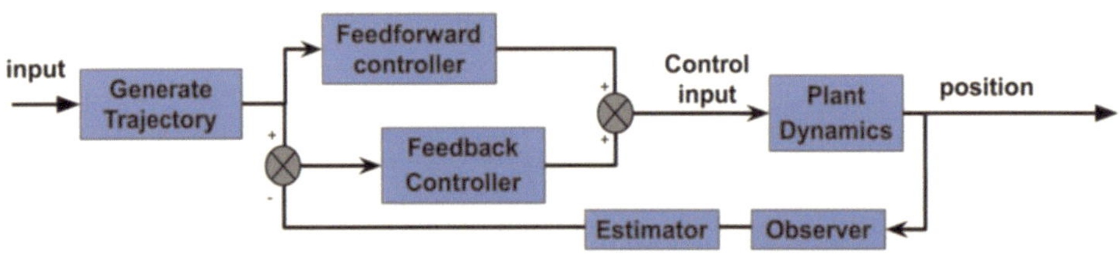

Figure 3.
Generic nonlinear feedforward/feedback control schematic.

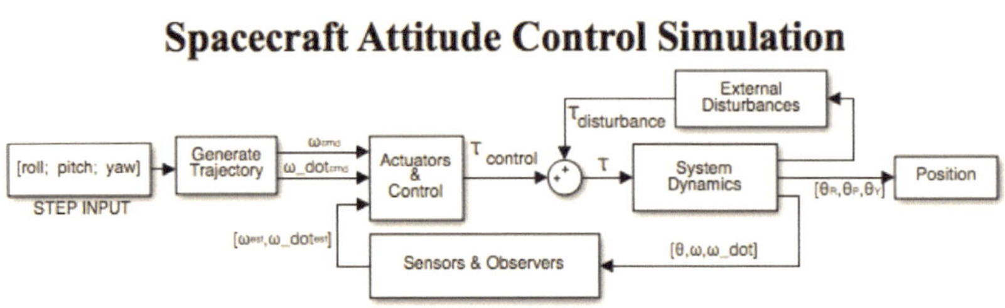

Figure 4.
Nonlinear feedforward/feedback spacecraft control schematic.

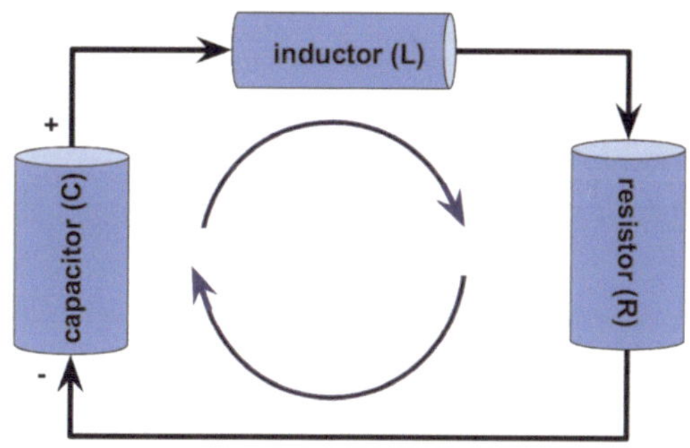

Figure 5.
RLC schematic for VDP derivation.

relaxation oscillators, what later became a description of what we now call limit cycles [22]. His initial investigation began with describing the human heartbeat, and later when turning towards the issues of radio communication [23–25] at the time (the result of deterministic chaos) and is illustrated with the resistor-inductor-capacitor (RLC) circuit shown in **Figure 5**.

The circuit in **Figure 5** represents a schematic for an RLC circuit comprised of a nonlinear resistor (R), an inductor (L), and a capacitor (C). This common circuit can be described by the differential equation [21] in Eq. (11):

$$\ddot{V} - \frac{1}{C}(\alpha - 3\gamma V^2)\dot{V} + \frac{1}{LC}V = 0, \tag{11}$$

where:

$$x = \sqrt{3\gamma/\alpha}V \text{, and } \mu = \sqrt{L/C}\alpha \text{, and } L/R \propto \mu\sqrt{LC}, \tag{12}$$

and where μ is the damping coefficient, and can be rearranged to get in the form of the differential equation that describes the Van der Pol equation for limit cycle oscillations in Eq. (13).

$$\frac{d^2x}{dt^2} - \mu(1 - x^2)\frac{dx}{dt} + x = 0, \tag{13}$$

By using the simplification assumption in Eq. (15), one can simulate the VPD as a plant to a controls simulation in MATLAB/Simulink structured around the model presented previously in **Figure 3**. The natural periodic oscillations in the phase portrait can be seen in **Figure 6**, which are shown to converge to the same limit cycle from any initial condition nearby (local). This model will be discussed in greater detail in Section 2.

Phase portraits are ways to represent the performance of a system, and to also analyze the expected stability within some local bounds usually determined by the anticipated operational bounds [10, 11, 23]. These portraits display the state of interest with respect to the derivative of that state. Ideally, the goal is such that the state is controllable enough so that the state can be forced to zero within a given time-constant. Sometimes, in a nonlinear system, just being able to prevent the state from growing unbounded (blowing up) and towards an arbitrary asymptotic limit is acceptable [11].

Taking the unforced VPD equation and adding a sinusoidal forcing function to Eq. (13) gives Eq. (14):

$$\frac{d^2x}{dt^2} - \mu(1 - x^2)\frac{dx}{dt} + x - A\sin(\omega t) = 0, \tag{14}$$

Using the forced VDP equation, and simplifying it by using the outlined assumptions in Eq. (15) to achieve a perfectly circular limit cycle:

$$\mu = 1, \quad \omega = 1, \quad A = 1, \tag{15}$$

to get Eq. (16):

$$\ddot{x} - (1 - x^2)\dot{x} + x - sin(t) = \ddot{x}_d - (1 - x_d^2)\dot{x}_d + x_d, \tag{16}$$

In order to implement the forcing function onto the VDP system, it is needed to invert the dynamics such that the VDP equation is used as the feedforward control signal, which will feed into the plant. The steady-state results can be seen in **Figure 7**, with a severe amount to transient phenomenon before reaching the perfectly circular limit-cycle steady-state response.

1.3 What are transient trajectories?

What are transient trajectories? This is a good question, and one with issues and difficulties that the reader may understand without explicitly realizing it. Transient trajectories are those trajectories that transition between the intended steady-state trajectories, and are often short lived [1, 10, 11, 26–28]. The most common types of transient trajectories are of the variety if initial start-up of a system [11]. For example; let us say we have a satellite pointing at some location (x1, y1) on Earth, and now it is needed to point a different location (x2, y2). The desired control and corresponding control trajectory (if a solely feedback control loop is not implemented) will comprise the transient trajectory. It starts at (x1, y1), ends at (x2, y2), and incorporates every point in the resulting path between those two

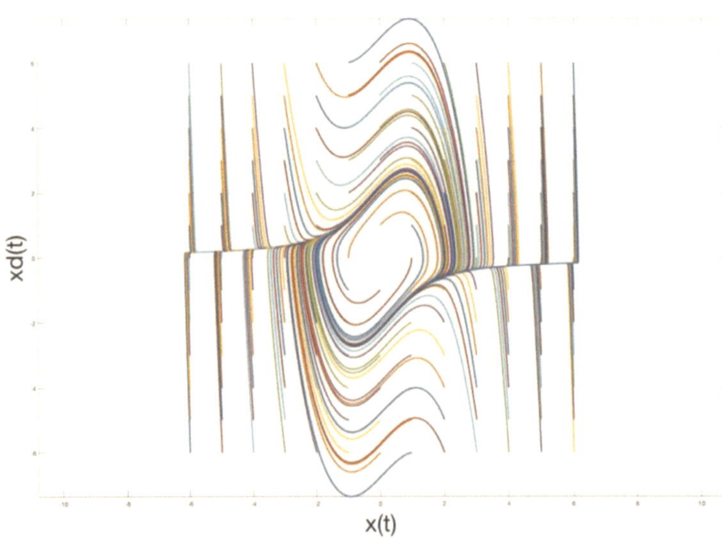

Figure 6.
Phase portrait illustration of unforced VDP system.

points that the platform takes to include the multiple controllable states of the system.

Figure 8 shows an example of a desired transient trajectory. In this example a satellite with an electro-optical telescope is being steered by directing the pointing vector of the staring sensor it employs. The sensor starts at a (0°, 0°, 0°) in the standard (roll, pitch, yaw) coordinate system, and then the user desires the sensor to move to (0°, 0°, 30°). The user inputs a command of 30° yaw to the system, and can be interpreted in many ways. The red, yellow, and blue lines represent different variations of the interpretation across the desired angle, angular rate, and angular acceleration. The trajectory in red represents a sinusoidal-based step function that takes on discontinuities in the angular rate and acceleration terms, whereas the trajectories in yellow and blue are entirely continuous.

The effects of transient trajectories can be illustrated via phase portraits like those presented in **Figures 6** and 7, with the main concern in affecting the stability of a system of interest. If the transients couple with the potential variations in initial conditions to produce deleterious effects on the stability, it will be illustrated very clearly in a phase portrait as it will likely grow unbounded. Another method on evaluating the performance of a system when evaluating the effects of transients is through the use of an object cost function [10]. A common approach is by using the root-mean-square (RMS) value between the desired trajectory and the measured trajectory to gain an RMS error value as shown in Eq. (17).

$$RMS_{error} = \lim_{T\to\infty} \sqrt{\frac{1}{T}\int_0^T [q(t) - \hat{q}(t)]^2\, dt}, \tag{17}$$

where $\hat{q}$ is the measured trajectory, and q is the desired trajectory.

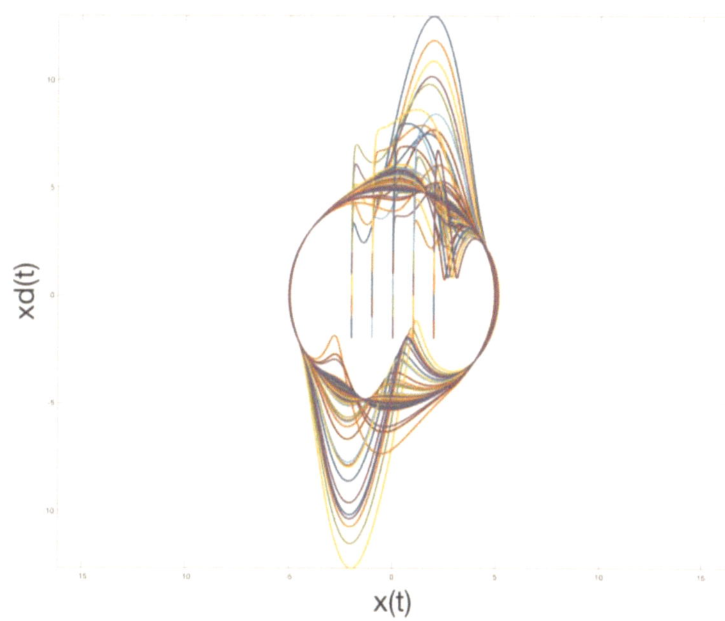

Figure 7.
Phase portrait illustration of forced VDP system.

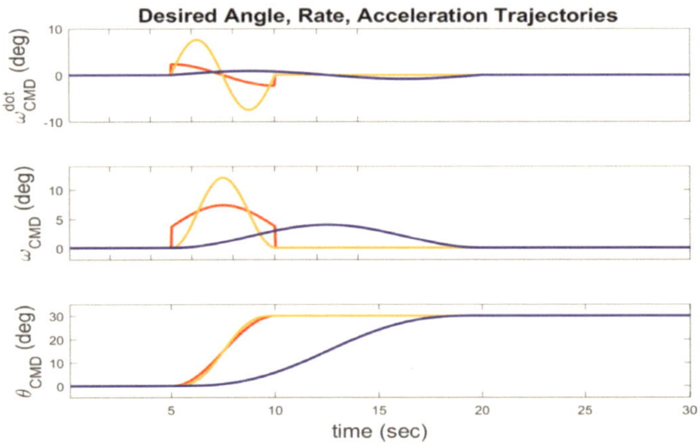

Figure 8.
Desired transient trajectory for a 30° yaw Maneuver of an optical pointing satellite vector.

2. Transient trajectory generation case study

At this point it is relevant to apply the basic components introduced in the previous section to the common nonlinear, and slightly chaotic VDP system to illustrate the benefits and highlight potential areas for further discussion.

Taking the Van der Pol oscillatory system as described by Eq. (16), and modeling it as the system plant we get the MATLAB/Simulink model in **Figure 9**. This model receives a control signal, and generates a new position. Inverting the dynamics result in a similarly defined model for a feedforward controller identified in **Figure 10**. Here, the model receives a defined trajectory vector comprised of the position, velocity, and acceleration ($x\dot{x}$, and $\ddot{x}$ respectively). Propagating those trajectories through the model creates an "ideal" control signal for the plant dynamics.

The plant dynamics and the feedforward controller form the heart of the simulation as the rest of the system parameters will change relative to the different approaches. Both of these models are incorporated in the high-level system diagram illustrated in **Figure 11**. The high-level diagram also shows the user input starting from the right-hand-side, which is fed in multiple trajectory generation functions.

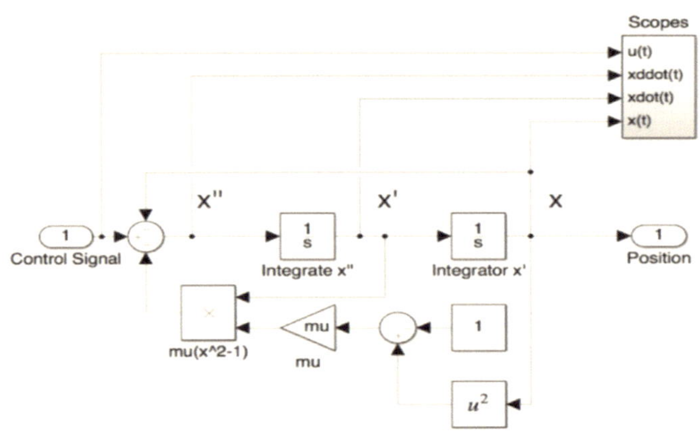

Figure 9.
Van der Pol plant dynamics.

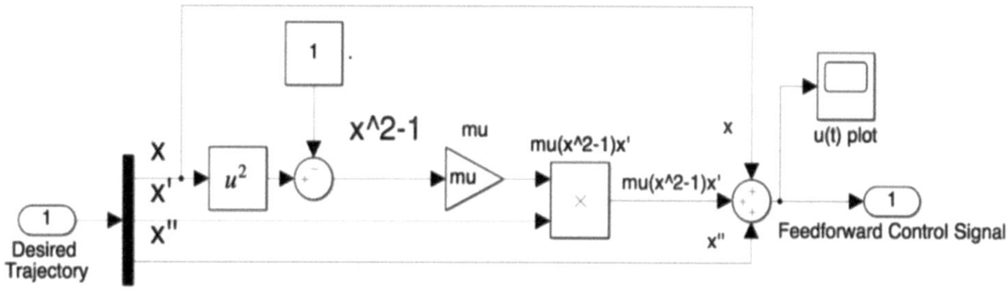

Figure 10.
Inverted Van der Pol system for feedforward controller.

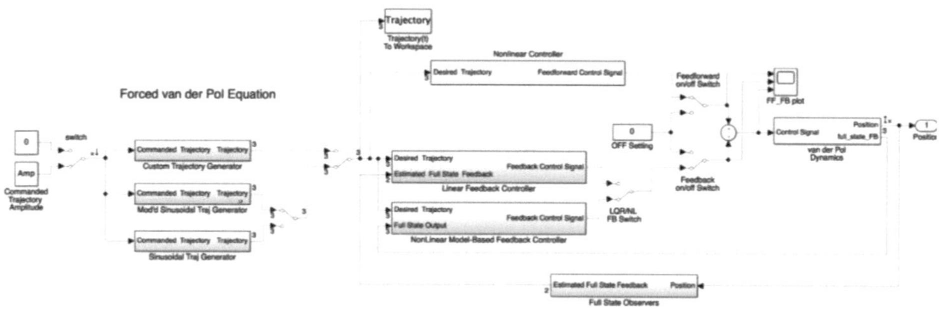

Figure 11.
High level system simulation in MATLAB/Simulink.

The output of the desired trajectory function is then fed into both the feedback and the feedforward controllers. Here, the output of the controllers can be turned on or off as desired to evaluate the performance of the controllers. For deterministic control algorithms it is necessary to assume either full-state feedback, or non-stochastic signals on the output.

2.1 Classical tuning method

One can apply classical tuning methods to the feedback controllers such as PID, and LQR to treat this nonlinear system as a linear system. The PID controller in **Figure 2** can serve as a foundation for multiple variants of a linear feedback controller by modifying the gain coefficients K_i, K_d, and K_p. Due to the ineffectiveness of linear control algorithms on the highly nonlinear VDP plant, the LQR feedback controller will be the only approach illustrated. Calculating the LQR coefficients are somewhat trivial in MATLAB/Simulink if the system description is in a compatible form and the MATLAB function call can be used: [K, S,e] = LQR (A,B,Q,R,N) [29], which gives the relevant K_d, and K_p values. In this instance, the system is described in state-space as shown in Eq. (18):

$$A = \begin{bmatrix} 1 & -1 \\ 1 & 0 \end{bmatrix}, \quad B = \begin{bmatrix} -1 \\ 0 \end{bmatrix}, \quad C = \begin{bmatrix} 0 & 1 \end{bmatrix}, \quad D = \begin{bmatrix} 0 \end{bmatrix} \tag{18}$$

to get a resulting control law of:

$$\frac{d^2x}{dt^2} - \mu(1 - x^2)\frac{dx}{dt} + x = -K_d(\dot{x}_d - \dot{x}) - K_p(x_d - x), \tag{19}$$

or Eq. (22) when coupling the ideal forced VDP feedforward controller with LQR:

$$\ddot{x} - (1 - x^2)\dot{x} + x = \ddot{x}_d - (1 - x^2)\dot{x}_d + x_d - K_d\left(\dot{x}_d - \dot{x}\right) - K_p\left(x_d - x\right), \tag{20}$$

The resulting phase portrait with only incorporating the LQR gains implemented in Eq. (19) are displayed in the left side of **Figure 12**. It can be seen that the stability is affected such that the system steadily grows unbounded and not to an asymptotic limit which is desired for illustrating stability. Investigating the nearby initial conditions does not identify any condition that produces a stable system.

The right side of **Figure 12** illustrates similar results from coupling the ideal nonlinear feedforward controller with the LQR feedback gains. Again, it can be seen that the system grows unbounded with no identified initial conditions providing stability. It can also be seen that the trends in the trajectories are influenced by both the LQR feedback only system and the ideal feedforward controller, although the feedforward controller in not robust enough to bring the system back to an asymptotic limit cycle.

2.2 Isolated trajectory fractionalization

With the results identified in Section 2.1 using linear feedback methods to compensate for trajectory tracking error of the nonlinear VDP system, it is necessary to try something different. One way is to incorporate isolated trajectory fractionalization (ITF). This train of thought assumes the ability of the transient trajectory to be fractured into sub components which can be elegantly stitched together to form the desired transient trajectory. There are many ways to stitch trajectories utilizing the mathematical principles of spline interpolation, Chebyshev polynomials, Lagrange polynomials, and the Runge Kutta methods [30] for example. Here we will illustrate the micro-transient generation to get a better performing transient trajectory via the 8-term Fourier Series fitting method. Under the theory that any periodic signal can be broken up to an infinite series of orthogonal basis functions based on a combination of sines and cosines [30] as defined by Eq. (21):

$$T_n = a_0 + \sum_{i=1}^{n} a_i cos(i\omega t) + b_i sin(i\omega t) \tag{21}$$

,

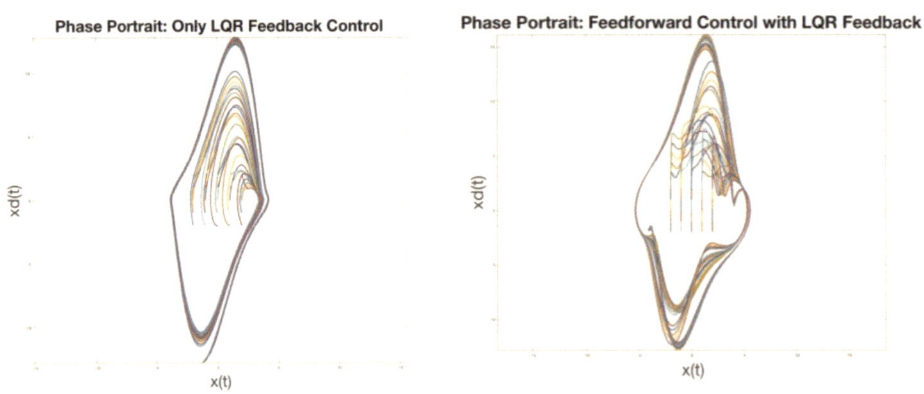

Figure 12.
Applying the optimal linear-quadratic-regulator feedback approach to the forced Van der Pol oscillator.

where T_n is the resulting sum of the functions used to replicate the originally desired trajectory. a_0 is a steady state offset, while a_i and b_i are the corresponding constant coefficients for each orthogonal basis set.

In the case of the sinusoidally forced VDP system illustrated in **Figure 7**, the unwanted transient response is primarily within the first few cycles of oscillations then after the sharp initial transients the tracking error slowly reduces over time until the trajectory is a perfect match to the desired trajectory. One way to split this desired trajectory is to heuristically describe the sinusoid function that will smoothly and quickly travel between the initial conditions and the desired steady state response. Taking advantage of the a-priori knowledge of how sinusoidal function performs with the VDP system a simple sine function with a phase shift is chosen as described by Eq. (22):

$$x_{01} = A_1 \sin\left(t - \frac{\pi}{2}\right), \tag{22}$$

where A_1 is a scaling coefficient proportional to the desired oscillatory radius in the phase plane. And the resulting derivative is:

$$\dot{x}_{01} = A_2 \cos\left(t - \frac{\pi}{2}\right), \tag{23}$$

resulting in a new scaling coefficient A_2. Using Eqs. (22) and (23) as the starting points, the steady state trajectory is then described by Eqs. (24) and (25) in order to match the initial conditions.

$$x_{23} = \frac{(A - 0.8)}{2} \sin\left(t - \frac{\pi}{2}\right) + \frac{\pi}{2} + 0.4, \tag{24}$$

$$\dot{x}_{23} = \frac{(A)}{2} \cos\left(t - \frac{\pi}{2}\right) \tag{25}$$

Next, by using the Fourier decomposition described in Eq. (21), the resulting trajectory can be planned as illustrated in **Figure 13**. This initial attempt is fairly close but still allows for large residual error. **Figure 13** displays the desired total trajectories for x_d and $\dot{x}_d$ with a Fourier fit line plotted for comparison. The Fourier fit line of the resulting trajectory using this transient trajectory fractionalization

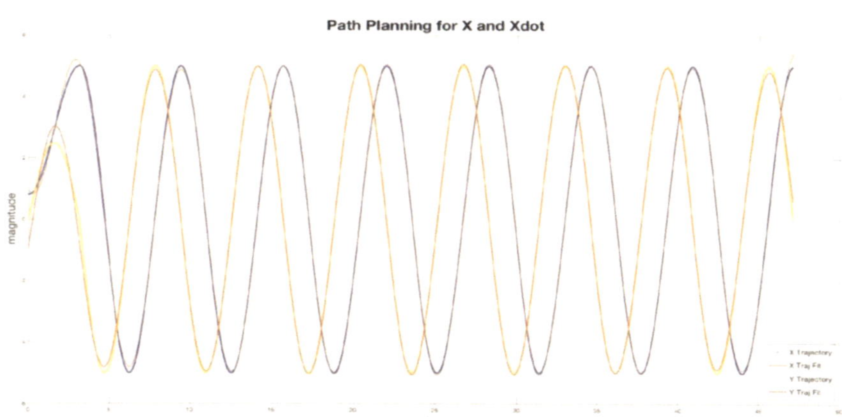

Figure 13.
Trajectory fractionalization via Fourier fitting.

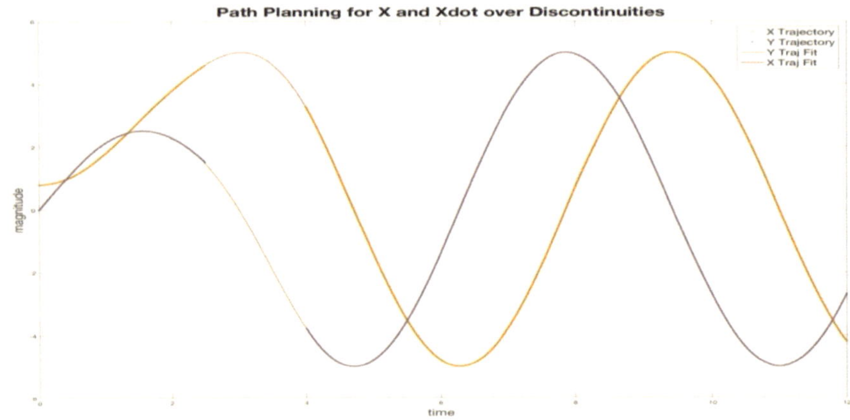

Figure 14.
Isolated trajectory fractionalization via Fourier fitting.

method. One way to mitigate this residual error is by given the fitting algorithm more "flexibility" to merge the trajectories.

To allow the fitting algorithm more flexibility, a large section isolated between the desired trajectories is introduced. The missing data is strategically placed such that the points where the 2nd derivative is zero. This allows for an extremely smooth function across the 1st derivative. Any sharp discontinuities can introduce large unwanted transients. The next iteration in the isolated trajectory fractionalization routine is illustrated in **Figure 14**.

The Fourier fit in **Figure 14** was built with the following parameters:

$$\delta_t = 0.001, t_0 = 0, t_1 = 2500, t_2 = 4000, t_3 = 12000 \tag{26}$$

where δ_t is the time step, t_0 is the initial time, t_1 is the end time of the first trajectory fraction, t_2 is the start of the 2nd trajectory fraction, and t_3 is the final time. The resulting parameters allow the fitting algorithm 1500 (1.5 second) time steps to find a sm0oth fit. The resulting trajectories form the desired phase plane trajectory being fed into the feedforward controller is illustrated on the left in **Figure 15**. The right side of **Figure 15** illustrates the actual results on the output of the VDP system.

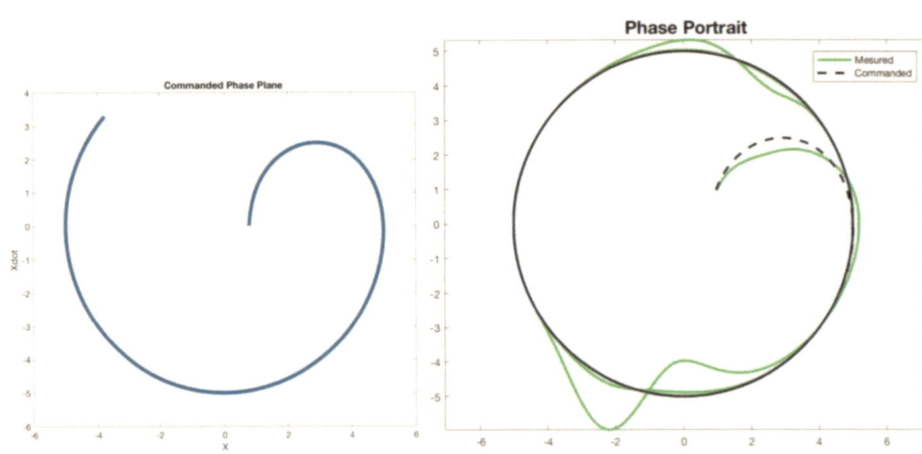

Figure 15.
Phase plane error in forced VDP system using isolated trajectory fractionalization via Fourier fitting.

The corresponding x, $\dot{x}$, and $\ddot{x}$ tracking error is illustrated in **Figure 16**. It's interesting to note that the large disturbance in the trajectories seen if **Figure 15** occur during the transition to the steady-state trajectory and that a spike in the $\ddot{x}$ error happens about 1 second later. The results shown here highlight the need to ensure that multiple derivative states are smooth when implementing the fitting algorithms, due to unforeseen perturbations. Even though the desired phase plane in **Figure 15** is perfectly smooth, the unidentified perturbations in the second derivative are affecting the results.

Utilizing the tracking error values along the entire transient trajectory an objective cost function can be defined and evaluated. In the case of the VDP system, the goal is to match the actual trajectory with the desired trajectory with respect to the phase plane. Therefore the parameters of interest are x, $\dot{x}$, and $\ddot{x}$ along the entire trajectory resulting in the objective cost function, J, in Eq. (27).

$$J = \sqrt{RMSe_x^2 + RMSe_{\dot{x}}^2 + RMSe_{\ddot{x}}^2}, \tag{27}$$

where RMSe is the RMS value of the error along the entire trajectory on each component. This provides a single metric to evaluate how well the actual trajectory fits to the desired trajectory. Once evaluated, a value of J = 1.0604 is achieved using the isolated trajectory fractionalization technique, whereas the objective cost function for the sinusoidal forced VDP system is J = 4.9603. This shows a 78% reduction in trajectory tracking error via this technique.

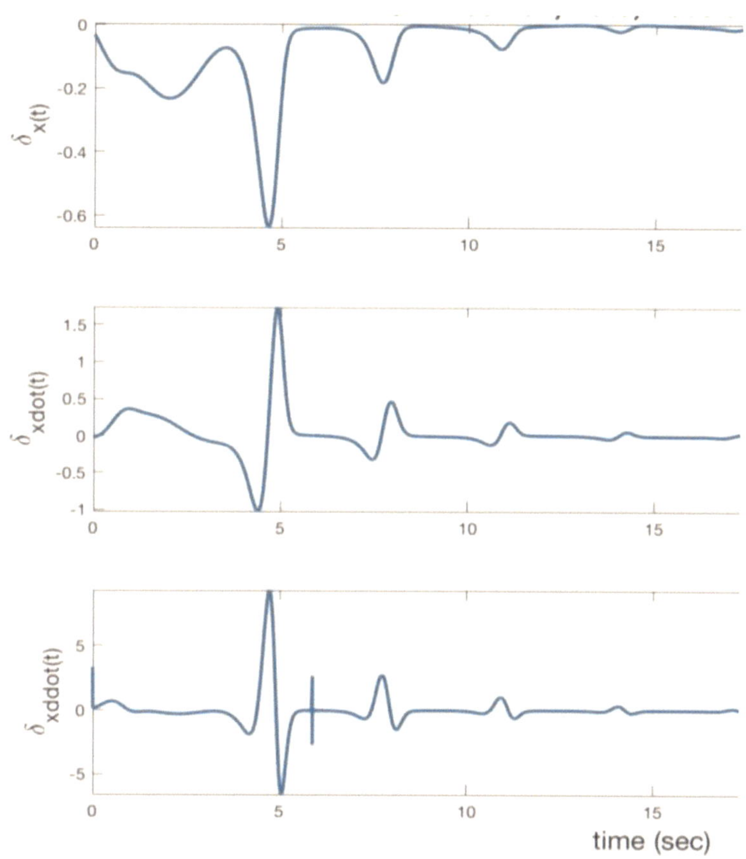

Figure 16.
Trajectory tracking error using ITF.

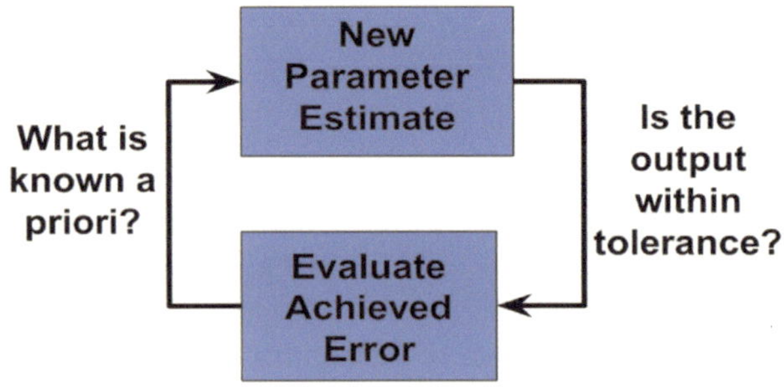

Figure 17.
Cyclical process of deterministic parameter tuning.

2.3 Targeted exponential weighting

2.3.1 1-term targeted exponential weighting

The targeted exponential weighting method is another technique to deterministically modify transient trajectories, and is ideally applied to the extrema in the transients via a-priori knowledge of the system characteristics. By taking advantage of the mathematical approach of exponential decay (or growth), one can modify an existing control trajectory via the cyclical parameter tuning process shown in **Figure 17**.

The parameter tuning process outlined in **Figure 17** starts with a-priori information of the system's characteristic behavior, this is then used to tailor a trajectory for the system. The trajectory is fed through the feedforward controller/plant. The output is then evaluated along the trajectory and compared to the desired. If the error is greater than a given tolerance value then the new information gained from the input parameters are compared to what was previously known and a new set of parameters are generated for the next evaluation. This is repeated until the error is within the given tolerance or until a pseudo-global minimum is found.

Considering the forced Van der Pol system, again it is now known that the initial conditions give rise to the largest perturbations to the ideal trajectory of a perfect circle in the phase plane. With this in mind the targeted exponential weighting technique will be targeted for those initial transient behaviors in order to minimize their impact.

For the forced VDP system under investigation, the initial configuration will take the original forcing function, x_d = Asin(t), as the ideal trajectory for the position. This will give the desired steady state response. Next, the derivative will be evaluated to get $\dot{x}_d$, and here we need to look at the trajectory error from the baseline forced VDP case to decide the next course of action. The tracking error can be found in **Figure 18**.

$$x_d = \text{Asin(t)}, \dot{x}_d = A\left(1 - e^{-10t}\right)\cos\left(\text{t}\right), \ddot{x}_d = \frac{dx}{dt}\dot{x}_d \tag{28}$$

It can be seen in **Figure 18** that the most severe trajectory transients are in the initial states of x, and $\dot{x}$, in addition to the transients on $\ddot{x}$ beyond t = 1 second. The first focus area will be on $\dot{x}$ because there is no desire to reduce x as that will help preserve the final desired trajectory. Additionally, the large transients are periodic in nature and therefore if the initial spike can be minimized then the following periodic spikes should be greatly reduced. In order to minimize the initial transients in $\dot{x}$ an increasing exponential will be used to force the derivative to zero at time = 0. The desired trajectory response will grow exponentially to the final state and the exponential rate will be tuned deterministically to get the resulting trajectory equations in Eq. (28). Taking the derivative of the tuned exponentially increase

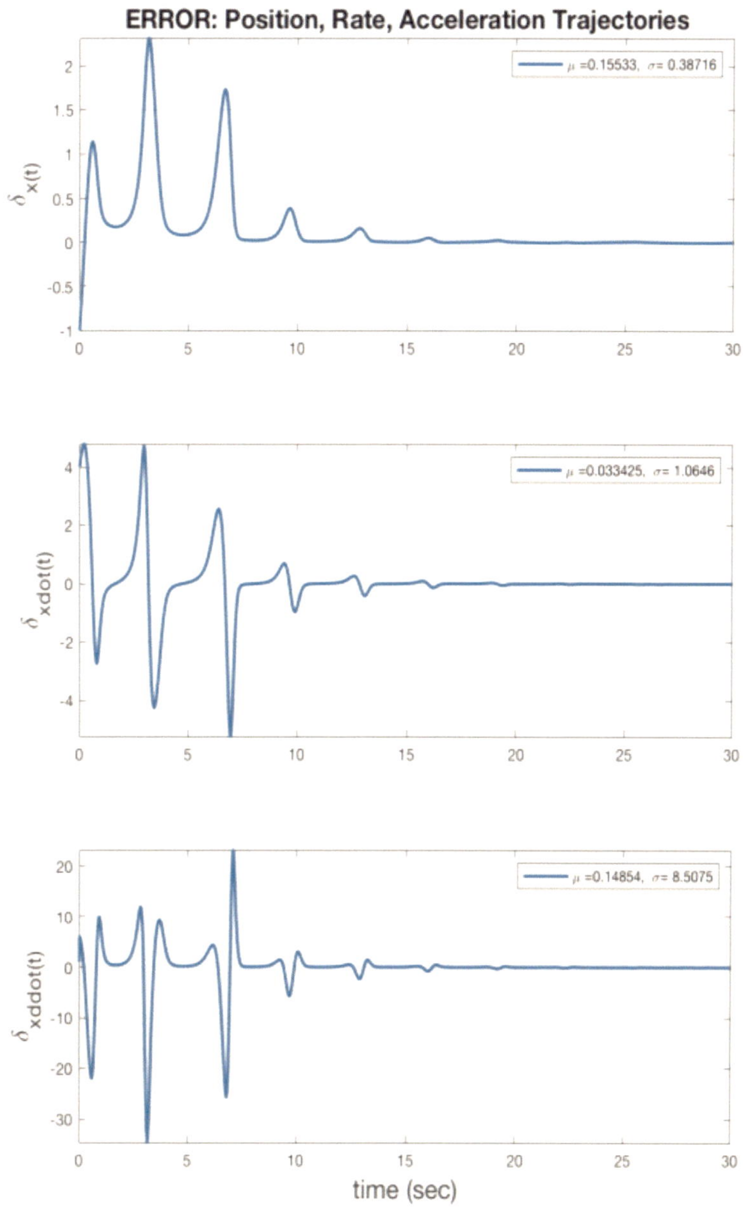

Figure 18.
Trajectory tracking error in forced VDP system.

trajectory will provide $\ddot{x}$. where A = 5, for an arbitrary circle radius of 5 in the phase plane.

This approach takes the ideal forcing function for the Van der Pol oscillator, Asin (ω t), and by modifying the nominal derivative, ω Acos(ω t), via an exponential dithering method $(1 - e^{-Bt})$ manipulates the targeted trajectory section (in this case where $t < 2$) in order to attempt to minimize the unwanted micro-transients. Generating the three trajectories in x, $\dot{x}$, and $\ddot{x}$ via the expressions in Eq. (28) result in a output phase portrait as illustrated in **Figure 19**, with the residual tracking error on each trajectory component in **Figure 20**.

The benefits by utilizing the targeted exponential weighting method are immediately noticeable when comparing the original phase portrait of the forced VDP system in **Figure 7**, and the results using the isolated trajectory fractionalization method in **Figure 15**. Additionally, the objective cost function, J, decreases from J = 4.9603, to J = 1.0604, to J = 0.6328 for an overall reduction of 87% from implementing target exponential weighting algorithm. The next step will be to implement the same methodology on $\ddot{x}$ to gain further improvement.

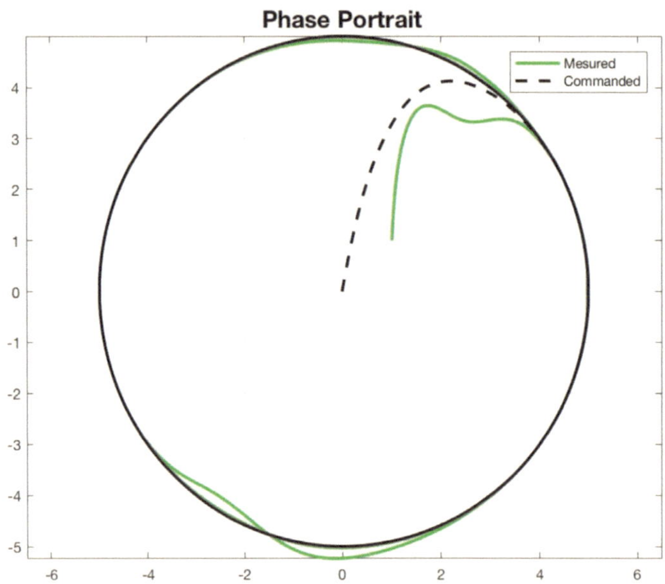

Figure 19.
Phase plane error in forced VDP system using 1-term targeted exponential weighting.

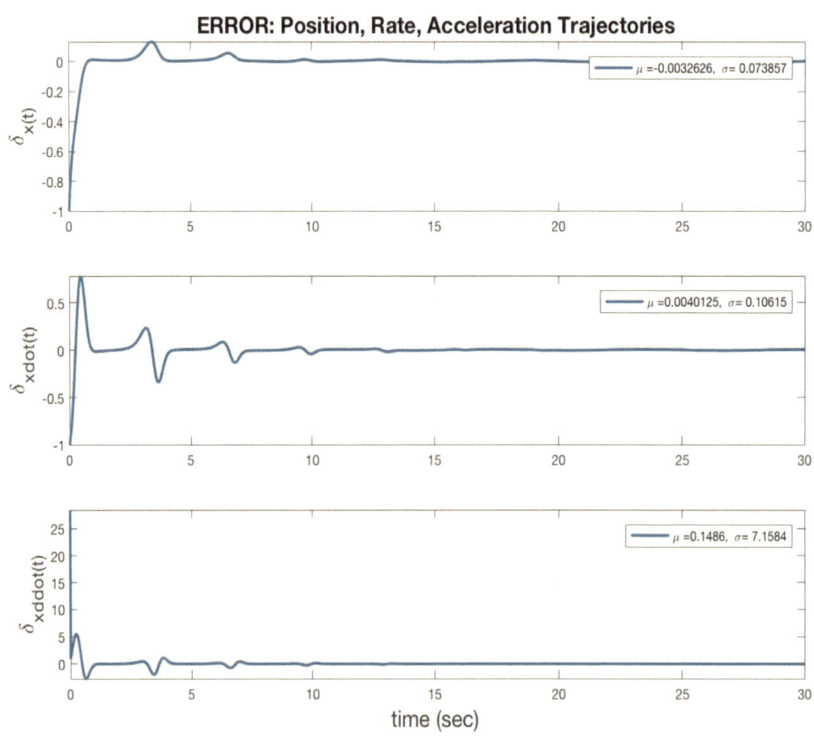

Figure 20.
Trajectory tracking error in forced VDP system using 1-term targeted exponential weighting.

2.3.2 2-term targeted exponential weighting

Using the same methodology in the 1-term method previously described, the exponential dithering will be applied to the 2nd derivative, $\ddot{x}_d$. Starting with Eq. (29) where x_d is of the form: $\mathrm{A}(1-\mathrm{e}^{-\mathrm{Bt}})\cos(\mathrm{t})$. The direct derivative is of the

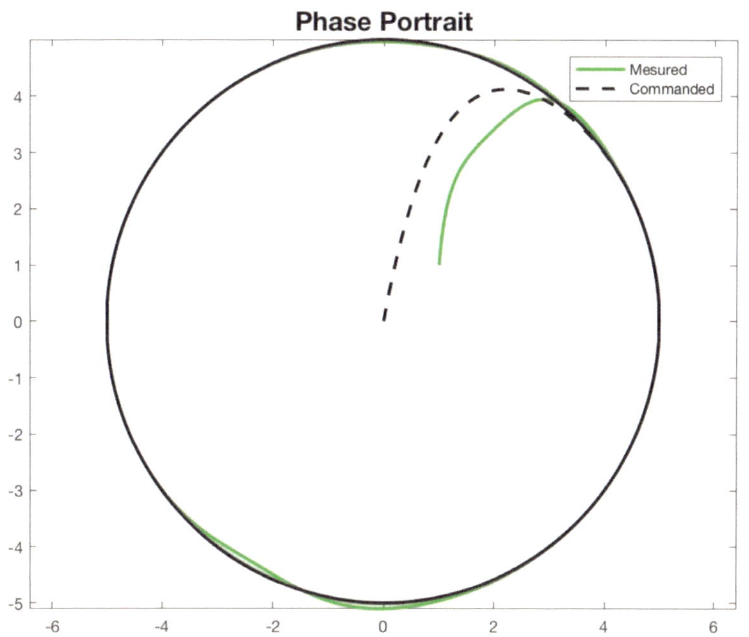

Figure 21.
Phase plane error in forced VDP system using 2-term targeted exponential weighting.

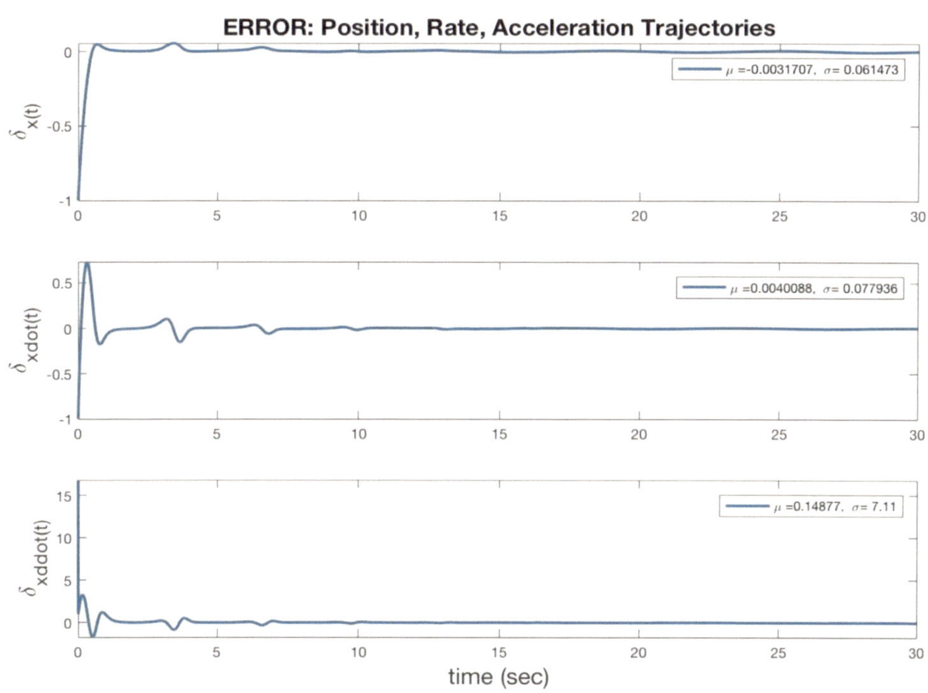

Figure 22.
Trajectory tracking error in forced VDP system using 2-term targeted exponential weighting.

form: $-Ae^{-Bt}((e^{-Bt} - 1)\sin(t) - B\cos(t))$. And making the assumption from a heuristic approach that $e^{-Bt} \approx Bt$ in the dithering sine term to get Eq. (30).

$$X_d = A\sin(t), \dot{x}_d = A\left(1 - e^{-5.5t}\right)\cos(t), \tag{29}$$

$$\ddot{x}_d = -Ae^{-3.17t}((3.17t - 1)\sin(t) - 3.17\cos(t)) \tag{30}$$

Generating the three trajectories in $x\,\dot{x}$, and $\ddot{x}$ via the expressions in Eqs. (29) and (30) result in a output phase portrait as illustrated in **Figure 21**, with the residual tracking error on each trajectory component in **Figure 22**.

The 2-term targeted exponential weighting method does indeed show an improvement over the 1-term variation. The resulting improvement based on the objective cost function shows an extra 5% decrease in trajectory tracking error to get J = 0.3758, which results in an overall reduction in tracking error on the order of 92% over the baseline forced Van der Pol system.

3. Conclusion

This chapter presented a small set of deterministic approaches to transient trajectory generation with particular interest in minimizing unwanted micro-transients that may cause havoc on a control system performance. Beginning with a brief introduction to control theory terminology which introduced state-space notation, transfer functions, feedback controllers, and the concept of observers for estimating unknown system states. From there the Van der Pol oscillatory equation was introduced and presented as a system under test to apply the deterministic trajectory generation techniques to.

Using the Van der Pol oscillator, feedforward controllers were introduced through the forced Van der Pol system and initial results of system performance were discussed and evaluated through the use of phase portraits. The micro-transients in the baseline case, the forced Van der Pol system using a forcing function in the form of Asin(t), were illustrated and compared to three different approaches. The first approach utilized a common feedback technique for linear system, the linear quadratic regulator (LQR). This was shown to be unstable.

	Sinusoidal (base)	**LQR FB**	**LQR w/ FF**	**Custom FF trajectory**	**Exp Xdot w/FF**	**Exp Xddot w/FF**
RMSe on x	0.4171	1.9181	0.9624	0.1044	0.0739	0.0616
RMSe on $\dot{x}$	1.065	3.1803	2.2486	0.2206	0.1062	0.078
RMSe on $\ddot{x}$	4.8266	13.8416	11.7283	1.0319	0.6194	0.3624
K_p		−2.6818	−2.6818			
K_d		−0.4142	−0.4142			
K_i		−0.2682	−0.2682			
$J(x, \dot{x})$	1.1438	3.7139	2.4459	0.2441	0.1294	0.0994
$J(x\,\dot{x}\,\ddot{x})$	4.9603	14.3312	11.9806	1.0604	0.6328	0.3758
% error reduction	0	n/a	n/a	78%	87%	92%

Table 1.
Summary of case study results.

The next approach utilized the isolated trajectory fractionalization technique which segmented the desired trajectory into sub-trajectories, and isolated the transition points and applying a Fourier fitting routine to stich the desired trajectories back together. This approach led to a reduction in trajectory error (as evaluated by an objective cost function) by 78%.

The final method was split into two slightly different variants. The first one presented was the 1-term targeted exponential weighting method. This method utilized a-priori knowledge of where the largest micro-transient response and applied dithering techniques to minimize those unwanted transients in the derivative of the desired trajectory. The second variation, the 2-term targeted exponential weighting method, applied a similar approach to the 2nd derivative of the desired trajectory. The resulting improvement over the baseline case was an 87, and 92% trajectory tracking error reduction.

For ease of comparison, the results are summarized in **Table 1**.

Acknowledgements

The author would like to acknowledge the technical guidance and leadership of Dr. Tim Sands, and the support of Air Force Research Laboratory during the research and writing of this chapter.

Conflict of interest

The authors declare no conflict of interest. The views expressed in this paper are those of the author, and do not reflect the official policy or position of the United States Air Force, Department of Defense, or the U.S. Government.

Author details

Matthew A. Cooper
Air Force Research Laboratory, Albuquerque, New Mexico, USA

*Address all correspondence to: matthew.cooper.17@us.af.mil

References

[1] Huibert K, Raphael S. Linear Optimal Control Systems. 1st ed. New York, NY, USA: Wiley-Interscience; 1972. ISBN 0-471-51110-2

[2] Sands T. Fine Pointing of Military Spacecraft [Ph.D. dissertation]. Monterey, CA, USA: Naval Postgraduate School; 2007

[3] Abdessemed F, Djebrani S. Trajectory generation for mobile manipulators. In: Jimenez A, Al Hadithi BM, editors. Robot Manipulators. Rijeka, Croatia: IntechOpen; 2010. DOI: 10.5772/9200

[4] Barrientos A, Gutierrez P, Colorado J. Advanced UAV trajectory generation: Planning and guidance. In: Lam TM, editor. Aerial Vehicles. Rijeka, Croatia: IntechOpen; 2009. DOI: 10.5772/6467

[5] Lim SJ, Yu SN, Han CS, Kang MK. Palletizing simulator using optimized pattern and trajectory generation algorithm. In: Di Paola AMD, Cicirelli G, editors. Mechatronic Systems. Rijeka, Croatia: IntechOpen; 2010. DOI: 10.5772/8929

[6] Jin TS, Hashimoto H. Trajectory generation and object tracking of mobile robot using multiple image fusion. In: Milisavljevic N, editor. Sensor and Data Fusion. Rijeka, Croatia: IntechOpen; 2009. DOI: 10.5772/6576

[7] Nemec B, Zlajpah L. Automatic trajectory generation using redundancy resolution scheme based on virtual mechanism. In: Rodi AD, editor. Contemporary Robotics. Rijeka, Croatia: IntechOpen; 2009. DOI: 10.5772/7809

[8] Ata AA, Johar H. Trajectory planning of a constrained flexible manipulator. In: Kordic V, Lazinica A, Merdan M, editors. Cutting Edge Robotics. Rijeka, Croatia: IntechOpen; 2005. DOI: 10.5772/4671

[9] Zhu ZH, Shi G. Piecewise parallel optimal algorithm. In: Valdman J, editor. Optimization Algorithms. Rijeka, Croatia: IntechOpen; 2018. DOI: 10.5772/intechopen.76625

[10] Slotine J. Applied Nonlinear Control, Chapter 9. Englewood Cliffs, NJ, USA: Prantice-Hall; 1991

[11] Ogata K. Modern Control Engineering. 5th ed. Upper Saddle River, NJ, USA: Prentice Hall PTR; 2009

[12] Nakatani S, Sands T. Autonomous damage recovery in space. International Journal of Control, Automation and Systems. 2016;**2**:31

[13] Nakatani S, Sands T. Simulation of spacecraft damage tolerance and adaptive controls. In: Proceedings of the 2014 IEEE Aerospace Proceedings, Big Sky; 1-8 March 2014; MT, USA. 2014

[14] Sands T. Physics-based control methods. In: Rushi G, editor. Advances in Spacecraft Systems and Orbit Determination. Rijeka, Croatia: In-Tech Publishers; 2012. pp. 29-54

[15] Cooper MA, Heidlauf PT. Nonlinear feed forward control of a perturbed satellite using extended least squares adaptation and a Luenberger observer. Journal of Aeronautics and Aerospace Engineering. 2018;7:205. DOI: 10.4172/2168-9792.1000205

[16] Sands T, Lorenz R. Physics-based automated control of spacecraft. In: Proceedings of the AIAA Space 2009 Conference and Exposition; 14-17 September 2009; Pasadena, CA, USA. 2009

[17] Sands T. Improved magnetic levitation via online disturbance decoupling. Physik Journal. 2015;**1**: 272-280

[18] Smeresky B, Rizzo A, Sands T. Kinematics in the information age. Mathematical Engineering, A Special Issue of Mathematics. 2018;**6**(9):148. DOI: 10.3390/math6090148

[19] Sands T, Bollino K, Kaminer I, Healey A. Autonomous minimum safe distance maintenance from submersed obstacles in ocean currents. Journal of Marine Science and Engineering. 2018; **6**(3):98

[20] Sands T, Bollino K. Autonomous underwater vehicle guidance, navigation, and control. In: Autonomous Vehicles. 2018. DOI: 10.5772/intechopen.80316. Available online at: https://www.intechopen.com/online-first/autonomous-underwater-vehicle-guidance-navigation-and-control [Accessed: 28 December 2018]

[21] Van der Pol B. A theory of the amplitude of free and forced triode vibrations. Radio Review. 1920;**1**: 701-710

[22] Van der Pol B. On “relaxation oscillations” I. Philosophical Magazine. 1926;**2**:978-992

[23] Van der Pol B. The nonlinear theory of electric oscillations. Proceedings of the IRE. 1934;**22**:1051-1086

[24] Van der Pol B, van der Mark J. Frequency de-multiplication. Nature. 1927;**120**:363-364

[25] Van der Pol B. Over relaxatie-trillingen. In: Tijdschrift van het Nederlandsch Radiogenootschap. Vol. 3. 1926. pp. 25-40

[26] Cooper M, Heidlauf P, Sands T. Controlling chaos—Forced van der Pol equation. Mathematics. 2017;**5**:70-80. DOI: 10.3390/math5040070

[27] Baker K, Cooper M, Heidlauf P, Sands T. Autonomous trajectory generation for deterministic artificial intelligence. Electrical and Electronic Engineering. 2018;**8**(3):59-68. DOI: 10.5923/j.eee.20180803.01

[28] Lobo K, Lang J, Starks A, Sands T. Analysis of deterministic artificial intelligence for inertia modifications and orbital disturbances. International Journal of Control Science and Engineering. 2018;**8**(3):53-62. DOI: 10.5923/j.control.20180803.01

[29] Linear-Quadratic Regulator (LQR) Design. Mathworks. Available from: https://www.mathworks.com/help/control/ref/lqr.html [Accessed: 27 December 2018]

[30] Trefethen LN. Approximation Theory and Approximation Practice (Other Titles in Applied Mathematics). Philadelphia, PA, USA: Soc. for Industrial and Applied Math; 2012

Chapter 7

Sinusoidal Trajectory Generation Methods for Spacecraft Feedforward Control

Kyle A. Baker

Abstract

The following is a brief walkthrough of material related to the modeling of spacecraft dynamics with feedforward control as the self-awareness declaration for deterministic artificial intelligence. Specifically, the focus will be on the analysis of various sinusoidal trajectory methods. The methods utilized are the basic MATLAB sine generation function, a Taylor series implementation, and two alternate algorithms for higher speed, lower precision and lower speed, higher precision implementations. The chapter features a brief summary of previous work investigating the impact of step size on Euler and Body angles. This is followed by a high level overview of Euler angle theory, quaternions, direction cosine matrices, kinematics, and dynamics to form a mathematical basis for the core material. With the numerical basis for the modeling efforts outlined, the results of running a SIMULINK model of spacecraft dynamics with feedforward control will be briefly analyzed and explored. The analysis will cover the impacts of varying step size with various sinusoidal trajectory generation methodologies.

Keywords: sine wave approximation, sinusoidal trajectory generation, feedforward control, Taylor Series approximation, spacecraft torque generation, space vehicle rotational mechanics, SIMULINK

1. Introduction

The study of spacecraft rotational mechanics includes three core functional areas: kinematics, dynamics, and disturbances. This chapter will be primarily focused on the trajectory generation methodology used to drive the space vehicle dynamics. In the model shown in **Figure 1**, a commanded spacecraft body movement is taken in and translated into both an input torque (T) and an angular velocity (ω) for the spacecraft body. A quaternion and direction cosine matrix are then calculated and employed to find Euler Angles for the spacecraft's attitude with respect to an inertial frame.

Previously unpublished academic work, based on the topology found in **Figure 1**, delved into the effects of varying time steps and maneuver time in feedforward control (everything to the left of dynamics) but considered only a single method of sinusoid generation. Eq. (1) is the idealized feedforward control for the simulation and it can additionally function as the self-awareness declaration for deterministic artificial intelligence [1–9]. In this chapter, the Torque generator

IntechOpen

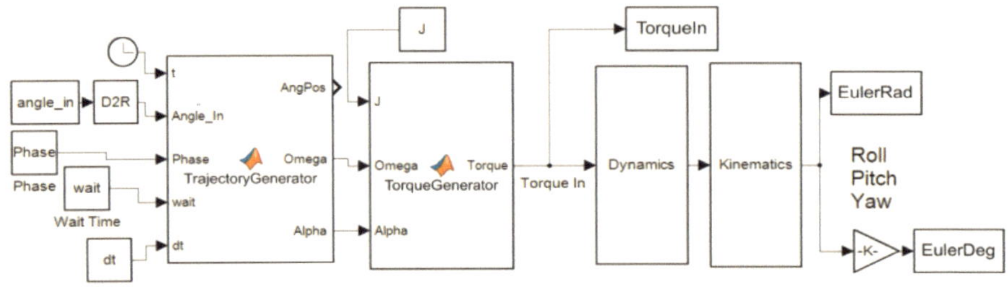

Figure 1.
Simulink model topology.

driven by Eq. (1) will remain unchanged but we will investigate the impact of four different sinusoid generation methods in the Trajectory generator, namely:

- MATLAB's sine function
- 4th order Taylor series approximation
- Low precision approximation algorithm
- High precision approximation algorithm

These methodologies require examination due to the inherent errors in an actual spacecraft's measurement apparatus. No onboard system can ever measure a spacecraft's angular position, velocity, or acceleration at infinite precision. Additionally, any disturbances accounted for in the coarse control from feedforward design implementations will still require additional feedback control for robust, fine tuning. As such, it may be more prudent to embrace a small amount of course control error in order to speed up overall computation time. In order to assess these methodologies, a SIMULINK model for each Trajectory generator method was created and their outputs were compared for error and computation time.

$$\begin{bmatrix} T_x \\ T_y \\ T_z \end{bmatrix} = \begin{bmatrix} J_{xx}\dot{\omega}_x + J_{xy}\dot{\omega}_y + J_{xz}\dot{\omega}_z - J_{xy}\omega_x\omega_z - J_{yy}\omega_y\omega_z - J_{yz}\omega_z^2 + J_{xz}\omega_x\omega_y + J_{zz}\omega_z\omega_y + J_{yz}\omega_y^2 \\ J_{yx}\dot{\omega}_x + J_{yy}\dot{\omega}_y + J_{yz}\dot{\omega}_z - J_{yz}\omega_x\omega_y - J_{zz}\omega_x\omega_z - J_{xz}\omega_x^2 + J_{xx}\omega_x\omega_z + J_{xy}\omega_z\omega_y + J_{xz}\omega_z^2 \\ J_{zx}\dot{\omega}_x + J_{zy}\dot{\omega}_y + J_{zz}\dot{\omega}_z - J_{xx}\omega_x\omega_y - J_{xz}\omega_y\omega_z - J_{xy}\omega_y^2 + J_{yy}\omega_x\omega_y + J_{yz}\omega_z\omega_x + J_{xy}\omega_x^2 \end{bmatrix} \tag{1}$$

2. Sinusoidal trajectory generation

In the previous work referred to in Section 1 of this chapter it was found that a sufficiently small time step size must be utilized in order to adequately model the commanded input as a sinusoid. This can be seen with a snapshot of the experimental results as shown in **Figure 2**.

These graphs were generated when the model shown in **Figure 1** was tested with a commanded input of $[0, 0, 30]^T$ which corresponds to zero roll, zero pitch, and a 30° yaw. This allowed analysis to focus on time step impacts to one axis of rotation of MATLAB sinusoidal generation methodology. The quiescent and post-maneuver timeframes were both set to 5 s and the maneuver was conducted over a 10 s interval. **Figure 2** shows the results of a time step of 1 s and a time step of 0.01 s,

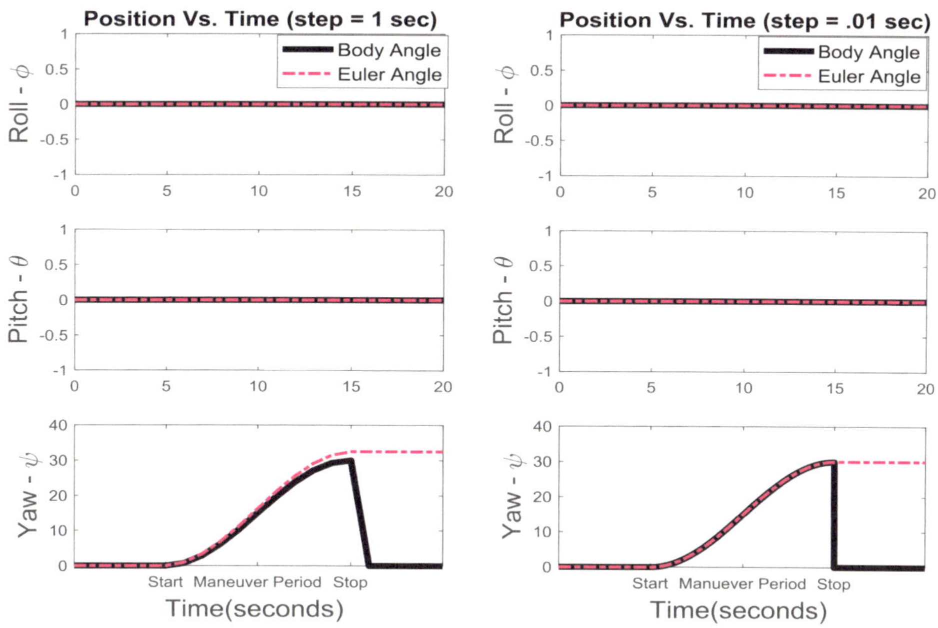

Figure 2.
Position vs. time graphs as a function of time step.

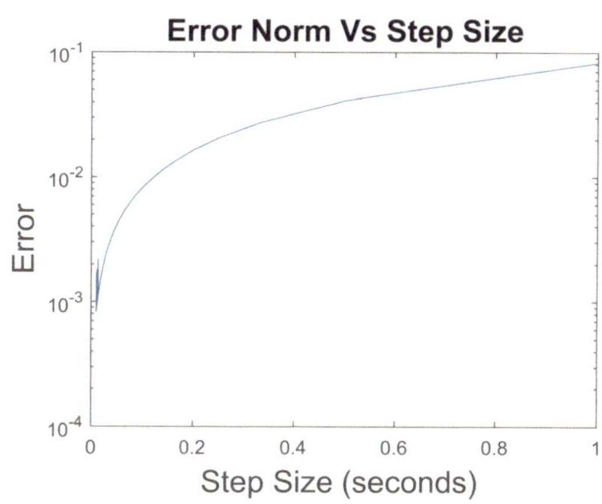

Figure 3.
Error vs. step size.

both using the Runge-Kutta solver. With the larger step size of 1 s, the Euler angles lost tracking and went slightly above the commanded angle while the smaller step size of 0.01 s afforded better tracking between Euler angle and Body angle. The main takeaway was that with finer step size resolution one could essentially equate the Euler and Body angles on a given model even though the former is in the inertial reference frame and the latter is in the spacecraft body reference frame.

Additionally, 100 iterations were run over a range of step sizes between 1 and 0.01 s to see what impact a chosen step size would have on error between Body and Euler Angles at the end of the maneuver phase. The results of this study can be seen below in **Figure 3**.

From this graph you can clearly see the benefit of reducing step size. It should be noted, however, that once step size was reduced to 0.01119 s the model reached a point where CPU and MATLAB precision comes into play and shrinking step size did not necessarily result in reducing error. This is noticeable with the erratic nature of the curve on the left side of the graph when approaching a much small step size.

Since it was found that we could adequately model our system with a small enough step size this allowed further investigation into other areas within the model which could be changed and optimized. This line of thought led us to create a new model which could be utilized to compare and contrast various sinusoidal generation methodologies. This new model's numerical basis and simulation results will be shown in the following two subsections.

2.1 Model creation

Before adding changes for various sinusoidal generation methodologies the mathematical basis and assumptions used in the previous model were re-verified. The first step used in model creation (and re-verification) was the implementation of a direction cosine matrix to numerically represent rotations about a set of axes to project a starting frame onto a desired reference frame in order to outline the system kinematics [10–14]. **Figures 4** and **5** provide visual depictions of the process driven by Eq. (2) through Eq. (4). Each direction cosine matrix equation takes an axial rotation as depicted by the series of rotations in **Figure 4** and represents it as an orthonormal matrix consisting of sines, cosines, zeroes, and ones per the trigonometry rules shown in **Figure 5**.

$$1\,RotationDCM = \begin{bmatrix} 1 & 0 & 0 \\ 0 & \cos\Phi & \sin\Phi \\ 0 & -\sin\Phi & \cos\Phi \end{bmatrix} \tag{2}$$

$$2\,RotationDCM = \begin{bmatrix} \cos\theta & 0 & -\sin\theta \\ 0 & 1 & 0 \\ \sin\theta & 0 & \cos\theta \end{bmatrix} \tag{3}$$

$$3\,RotationDCM = \begin{bmatrix} \cos\Psi & \sin\Psi & 0 \\ -\sin\Psi & \cos\Psi & 0 \\ 0 & 0 & 1 \end{bmatrix} \tag{4}$$

For more complicated movements, direction cosine matrices are multiplied together resulting in a more intricate matrix. Eq. (5) is an example of this for a 3-2-1 Rotation. This direction cosine matrix sequence and others are provided a more in depth treatment in Refs. [14-16] and as well as other chapters in this book. Note that in Eq. (5), the "C" and "S" characters are utilized as shorthand for the sine and cosine trigonometric functions.

$$321\,DCM\ Rotation = \begin{bmatrix} C\theta C\Psi & C\Phi S\Psi & -S\theta \\ S\Phi S\theta C\Psi - C\Phi S\Psi & S\Phi S\theta S\Psi + C\Phi C\Psi & S\Phi C\theta \\ C\Phi S\theta C\Psi + S\Phi S\Psi & C\Phi S\theta S\Psi - S\Phi C0 & C\Phi C\theta \end{bmatrix} \tag{5}$$

The other major workhorse of the model's kinematics is the orthonormal quaternion matrix [17–19], which accomplishes the same feat as the direction cosine matrix but with intrinsic divide by zero protection. The particular quaternion calculation format implemented in the model can be seen in Eq. (6).

$$\dot{q} = \begin{bmatrix} 0 & \omega 3 & -\omega 2 & \omega 1 \\ -\omega 3 & 0 & \omega 1 & \omega 2 \\ \omega 2 & -\omega 1 & 0 & \omega 3 \\ -\omega 1 & -\omega 2 & -\omega 3 & 0 \end{bmatrix} \begin{bmatrix} q1 \\ q2 \\ q3 \\ q4 \end{bmatrix} \tag{6}$$

To find the quaternion from Eq. (6), it is a simple matter of initializing the quaternion vectors with an orthonormal set (i.e., $[0,0,0,1]^T$) and integrating the output.

The final matrix utilized, shown in Eq. (7), is an equation equivalent to the previously shown 3-2-1 rotational matrix Eq. (5) but written in terms of quaternion elements. This quaternion based 3-2-1 rotation is depicted below in Eq. (7).

$$321\ DCMRotation = \begin{bmatrix} 1-2(q_2^2+q_3^2) & 2(q_1q_2+q_3q_4) & 2(q_1q_3-q_2q_4) \\ 2(q_1q_2-q_3q_4) & 1-2(q_1^2+q_3^2) & 2(q_2q_3+q_1q_4) \\ 2(q_1q_3+q_2q_4) & 2(q_3q_2-q_1q_4) & 1-2(q_1^2+q_2^2) \end{bmatrix} \tag{7}$$

In actual implementation, the SIMULINK model uses Eq. (7) but for calculation purposes takes advantage of Eq. (5). Combining terms leaves us with Eq. (8) through Eq. (10) for Euler Angles:

$$\theta = \sin^{-1}(1-2(q_2^2+q_3^2)) \tag{8}$$

$$\Phi = \mathrm{atan2}(2(q_2q_3+q_1q_4)/1-2(q_1^2+q_2^2)) \tag{9}$$

$$\Psi = \mathrm{atan2}(2(q_1q_2+q_3q_4)/1-2(q_2^2+q_3^2)) \tag{10}$$

Referring back to **Figure 1**, the Dynamics block is driven by Eq. (11) (the Euler moment equation) when a torque is provided by the Feedforward Control section's Torque generator.

$$\sum T = \dot{H} = J\dot{\omega} + \omega \times J\omega \tag{11}$$

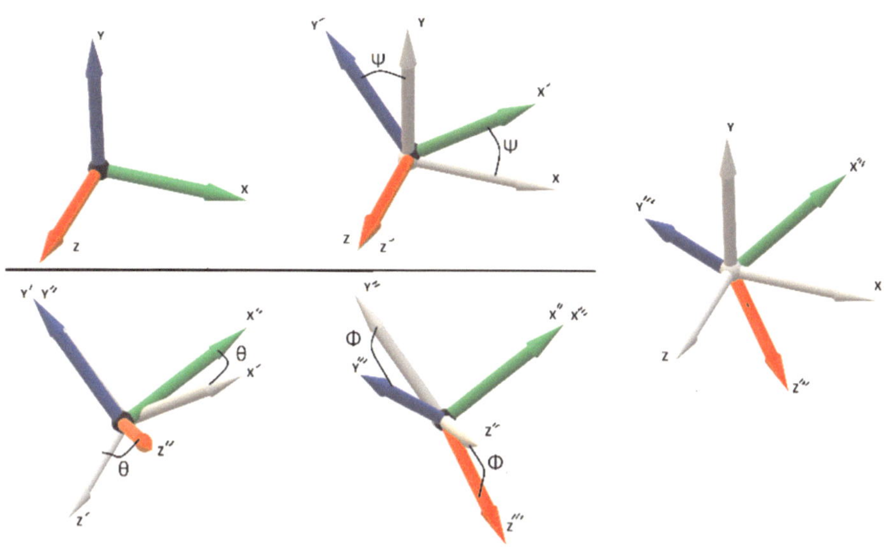

Figure 4.
Simple 3-2-1 rotation.

To derive the angular velocity of the body (ω_{BODY}) fed from dynamics to kinematics, we multiply moment of inertia (J) by the time derivative of angular velocity, i.e., angular acceleration ($\dot{\omega}$). This $J\dot{\omega}$ term is multiplied by the inverse of J and then integrated as per Eq. (12).

$$\int (J^{-1} * J\dot{\omega})dt = \omega_{BODY} \tag{12}$$

Afterwards, the ω_{BODY} is used to obtain the spacecraft attitude's Euler angles.

The feedforward control blocks in **Figure 1** contain the Trajectory generator and the Torque generator. The Trajectory generator takes in a commanded body angle and then uses a sine wave in order to approximate the commanded maneuver. To help elaborate on this point, **Figure 6** shows a square wave and a sine wave, both shifted up in amplitude such that they operate from zero to two instead of between negative and positive one.

We can see that if a square wave was used to approximate the commanded maneuver, the spacecraft would essentially be expected to transition from the zero position up to its max amplitude at the two positions instantaneously. This is a physical impossibility. With the sine wave in the same figure we can see that the

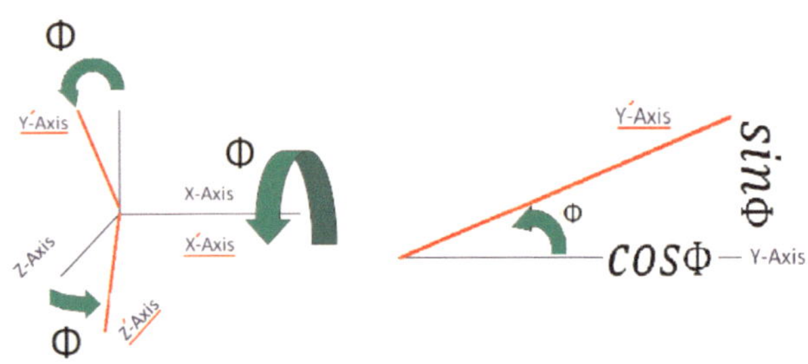

Figure 5.
Depiction of a Φ rotation about the X axis.

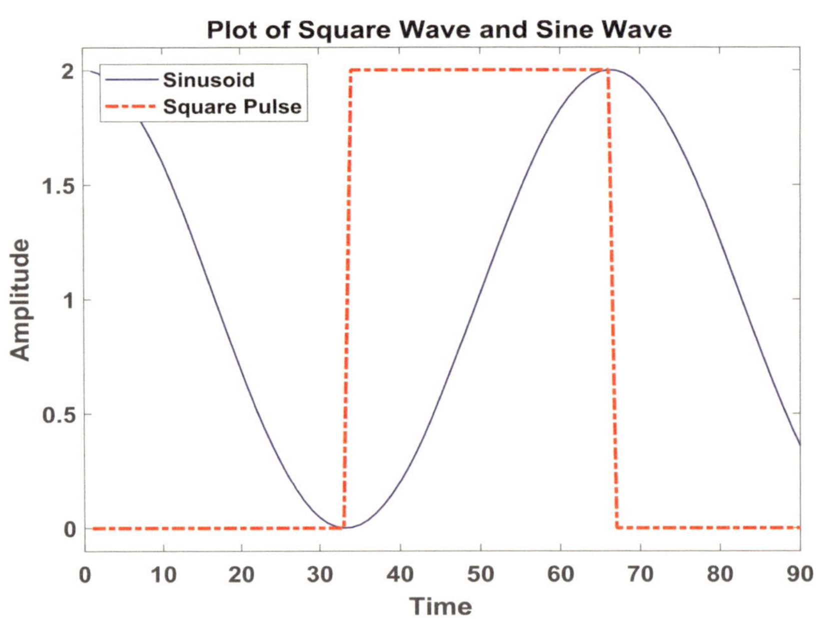

Figure 6.
Visual depiction of square and sine waves.

spacecraft machinery is afforded a ramp up and slow down period along with a relatively linearly slope in the middle. Basically, the half period of sinusoid within the square pulse of **Figure 6** is used to provide a smooth, achievable input to the system.

Our original model's Trajectory generator follows Eq. (13) through Eq. (15) to approximate the commanded maneuver for angular position, angular velocity (ω), and angular acceleration ($\dot{\omega}$) via the MATLAB sine wave function.

$$AngularPosition = \frac{1}{2}\left(A + A * \sin\left(\left(\frac{\pi}{\Delta t}\right)(t - t_{wait}) - \frac{\pi}{2}\right)\right) \tag{13}$$

$$AngularVelocity = \frac{1}{2}A * \left(\frac{\pi}{\Delta t}\right)\cos\left(\left(\frac{\pi}{\Delta t}\right)(t - t_{wait}) - \frac{\pi}{2}\right) \tag{14}$$

$$AngularAcceleration = -\frac{1}{2}A * \left(\frac{\pi}{\Delta t}\right)^2 \sin\left(\left(\frac{\pi}{\Delta t}\right)(t - t_{wait}) - \frac{\pi}{2}\right) \tag{15}$$

Eq. (13) models the input command, where "A" is the maneuver's commanded angle. The base frequency of the sinusoid (ω_{sine}) is $\left(\frac{\pi}{\Delta t}\right)$ where (Δt) is the desired maneuver time. The t_{wait} term allows for a quiescent period and $-\frac{\pi}{2}$ term allows for a proper phase shift to implement the sinusoidal half period of **Figure 4**. The effect of this can be seen later on in **Figure 7**. Eqs. (14) and (15) are just successive derivatives of Eq. (13) used to generate angular velocity and acceleration which are fed into Eq. (1) in the Torque generator from **Figure 1**. This produces an output torque which drives the dynamics.

From Eq. (13) through Eq. (15) it can be clearly seen that the argument of the sine and cosine terms always follows the form of Eq. (16). We can use this to implement our Taylor series and the other two other algorithms on equal footing.

$$Arg = \left(\frac{\pi}{\Delta t}\right)(t - t_{wait}) - \frac{\pi}{2} \tag{16}$$

The Taylor series, as detailed in Ref. [20], is a numerical method that can be used to approximate other functions. In our model we substitute the sine and cosine in Eq. (13) through Eq. (15) with Eqs. (17) and (18).

$$Taylor\ Sin = Arg - \frac{Arg^3}{3!} - \frac{Arg^5}{5!} - \frac{Arg^7}{7!} \tag{17}$$

$$Taylor\ Cos = 1 - \frac{Arg^2}{2!} - \frac{Arg^4}{4!} - \frac{Arg^6}{6!} \tag{18}$$

The Taylor series is a power series and additional terms could be included ad infinitum for greater precision; however, initial testing found that four series terms provided a reasonable approximation while maintaining a viable runtime. Additionally, it was found that pre-calculating the factorial terms sped up computation time.

The last set of sinusoidal generation methodologies tested was the low precision (LP) and high precision (HP) algorithms. These were found to be used in many applications, especially ones which limited by lower processing power such as mobile gaming. Refs. [21, 22] provided the baseline for adaptation of the baseline Eqs. (19) and (20). Note that the same equation is used for sine and cosine except that the argument term is given a positive $\frac{\pi}{2}$ phase shift when applied to the cosine in Eq. (14). In Eq. (19), $(+/-)$ indicates that a plus is used if Arg is less than zero and a minus is used otherwise.

$$LP = 1.27323954 * Arg\ (+/-)\ 0.405284735 * Arg^2 \quad (19)$$

$$HP = .225 * [LP * abs(LP) - LP] + LP \quad (20)$$

Eq. (20) provides additional smoothing to Eq. (16) at the cost of computation time to implement a high precision mode. This equation could be implemented such that "$LP * abs(LP)$" essentially become the magnitude of LP^2. While this analysis used "if then" statements, there may be more efficient ways to implement Eqs. (19) and (20) depending on the software package being utilized.

2.2 Model simulation and analysis

For the purpose of model verification, commands are initially held constant at zero resulting in zero torque to allow us to evaluate model operation during a quiescent period. With zero input torque, Eq. (11) shows us that the change in angular momentum should be zero as well; therefore the model should not change. After a 5 s quiescent period, a 30° yaw maneuver was input into each model and the maneuver was conducted over a 10 s period at which point the commanded body angle went to zero (indicating no more change required). Afterwards the output Euler angles should remain constant with the spacecraft's new attitude. The results of this test were plotted in **Figure 7**. Additionally, note that the model was setup with an arbitrary diagonalized inertia matrix (J) per Eq. (21). The roll and pitch Euler angles remained at zero, as they should have, and as such are not shown.

$$J = \begin{bmatrix} 150 & 0 & 0 \\ 0 & 90 & 0 \\ 0 & 0 & 35 \end{bmatrix} \quad (21)$$

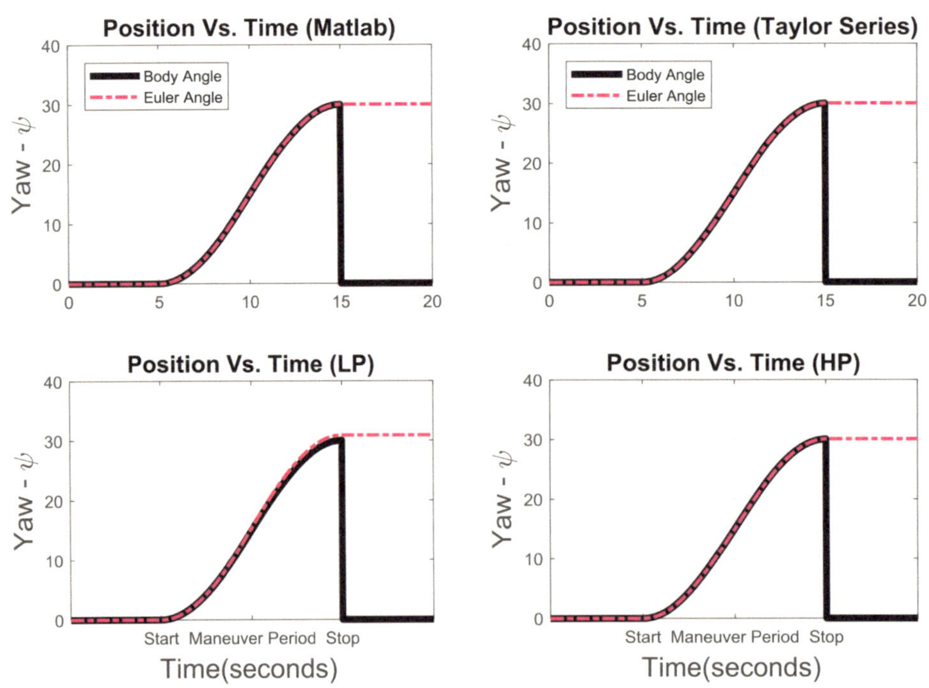

Figure 7.
Feedforward control for 30° yaw maneuver.

From a qualitative standpoint you can see that each sine generation algorithm created the intended Euler angle movement shown earlier in **Figure 4**. Upon closer examination the only algorithm that appeared to lose tracking on the body angle was the low precision algorithm. Since we achieved the basic shape from each method, we now turn our attention to analyzing the error and computation time associated with each for a given time step interval.

In the previous work addressed in the beginning of Section 2 of this we found that for a Runge-Kutta solver with step size of 0.01119, the MATLAB sine function reached a point where CPU and MATLAB precision started to affect the gains offered by shrinking step size. With this in mind, step sizes of 0.1, 0.05, and 0.1 s were chosen for analysis, results of which can be seen in **Figure 8** and **Table 1**.

One major inference to be drawn from **Table 1** is that the normalized error columns show Taylor, LP, and HP algorithms are roughly step-size invariant within our test range; only the MATLAB function's error reduces with step size in our model. Interestingly, the LP and HP functions can be more accurate than Taylor but we are more concerned with the final angle in coarse control (corresponding to the peak of sine curve) rather than the intermediate steps—so in this case, the Taylor series is considered more accurate.

The other major item of note is the difference in average computation time. While the MATLAB command is ultimately the most accurate at all step sizes, we can see that the LP and HP algorithms generally run faster. It should be noted that results were relatively inconsistent when run below 200 iterations but at 500

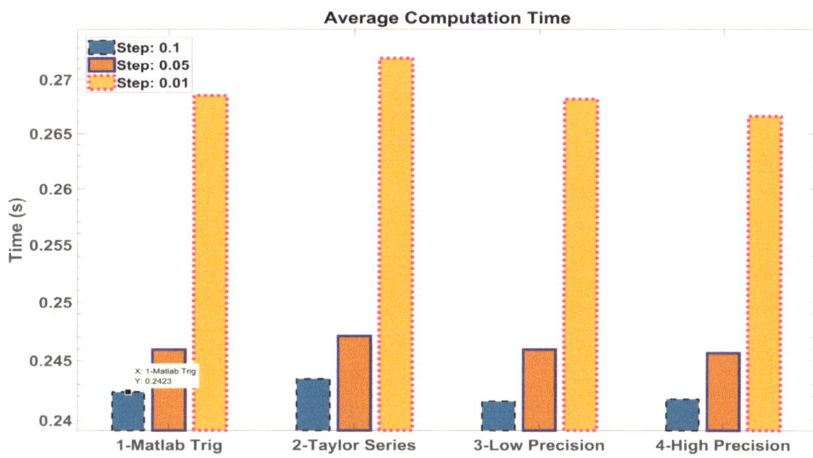

Figure 8.
Computation time results.

Method	Step size		Step size		Step size	
	0.01 s		0.5 s		0.1 s	
	Time(s)	Error	Time(s)	Error	Time(s)	Error
1-MATLAB	0.2423	1.02E-9	0.2459	6.36E-11	0.2685	1.02E-13
2-Taylor	0.2434	3.53E-5	0.2471	3.53E-5	0.2720	3.53E-5
3-LP	0.2416	2.81E-2	0.2459	2.81E-2	0.2682	2.81E-2
4-HP	0.2417	3.25E-4	0.2456	3.25E-4	0.2666	3.25E-4

Time and error results averaged over 500 iterations per model.

Table 1.
Timing and error results.

iterations they stabilized with HP and LP usually running faster during a given test. Since HP would run faster than LP sometimes and vice versa, even at greater iterations; it is believed that this may come down to specific CPU architecture used and how a dual core processor handles calculations.

3. Conclusions

When it comes to sinusoidal trajectory generation, if your spacecraft design has accurate fine control (e.g., robust feedback mechanisms) and can handle coarse control error on the order of 10^{-4}, then it may be more prudent to utilize the HP algorithm. This would allow you to reduce processing power and time resulting in lower power requirements and faster onboard calculations. A fourth order Taylor series would not be beneficial due to longer computation times and less accuracy than the MATLAB function; extending the order of the series would increase accuracy but also extend its runtime, thereby, losing viability. Additionally, simulation results reveal that the fastest methodology may vary with CPU architecture indicating that there may not be a definitive answer for "best" trajectory generation method. This should be evaluated within the specific spacecraft design trade space. Very little information is available on the proprietary MATLAB sine calculations but future testing will investigate the LP and HP algorithms against MATLAB on a variety of CPU architectures and organic sinusoidal generation on other platforms such as PYTHON.

Author details

Kyle A. Baker
Department of Mechanical and Aerospace Engineering, Naval Postgraduate School, Monterey, CA, USA

*Address all correspondence to: kabaker@nps.edu

References

[1] Lobo K, Lang J, Starks A, Sands T. Analysis of deterministic artificial intelligence for inertia modifications and orbital disturbances. International Journal of Control Science and Engineering. 2018;**8**(3):53-62

[2] Sands T. Electric vehicle sales catastrophe averted by deterministic artificial intelligence methods. Applied Sciences. 2018;**8**:2081

[3] Nakatani S. Simulation of spacecraft damage tolerance and adaptive controls. In: 2014 IEEE Aerospace Conference. 2014. pp. 1-16. DOI: 10.1109/AERO.2014.6836260

[4] Nakatani S. Autonomous damage recovery in space. International Journal of Automation, Control and Intelligent Systems. 2016;**2**(2):22-36. ISSN Print: 238175

[5] Nakatani S. Battle-damage tolerant automatic controls. Electronics and Electrical Engineering. 2018;**8**:10-23. DOI: 10.5923/j.eee.20180801.02.

[6] Heidlauf P, Cooper M. Nonlinear Lyapunov control improved by an extended least squares adaptive feed forward controller and enhanced Luenberger observer. In: Proceedings of the International Conference and Exhibition on Mechanical & Aerospace Engineering; 2-4 October 2017; Las Vegas, NV, USA. 2017

[7] Cooper M, Heidlauf P, Sands T. Controlling chaos—Forced van der pol equation. Mathematics on Automation Control Systems, A Special Issue of Mathematics. 2017;**5**:70-80. DOI: 10.3390/math5040070

[8] Sands T. Phase lag elimination at all frequencies for full state estimation of spacecraft attitude. Physics Journal. 2017;**3**(1):1-12

[9] Sands T. Nonlinear-adaptive mathematical system identification. Computation. 2017;**5**:47-59. DOI: 10.3390/computation5040047

[10] Wright T. Elements of Mechanics Including Kinematics, Kinetics, and Statics, With Applications. New York: Nostrand; 1909

[11] Eduard Study (D.H. Delphenich Translator). Foundations and goals of analytical kinematics. Berlin Mathematical Society. Sitzber. d. Berl. Math. Ges. 1913;**13**:36-60. Available from: http://neo-classical-physics.info/uploads/3/4/3/6/34363841/study-analytical_kinematics.pdf [Accessed: 14 April 2017]

[12] Gray A. A Treatise on Gyrostatics and Rotational Motion. London: MacMillan; 1918. ISBN 978-1-4212-5592-7

[13] Fung AC, Zimmermun BG. Digital simulation of rotational kinematics. In: NASA Technical Report NASA TN D-5302; October 1969; Washington, DC. 1969. Available from: https://ntrs.nasa.gov/archive/nasa/casi.ntrs.nasa.gov/19690029793.pdf

[14] Smeresky B, Rizzo A, Sands T. Kinematics in the information age. Mathematical Engineering, A Special Issue of Mathematics. 2018;**6**(9):148. DOI: 10.3390/math6090148

[15] Wie B. Space Vehicle Dynamics and Control. 1st ed. Reston, VA, USA: AIAA, McGraw-Hill; 1998. pp. 310-327. DOI: 10.2514/4.103803

[16] Slabaugh GG. Computing Euler Angles From a Rotation Matrix. 1999;6 (2000).pp. 39-63. Available form: h ttp://www.close-range.com/Docspacec raftomputing_Euler_angles_from_a_rotation_matrix.pdf [Accessed: January 1999]

[17] Henderson DM. Euler Angles, Quaternions, and Transformation Matrices—Working Relationships. McDonnell Douglas Technical Services Co. Inc., as NASA Technical Report NASA-TM-74839. 1977. Available from: https://ntrs.nasa.gov/archive/nasa/casi.ntrs.nasa.gov/19770024290.pdf

[18] Henderson DM. Euler Angles, Quaternions, and Transformation Matrices for Space Shuttle Analysis. McDonnell Douglas Technical Services Co. Inc., Houston Astronautics Division as NASA Design Note 1.4-8-020. 1977. Available from: https://ntrs.nasa.gov/archive/nasa/casi.ntrs.nasa.gov/19770019231.pdf

[19] Kuipers J. Quaternions and Rotation Sequences, Geometry, Integrability, and Quantization; 1-10 September 1999; Varna, Bulgaria. Sofia: Coral Press; 2000

[20] Weisstein EW. Taylor Series. From MathWorld—A Wolfram Web Resource [Internet]. 2018. Available from: http://www.mathworld.wolfram.com/TaylorSeries.html [Accessed: 21 June 2018]

[21] Baczynski M. Fast and Accurate Sine/Cosine Approximation [Internet]. 2007. Available from: http://www.lab.polygonal.de/2007/07/18/fast-and-accurate-sinecosine-approximation/ [Accessed: 21 June 2018]

[22] Climatiano M. Faster Sine Approximation Using Quadratic Curve [Internet]. 2014. Available from: http://www.mclimatiano.com/faster-sine-approximation-using-quadratic-curve/ [Accessed: 21 June 2018]

Chapter 8

Modern Control System Learning

Brendon Smeresky and Alex Rizzo

Abstract

This manuscript will explore and analyze the effects of different controllers in an overall spacecraft's attitude determination and control system (ADCS). The experimental setup will include comparing an ideal nonlinear feedforward controller, a feedback controller, and a combined ideal nonlinear feedforward + feedback controller within a Simulink simulation. A custom proportional, derivative, integral controller was implemented in the feedback control, adding an additional term to account for the nonlinear coupled motion. Consistent proportional, derivative, and integral gains were used throughout the duration of the experiment. The simulated results will show that the ideal nonlinear feedforward controller lacked an error correction mechanism and took extra time to execute, the feedback controller faired only slightly better, but the combined ideal nonlinear feedforward controller with feedback correction yielded the highest accuracy with the lowest execution time. This highlights the potential effectiveness for a learning control system.

Keywords: control systems, feedforward, feedback, learning systems

1. Introduction

The goal of a spacecraft's attitude determination and control system (ADCS) is to have a system that can move to and hold a specific orientation in three-dimensional space, relative to an inertial frame. This project can be viewed through three different lenses: classical control, modern control, and/or machine learning. These lenses explain the same control theory in three different contexts. For all the control theories, the ADCS considers the kinetics, kinematics, disturbances, controls, and actuators that dictate the system's motion [1]. Specifically, with regard to classical control, both feedforward and feedback controller are implemented in order to eliminate the error between a desired and commanded signal [1]. With regard to modern control, a similar estimation and correction method is implemented using either an extended Kalman controller, which relies upon on a nonlinear control estimator coupled with a linear control corrector, or an unscented Kalman controller, which uses both a nonlinear control estimator and nonlinear control corrector, in order to reduce error [2–6]. The third context relates control systems to deterministic artificial intelligence and machine learning. The control estimate derives from self-awareness of its own attributes that update every time-step with new information. This self-updating learning mechanism can be viewed akin to the update cycle used by supervised learning algorithms to model a system's performance. As an example, the updating mechanism is either a linear or nonlinear method to update an unknown inertia matrix for a spacecraft [7–13].

Figure 1 depicts the topology of the computational steps that take desired angle inputs and calculates Euler angle outputs: φ, θ, and ψ. The desired angle inputs are

IntechOpen

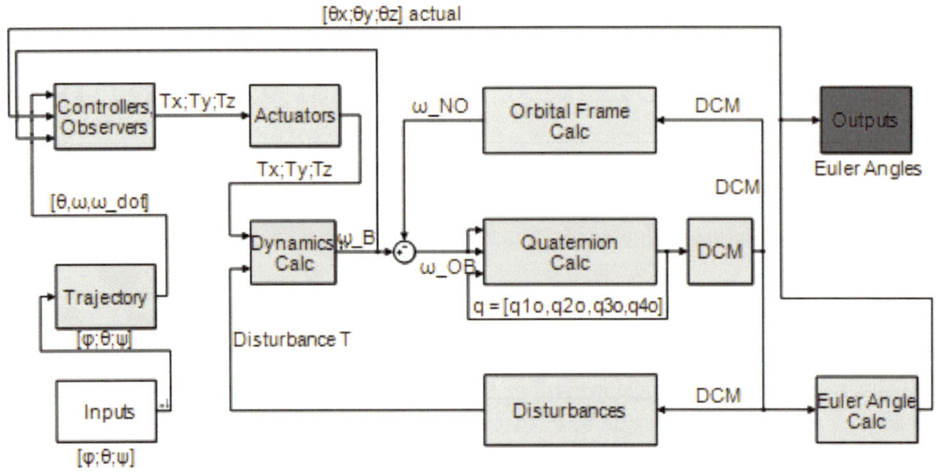

Figure 1.
The overview of the control system from the desired φ, θ, and ψ inputs (white box), through calculations steps (light gray boxes) to φ, θ, and ψ Euler angle outputs (dark gray box).

processed through the trajectory, controls, actuators, dynamics, and disturbances blocks. Section II will explain the theory behind the overall control system, Section III will detail the experimental setup, Section IV will show the results, and Section V will conclude this paper.

2. Background and theory

The rotation maneuver from one position to another is measured from the inertial reference frame or $[X_I, Y_I, Z_I]$ to the final position, the body reference frame or $[X_B, Y_B, Z_B]$, as depicted in **Figure 2**. For this simulation, a model was created to rotate from orientation A, $[X_A, Y_A, Z_A]$, to orientation B, $[X_B, Y_B, Z_B]$. The kinetics, kinematics, orbital frame, and disturbance calculations are explained in Ref. [1]. This paper focuses on a combined feedforward plus feedback controller as an error estimation and correction mechanism. This simulation utilizes three control moment gyroscopes (CMG) that are responsible for physically moving the system according to the inputted control signal. Additionally, this paper will focus on how the control system implementation affects the rotational maneuver and final orientation of a spacecraft.

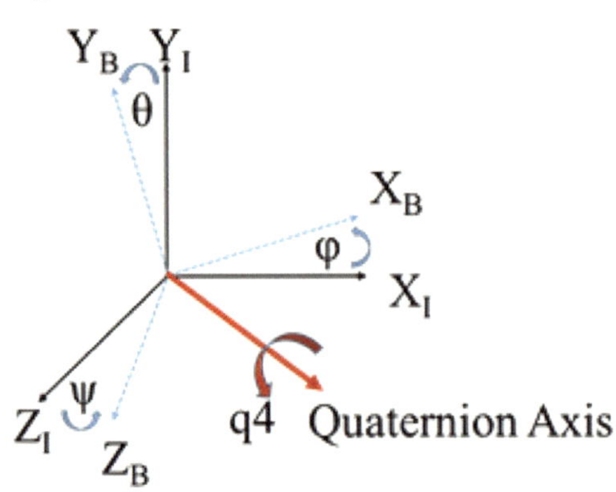

Figure 2.
Execution of a rotation from XI to XB; blue arrows denote angle rotations which can be seen to rotate around the quaternion axis, q4 in red.

2.1 Control moment gyroscopes

A CMG acts like a large reaction wheel spinning at a constant speed that transfers energy by changing its orientation. It successfully induces motion by following the governing equations of rotational mechanics, detailed in Eqs. (1) and (2):

$$T = \dot{H}_s + \omega \times H_s = u^* = \dot{H} \tag{1}$$

$$H_s = J\omega + h \tag{2}$$

These governing equations apply to any rotating, rigid body of mass. T represents the torque which is equal to the optimal control, u^*; H_s represents the total system's angular momentum; ω represents the angular velocity of the body; J is the inertia matrix for the entire body, including the CMGs; and h is the momentum produced by the CMGs. All these variables are expressed in the body frame of the spacecraft.

Physically on a spacecraft, the CMGs are typically one of several cylinders located at different orientations within the spacecraft's bus, used to perform reorientation maneuvers. In **Figure 1**, the CMGs are represented within the actuators block, which is directly before the dynamics block. The actuator input is a commanded torque $u = \dot{H}$, and the output is an actual torque that is fed to the system using a sinusoidal trajectory described in [14].

The method of transforming a commanded torque, T, into an actual torque using the CMGs is described in Eqs. (3), (4), and (5). In these equations, the variable θ_i is the rotation about the gimbal axis, and β is the skew angle orientation of the respective CMG. The notations have also been shortened so that sine and cosine trig functions are "s" and "c," respectively:

$$[A] = \frac{\delta H}{\delta \theta} = \begin{bmatrix} \sin\theta_1 & \cos\beta_2 \cos\theta_2 & -\sin\theta_3 \\ -\cos\beta_1 \cos\theta_1 & \sin\theta_2 & \cos\beta_3 \cos\theta_3 \\ \sin\beta_1 \cos\theta_1 & \sin\beta_2 \cos\theta_2 & \sin\beta_3 \cos\theta_3 \end{bmatrix} \tag{3}$$

$$[A]^{-1}\dot{H} = [A]^{-1}[A]\{\dot{\theta}\} = \{\dot{\theta}\} \tag{4}$$

$$[A]^{-1} = \begin{bmatrix} \dfrac{c(\theta_3)}{c\theta_1 s\theta_3 + s\theta_1\theta_3} & \dfrac{-s(\theta_3)}{(c\theta_1 s\theta_3 + s\theta_1\theta_3)t\theta_2} & \dfrac{s(\theta_3)}{c\theta_1 s\theta_3 + s\theta_1\theta_3} \\ 0 & \dfrac{1}{s\theta_2} & 0 \\ \dfrac{-c(\theta_1)}{c\theta_1 s\theta_3 + s\theta_1\theta_3} & \dfrac{-s(\theta_1)}{(c\theta_1 s\theta_3 + s\theta_1\theta_3)t\theta_2} & \dfrac{s(\theta_1)}{c\theta_1 s\theta_3 + s\theta_1\theta_3} \end{bmatrix} \tag{5}$$

The first step is to build $[A]$, commonly referred to as the Jacobian matrix or the spatial matrix. This matrix takes the angular changes in H and compares them to the changes in θ_i. This concept is visually represented in **Figure 3**, given a fixed β and fixed θ_i from (3).

The second step is based on the "so-called" inverse steering law, which is represented in (4). This equation relates the commanded torque to the gimbal rate, where the commanded torque is also known as the rate of change of the angular momentum. This calculation can be done with a variety of methods. A few potential methods for inversion include singular value decomposition, matrix inversion for square matrices, matrix pseudo-inversion for non-square matrices, or element by element in $[A]^{-1}$ as defined in (5). Each of these methods yields a commanded gimbal rate, $\dot{\theta}$. For simplification, the actuator is assumed to be perfect and produces the actual gimbal rate commanded without error or loss.

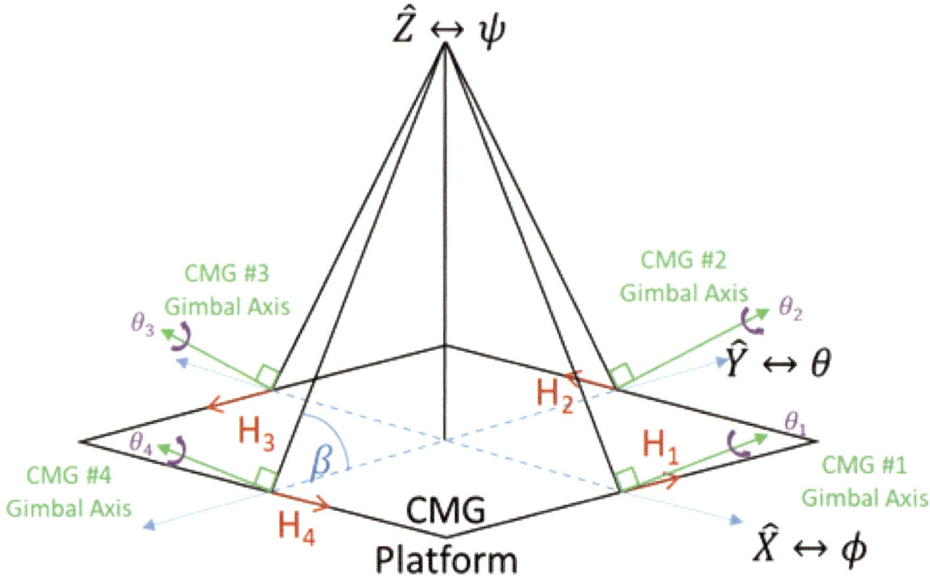

Figure 3.
CMG diagram with blue for axes and β angles, red for angular momentum vectors, green for θ rotation axes, and purple for the direction of θ rotation.

The last step is to invoke the inverse steering law in (6) to relate the Jacobian matrix to the actual gimbal rate and determine the actual torque produced. This can be completed using decoupled equations, as shown in [15]:

$$T = [A]\{\dot{\theta}\} = \dot{H} \tag{6}$$

Alternatively, Eqs. (4), (5), and (6) can be combined algorithmically and solved for using Eq. (7):

$$\begin{aligned} \boldsymbol{det}|\boldsymbol{A}| = & s\theta_1(s\theta_2 s\beta c\theta_3 - c\beta c\theta_3 s\beta c\theta_2) + c\beta c\theta_2(c\beta c\theta_1 s\beta c\theta_3 + c\beta c\theta_3 s\beta c\theta_1) \\ & + s\theta_3(c\beta c\theta_1 s\beta c\theta_2 + s\theta_2 s\beta c\theta_1) \; where \; \beta_1 \neq \beta_2 \neq \beta_3 \end{aligned} \tag{7}$$

In one calculated step, an output torque is yielded. This torque will feed into the dynamics as described in (1), using the process detailed above and in [1].

2.2 Singularities

A singularity occurs when an element in the Jacobian matrix, from (3), is resolved to an undefined value. This is caused by a zero existing within the denominator of (5), which complicates the calculation when solving for the determinant of $[A]$. Eq. (7) shows that singularities depend upon θ_1, θ_2, θ_3, β_1, β_2, and β_3 values. Conceptually, this occurs at certain θ and β combinations because infinite torque is required to move the CMG when the torque vector is orthogonal to the gimbal axis. Trying to do so is impossible and yields unstable behavior as the CMG acts erroneously and tries to resolve a 1/0 calculation and command an undefined torque. Furthermore, when all the β angles are equal, $\beta_1 = \beta_2 = \beta_3$, (7) simplifies further but is depicted as is for thoroughness.

This analysis is completed by taking (7) and stepping through θ and β combinations to verify which yield a zero determinant. For example, with sin θ_1, cos β_2, cos θ_2, and sin θ_3 all equal 0, the determinant of $[A]$ is zero, yielding a possible solution of $\theta_1 = \theta_2 = \theta_3 = 0°$. However, this is a long process with the many permutations of solutions, which are omitted in this manuscript [15].

2.3 Controllers and observers

The input to a CMG is a torque vector, $[T_x, T_y, T_z]$, which is a signal generated by the trajectory block in **Figure 1**. However, this signal is not tuned to adjust to real world influences, where mechanical hardware can introduce errors due to incorrectly or un-modeled attributes, noise, etc. In order to overcome these losses, either a feedforward controller, a feedback controller, or a combination of both controllers can be used to counter introduce errors. More specifically, proportional, integral, and derivative (PID) gains are correlated to the position error generated when moving from one position to another position to correct the errors. However, using only the position error e_θ, its integral $\int e_\theta dt$ and its derivative $\frac{d}{dt} e_\theta$ result in inaccuracies. This is due to the derivative calculation, which is both inefficient and inaccurate as a result of the virtual-zero reference created in the cascaded topology of a PID controller when the computation is initialized [16–19]. This inaccuracy can be prevented by sending in both the position error and the velocity error, which has been done in this experiment via an enhanced Luenberger proportional, derivative,

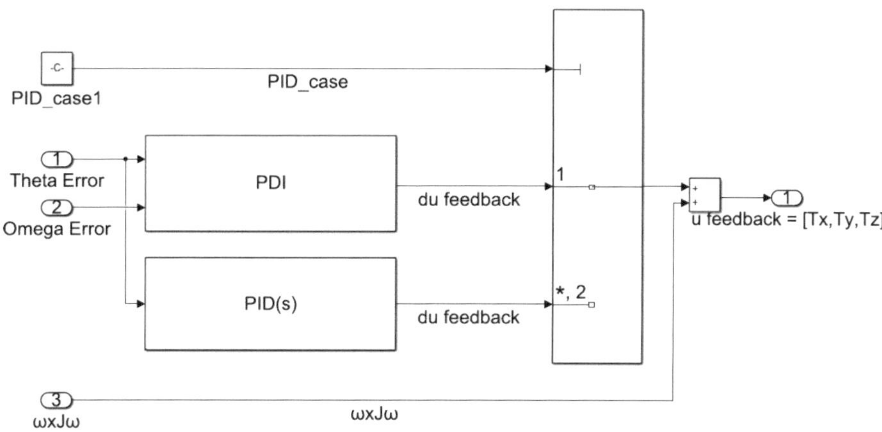

Figure 4.
Topology of a feedback controller with two methods of control: A classic PID controller or an enhanced Luenberger PDI controller.

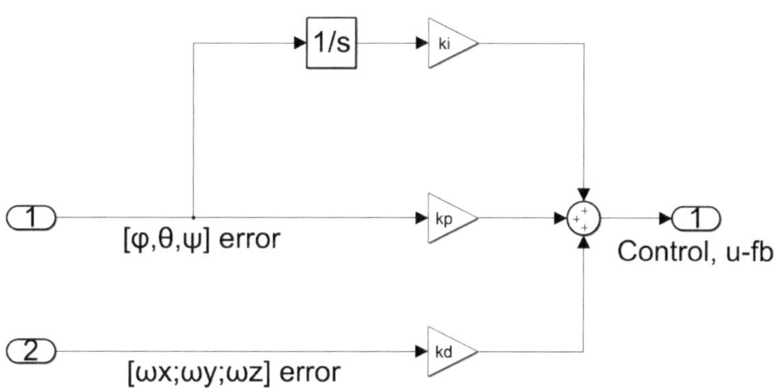

Figure 5.
PDI controller with ω input to remove virtual-zero reference with K_p, K_d, and K_i gains.

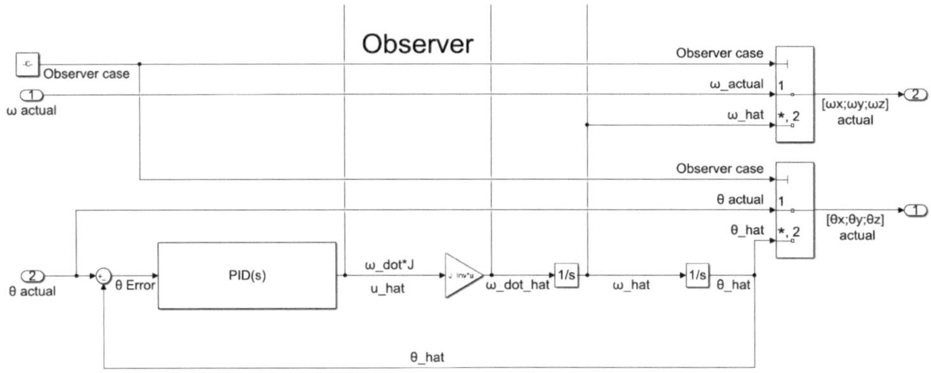

Figure 6.
Topology of an observer based upon a PID controller and two sets of differentiation to yield full-state knowledge.

integral (PDI) controller [16–19]. Additionally, the enhanced Luenberger controller differs from the conventional PID controller which only receives a position error. The result is a controller that outputs a commanded torque to the actuator block in **Figure 1**. Topologies are shown of the overall feedback controller in **Figure 4**, and the enhanced Luenberger PDI controller in **Figure 5**.

The simulation in this experiment utilized an observer to eliminate the virtual-zero reference described above. An observer is comparable to a controller as they both take in a position via system sensors and output a twice differentiated term to produce full-state feedback knowledge. However, it provides an advantage: because it is not implemented on a specific piece of hardware, much higher gains can be utilized than can be used otherwise. A topology of the observer is shown in **Figure 6** in the controller/observer block.

2.4 Control system learning

A control system is capable of learning by estimating its desired position and then updating the control to correct for errors. In a learning control system, the control estimator is the feedforward controller defined by (8), and the corrector or learning mechanism is the feedback controller defined by (9), where Φ and Θ are defined by (10) and (11), respectively. The feedback controller can also be written in terms of the gains and the position error, e_θ, as shown in (12). Combining (8) and (9) yields a learning system that develops a more accurate control over time through (13):

$$u_{ff} = \sum T = J\dot{\omega}_d + \omega_d \times J\omega_d = \Phi\Theta \tag{8}$$

$$u_{fb} = [\Phi]\{\hat{\Theta}\} = \Phi\left(\Phi^T\Phi\right)^{-1}\Phi^T\delta u \tag{9}$$

$$\Phi = \begin{bmatrix} \dot{\omega}_x & \dot{\omega}_y & \dot{\omega}_z & -\omega_y\omega_z & 0 & \omega_z\omega_y \\ \omega_x\omega_z & \dot{\omega}_x & 0 & \dot{\omega}_y & \dot{\omega}_z & -\omega_z\omega_x \\ -\omega_x\omega_y & 0 & \dot{\omega}_x & \omega_y\omega_x & \dot{\omega}_y & \dot{\omega}_z \end{bmatrix} \tag{10}$$

$$\Theta = \left\{J_{xx}, J_{xy}, J_{xz}, J_{yy}, J_{yz}, J_{zz}\right\}^T \tag{11}$$

$$u_{fb} = k_p e_\theta + k_d \dot{e}_\theta + k_i \int e_\theta \tag{12}$$

$$
\begin{aligned}
u_{tot} &= u_{ff} + u_{fb} \\
&= J\dot{\omega}_d + \omega_d \times J\omega_d + \Phi\left(\Phi^T\Phi\right)^{-1}\Phi^T\delta u \\
&= \Phi\Theta + \Phi\left(\Phi^T\Phi\right)^{-1}\Phi^T du = \Phi\left[\Theta + \left(\Phi^T\Phi\right)^{-1}\Phi^T\delta u\right]
\end{aligned}
\tag{13}
$$

Overall, the term "$[\Phi]\{\hat{\Theta}\}$" in (9) represents the self-awareness statement. The nonlinear state transition matrix, $[\Phi]$, was built by knowing the dynamics of the system, and $\{\hat{\Theta}\}$ is the vector of unknown variables. Another application includes analyzing a changing inertia matrix, where it is assumed that the mass of the system is varying. The vector of unknowns, $\{\hat{\Theta}\}$, is the learned moment of inertia that is recalculated at every iteration of the model and determining its new mass [9].

3. Experimental setup

This manuscript documents the implementation of three different control algorithm combinations to induce a yawing motion on a spacecraft by generating the commanded torque to a three-gimballed spacecraft ACS. The three cases are a nonlinear feedforward control (case 1), a linear feedback control (case 2), and a combination of both nonlinear feedforward + linear feedback (case 3). The gains for these controllers are found in **Table 1**.

The model in this manuscript was built in MATLAB and Simulink, where integrations were calculated using the ode45 with the Runge–Kutta solver and a fixed time-step. Euler angles were resolved using a 3-2-1 rotation sequence with the atan2 trigonometry function.

As per [1], initialized values include torque = [0,0,0] and quaternion = [0,0,0,1]. The spacecraft's inertia matrix is J = [10,0.1,0.1; 0.1,10,0.1; 0.1,0.1,10]. The disturbances are defined in [1]. The orbital altitude was set at 150 km with a drag coefficient of 2.5 and orbital motion off. Each simulation executed over a five-second quiescent period, five-second maneuver time, and five-second post-maneuver observation period, totaling 60 seconds and yielding a $\omega_f = \pi/2$ and $\varphi = \pi/2$ for the sinusoidal trajectory of the controller.

	K_p gain	K_d gain	K_i gain
PDI controller	1000	10	0.1
Observer	100,000	500	0.1

Table 1.
Tuned gain values for the PDI controller and observer.

4. Experimental results and analysis

4.1 Time-step analysis

Time-step analysis was completed to determine whether reducing the time-step would help minimize the body frame to the inertial frame error deviations.
The results of executing a maneuver with a feedforward + feedback controller utilizing two different time-steps are depicted in **Figure 7**. Expectations were that a smaller time-step would result in more precise results, meaning a smaller deviation

between the commanded and executed Euler angles. However, comparing the red and blue trajectories within each of the three plots in **Figure 7** shows that although some refinement is gained by decreasing the time-step, the gain is minimal. Therefore, a larger time-step can be used without losing much accuracy.

Comparing the $\theta_{actual} - \theta_{desired}$ and $\omega_{actual} - \omega_{desired}$ errors for time-steps of 0.01 and 0.001 in **Figure 8** yielded a similar result. The θ_z channel did receive the greatest amount of refinement with a smaller time-step, but no order of magnitude increase resulted. Therefore, these results confirm that varying the time-step has limited impact on the trajectories. Therefore, for the gains in **Table 1**, a minimum time-step of 0.01 is recommended, and decreasing it provides no additional benefit.

4.2 Control implementation

The performance of the three control system implementations is depicted in **Figure 9**. Comparing the three cases allowed further analysis on the differences between feedforward, feedback, and the combined feedforward + feedback control system. The feedforward and feedforward + feedback controllers are more precise than the feedback method. This is because it is based off an exact control equation, Eq. (8). Conversely, the feedback controller is based off a PDI controller that has one time-step of induced lag and is therefore less precise. Additionally, the gains in a PDI or PID controller must be finely tuned with predetermined gain values, which can be an iterative and time-consuming task because controller performance varies greatly depending on the values. Lastly, the combined controller configuration represents an error combination of both the feedforward and feedback plots. It allows the analytical accuracy of the feedforward equation to be updated with the responsiveness of the feedback correction, but too little error exists in this case for the results to be visible.

Figure 10 shows the error of the commanded Euler angle over time. The two left-most plots in **Figure 10** show that the error is different for each controller. The

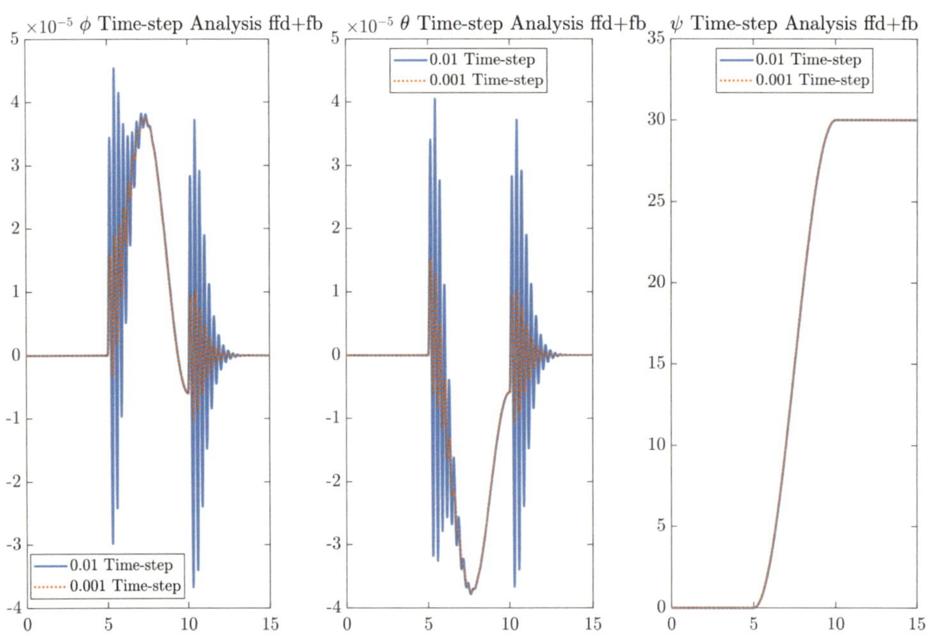

Figure 7.
Time-step analysis for the ϕ, θ, and ψ Euler angles for two time-steps.

DOI: http://dx.doi.org/10.5772/intechopen.90198

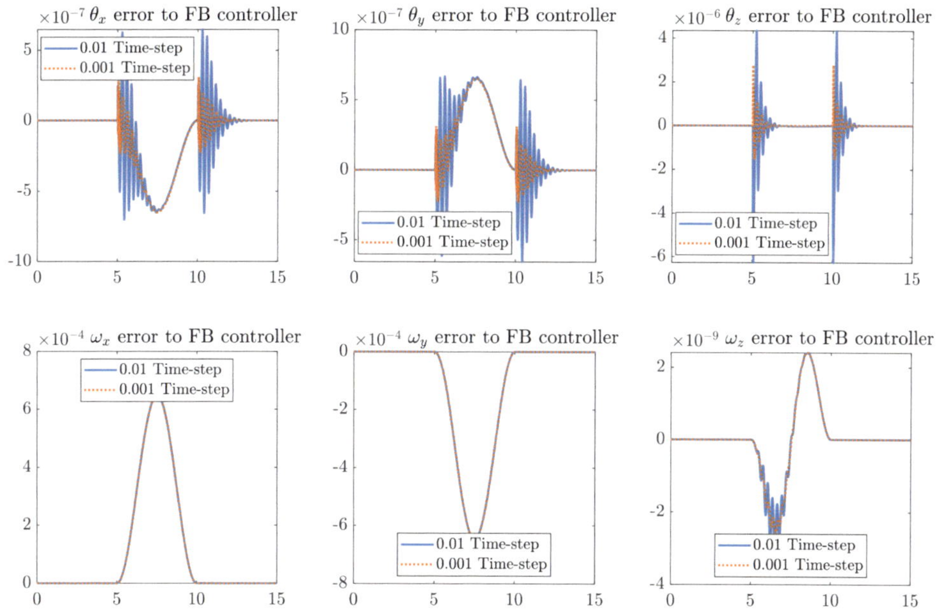

Figure 8.
Time-step analysis comparing θactual−θdesired and ωactual−ωdesired errors.

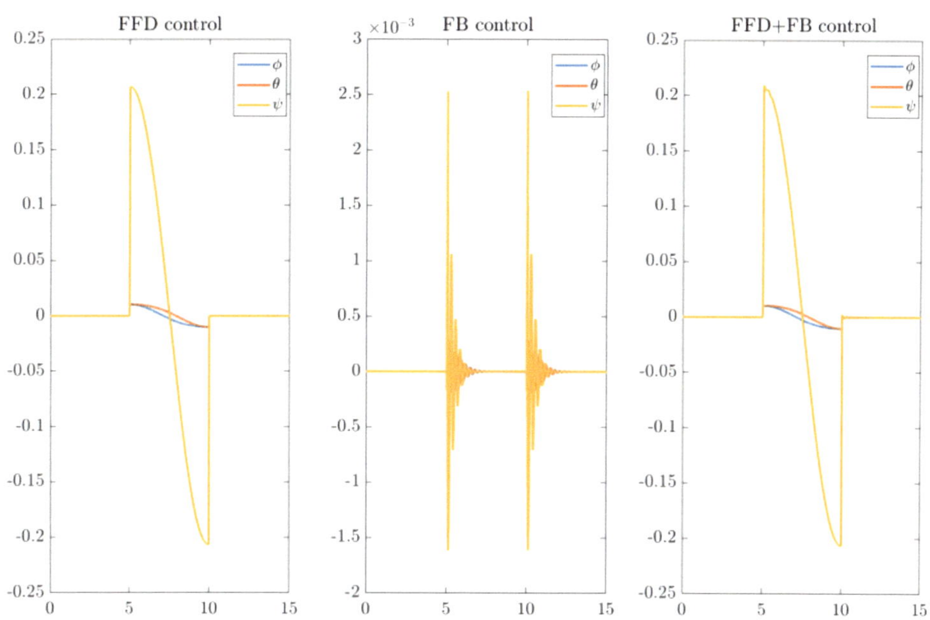

Figure 9.
Controller error over time for the three configurations.

feedback controller fluctuates initially as it corrects to minimize error over time. The feedforward controller is excellent initially but slowly deviates as error accrues without correction. Lastly, the combined controller is the best of both and starts with minimal error but then corrects that error over time. However, note that the error is minimal because no movement was commanded in either the φ or θ channels; the residual error exists because of cross-chatter between channels resultant from Eqs. (3) and (5).

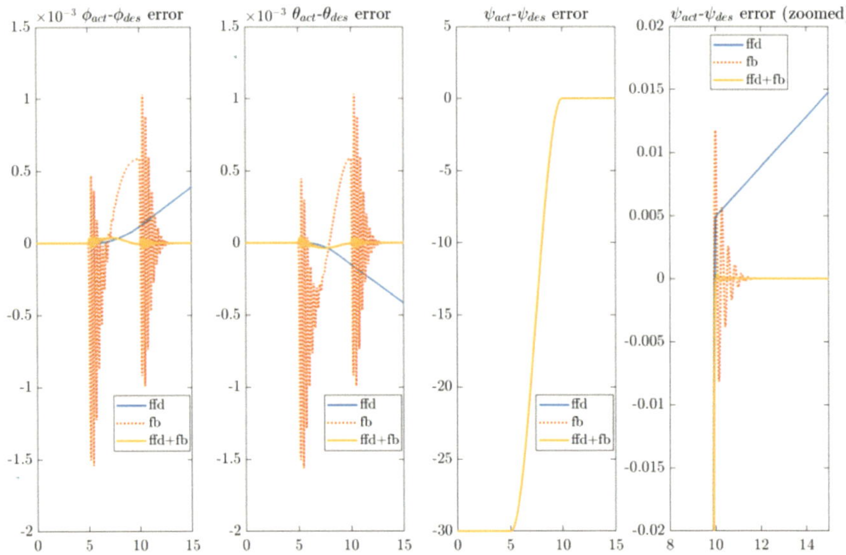

Figure 10.
Euler angle error for the three controller configurations.

	$\varphi_{actual} - \varphi_{desired}$	$\theta_{actual} - \theta_{desired}$	$\psi_{actual} - \psi_{desired}$	Run time (seconds)
u_{ff}	−3.93e-04°	4.18e-04°	−1.48e-02°	20.7
u_{fb}	6.03e-09°	−9.01e-08°	4.66e-08°	20.5
u_{ff+fb}	1.06e–08°	−7.94e-09°	4.38e-09°	20.3

Table 2.
The actual-desired Euler angle errors for the three cases using a 0.001 time-step and their associated run times.

The third plot from the left shows the position error in the ψ channel, which is the channel in which a 30-degree maneuver was commanded. Before the maneuver was started, the desired versus commanded error starts at 30°. At each time-step, the position is updated and the error decreases. Due to the scale of the maneuver, all three controllers appear to do well during the maneuver. To better understand the performance, the fourth and right-most plot is a zoom-in of the third plot, illustrating the accuracies of the feedforward controller due to the forward propagation accuracy of (8), the lag induced error and imperfect gain tuning of the feedback controller, and the results of the combined feedforward + feedback controllers. It is a better example of how each controller operates: the feedforward controller again starts off with minimal error before deviating over time, the feedback controller starts with the greatest amount of error that is overshot and damped, and the combined controller, which is the best of both the minimal starting error and correction capability of the other controllers.

Lastly, **Table 2** compares the boundary condition satisfaction at the final time of the maneuver. The results show that the feedforward + feedback controller has both the least amount of error and the shortest runtime. Conversely, the feedforward controller is the worst in both accuracy and runtime but only by a small margin compared to the feedback controller. The feedforward controller is hypothesized to perform worse because (12) tries to model (1) but can only poorly approximate it, yielding inaccuracies, which accrue over time.

Figure 11 is a revisualization of the data in **Figure 10**. This depiction is more intuitive and breaks down the change in angular position over time for each

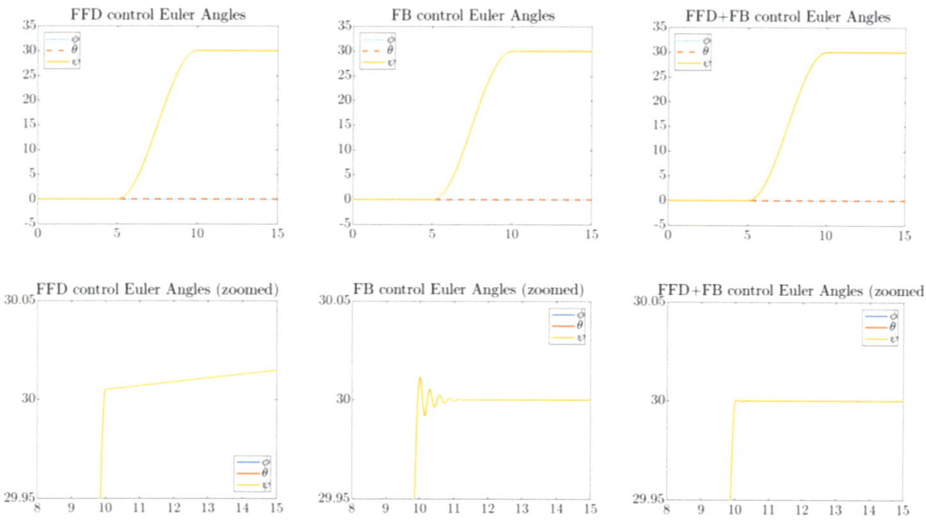

Figure 11.
Change in angular position for all three controller configurations.

controller, as well as magnifying the post-maneuver oscillations and damping. Commanding [0;0;30], we see that all controller configurations are responsive to this input, with the expected differences. The accuracy of the feedforward control in the left-most plots, combined with the undamped response of feedback control of the middle plots, gives dampened response of the combined controller in the right-most plots.

5. Conclusion

This experiment implemented and compared the effects of a feedforward, feedback, and a combined forward + feedback control system. A yaw maneuver was commanded, and the response was measured to show that an ADCS can estimate and then update its control over time, similar to a feedforward and feedback learning mechanism. The results showed that the feedforward controller lacks a correction mechanism that accrues error and takes time; the feedback system is slightly better in both metrics, but the combined feedforward + feedback system combines the best of both systems for superior accuracy in the shortest time. Therefore, the combined system is the best choice for its accuracy and adaptability. However, this combined system needs to be further researched by subjecting the system to noise and induced disturbances to validate the combined system's responsiveness.

Acknowledgements

We would like to thank our teacher, Dr. Timothy Sands, for his guidance in developing this work, as well as our families for their support while we spent our time away from them developing this research, so thank you.

Conflict of interest

The authors declare no conflict of interest.

Author details

Brendon Smeresky* and Alex Rizzo
Naval Postgraduate School Monterey, California, United States

*Address all correspondence to: bpsmeres@nps.edu

References

[1] Smeresky B, Rizzo A, Sands T. Kinematics in the information age. Mathematics. 2018;**6**(9):148

[2] Kalman RE. A new approach to linear filtering and prediction problems. Journal of Basic Engineering. 1960;**82**: 35-45

[3] McElhoe BA. An assessment of the navigation and course corrections for a manned flyby of Mars or Venus. IEEE Transactions on Aerospace and Electronic Systems. 1966;**2**(4):613-623

[4] Julier SJ, Uhlmann JK, UKF. New extension of the Kalman filter to nonlinear systems. In: Signal Processing, Sensor Fusion, and Target Recognition VI. Proceedings of SPIE. 3. pp. 182-193

[5] Sands T. Nonlinear-adaptive mathematical system identification. Computation. 2017;**5**:47

[6] Kalman RE. Contributions to the theory of optimal control. In: Boletín de la Sociedad Matemática Mexicana. 1960; **5**(2). pp. 102-119

[7] Nakatani S, Sands T. Battle-damage tolerant automatic controls. Electrical and Electronic Engineering. 2018; **8**(1):23

[8] Nakatani S, Sands T. Simulation of spacecraft damage tolerance and adaptive controls. IEEE Aerospace. 2014;**1-16**:2014

[9] S Nakatani T. Sands, nonlinear adaptive control: Autonomous damage recovery in space. International Journal of Control, Automation and Systems. 2016;**2**:23-36

[10] Sands T, Kim JJ, Agrawal BN. Spacecraft fine tracking pointing using adaptive control. In: Proceedings of 52th International Astronautical Congress; 2007

[11] Sands T, Kim JJ, Agrawal B. Spacecraft Adaptive Control Evaluation. Infotech@ Aerospace 2012, 2476

[12] Sands T, Kim JJ, Agrawal BN. Improved Hamiltonian adaptive control of spacecraft. In: 2009 IEEE Aerospace Conference. 1-10; 2009

[13] Cooper M, Heidlauf P, Sands T. Controlling chaos – Forced van der pol equation. Mathematics. 2017;**5**(4):70

[14] Baker K, Cooper M, Heidlauf P, Sands T. Autonomous trajectory generation for deterministic artificial intelligence. Electrical and Electronic Engineering. 2018;**8**:59-68. DOI: 10.5923/j.eee.20180803.01

[15] Sands TA, Kim JJ, Agrawal B. Control moment gyroscope singularity reduction via decoupled control. In: IEEE SEC 2009, 388-391; 2009

[16] Sands T., Lorenz R. Physics-based automated control of spacecraft. In: Proceedings of the AIAA Space Conference & Exposition; Pasadena, CA, USA; 14–17 September 2009

[17] Sands TA. Physics-based control methods. In: Advances in Spacecraft Systems and Orbit Determination. London, UK: InTech Publishers; 2012. pp. 29-54

[18] Sands T. Improved magnetic levitation via online disturbance decoupling. Physics Journal. 2015;**1**: 272-280

[19] Sands T. Phase lag elimination at all frequencies for full state estimation of spacecraft attitude. Physics Journal. 2017;**3**(1):1-12